North Korea in the World Economy

North Korea evokes images of nuclear confrontation, famine, isolation, and economic failure. The country also poses major foreign policy dilemmas for the international community. Nonetheless, Pyongyang seems to have belatedly recognized some of the challenges it faces and has begun to grapple with them – for example, by implementing economic reforms.

North Korea in the World Economy brings together a selection of many of *the* world experts on the North Korean economy and covers such important issues as:

- possible unification with South Korea;
- the significance of China's economic success;
- the role of Europe and the United States in North Korea.

This book provides an accessible, well-written and comprehensive account of this unique country and its economy. It will be extremely useful not only for students and academics with an interest in Korean studies, international finance and transition economies but also for those interested in international economics.

E. Kwan Choi is Professor of Economics at Iowa State University and served as President of the Korea-America Economic Association in 2001. **E. Han Kim** is Professor of Economics at the University of Michigan. **Yesook Merrill** is Assistant Director for Economics at the US General Accounting Office.

RoutledgeCurzon Advances in Korean Studies

1. The Politics of Economic Reform in South Korea
A Fragile Miracle
Tat Yan Kong

2. Market and Society in Korea
Interest, Institution and the Textile Industry
Dennis McNamara

3. Social and Economic Policies in Korea
Ideas, Networks and Linkages
Dong-Myeon Shin

4. North Korea in the World Economy
Edited by E. Kwan Choi, E. Han Kim and Yesook Merrill

North Korea in the World Economy

Edited by E. Kwan Choi, E. Han Kim and Yesook Merrill

RoutledgeCurzon
Taylor & Francis Group
LONDON AND NEW YORK

First published in 2003 by RoutledgeCurzon
11 New Fetter Lane, London EC4P 4EE

Simultaneously published in the USA and Canada
by RoutledgeCurzon
29 West 35th Street, New York, NY 10001

RoutledgeCurzon is an imprint of the Taylor & Francis Group

Typeset in Baskerville by LaserScript Ltd, Mitcham, Surrey
Printed and bound in Great Britain by
Antony Rowe Ltd, Chippenham, Wiltshire

British Library Cataloguing in Publication Data
A catalogue record for this book is available from the British Library

Library of Congress Cataloging in Publication Data
North Korea in the world economy / [edited by] E. Kwan Choi, E. Han Kim & Yesook Merrill.
p. cm.
Papers from the August 2001 conference on 'North Korea in the World Economy' held in Washington, D.C.
1. Korea (North) – Economic conditions – Congresses. 2. Korea (North) – Economic policy – Congresses. 3. Korean reunification question (1945-) – Congresses. 4. Korea (North) – Foreign economic relations – Congresses. I. Choi, Eun Kwan. II. Kim, Ung-han. III. Merrill, Yesook.

HC470.2.N668 2003

2002036917

ISBN 0–415–30429–6

Contents

Figures

Tables

Contributors

Joachim Ahrens is professor of economics at the European Business School in Oestrich-Winkel, Germany. Previously, he was associate professor at the University of Goettingen in Germany, Research Associate at the Department of Economics, University of California at Berkeley, a Visiting Scholar at the Hoover Institution of Stanford University, and an economist at the Asian Development Bank.

Bradley O. Babson is a Senior Advisor on North Korea to the World Bank and consultant on Asian affairs.

Nakki Baek is the Chief Researcher at the Korea Institute for Industrial Economics, Korea.

E. Kwan Choi is Professor of Economics at Iowa State University and served as President of the Korea-America Economic Association in 2001.

Donald P. Gregg is President and Chairman of the Korea Society, New York, USA. He served as American Ambassador to Korea from 1989–1993.

Jang C. Jin is Professor of Economics at the Chinese University of Hong Kong.

Won Bae Kim, is Senior Fellow at the Korea Research Institute for Human Settlements.

Myong Chol Kim is Executive Director of the Center for Korean-American Peace in Japan.

E. Han Kim is Professor of Economics at the University of Michigan.

Seon Lee is Professor of Economics at Kyung-Hee University, Korea.

Kenneth Lieberthal holds several positions at the University of Michigan: Distinguished Fellow and Director for China at the William Davidson Institute, Professor of Political Science, William Davidson Professor of Business Administration, and Research Associate of the Center for Chinese Studies.

Borje Ljunggren, is Swedish Ambassador to China. His career at the Swedish Ministry of Foreign Affairs include Deputy Director General and Head of the Department of Asia and the Pacific and Swedish Ambassador to Vietnam during 1994–97.

Felix Philipp Lutz heads the Future Trends/Markets and Politics Department in the Berlin office of Prognos, a consulting company based in Basel, Switzerland. Felix Lutz is also a Professor of International Relations and Business Administration at SIU-Schiller International University in Heidelberg, an American institution.

Thomas F. McCarthy has worked for over twenty-five years as a consultant in agriculture and rural development. He has undertaken ten extended missions in the DPRK, including work for the International Fund for Agricultural Development (IFAD), the UN Development Program, and the Food and Agriculture Organization.

Ronald Meinardus is the Resident Representative of the Friedrich-Naumann-Foundation in the Philippines. Before moving to Manila in early 2002, he served his organization in South Korea for nearly six years, where he also taught at Hanyang University.

John Merrill is Chief of Northeast Asia Division in the US Department of State's Bureau of Intelligence and Research.

Yesook Merrill, is Assistant Director for Economics at the US General Accounting Office.

C. Kenneth Quinones is co-director of Korean Peninsula Projects at the International Center in Washington, D.C.

Bertrand Renaud is an international specialist in housing finance, real estate and urban development. Dr. Renaud is a long-term student of Korean development and has published extensively on Korean economic issues.

In Je Rhee is a member of the Supreme Council and the Millennium Democratic Party, Korea.

Wolfgang Röhr is Head of the East Asia Division of the German Foreign Ministry.

Bernhard Seliger is resident representative of Hanns Seidel Foundation in Seoul and research fellow at the Institute for Research Into Culture and Economic Systems, University of Witten in Herdecke, Germany.

William J. Taylor is a former Director of National Security Studies at West Point and Senior Executive with the Center for Strategic and International Studies, is president of TAI, a Washington area-based consulting firm and an Adjunct Professor at the Georgetown University School of Foreign Service, Washington, DC.

Georgi Toloraya is Deputy Director General, First Asian Department, Ministry of Foreign Affairs of Russia, Moscow.

Erich Weingartner is an independent consultant on international and humanitarian affairs specializing in DPRK and the Editor of CanKor, the Canada-DPR Korea e-clipping service.

Preface

North Korea today evokes many unflattering images: famine, poverty, a rogue state, the last vestiges of the Cold War, weapons of mass destruction, human rights crises, totalitarian regime, isolation, refugees, etc. President Bush's State of the Union address in January 2002 added yet another negative image to the list when he branded North Korea as part of an "axis of evil" along with Iran and Iraq. During his visit to Seoul, South Korea, a month later, however, President Bush expressed support for Seoul's policy of reconciliation and engagement with North Korea. He added that the United States has no intention of attacking North Korea, is ready to talk, and will continue giving food aid to North Korea. The seemingly conflicting messages offered in the State of the Union speech and during his visit to South Korea illustrate the depth of the foreign policy challenge North Korea poses for the United States.

North Korea has been in dire economic straits for almost a decade and continues to face very difficult economic challenges. Throughout the past decade, North Korean gross domestic product (GDP) had a negative growth rate, contracting by as much as 50 percent in the mid-1990s by some estimates. Factories are operating at only 20 to 30 percent of capacity. Industrial infrastructure is devastated. Severe shortages of food and energy continue. In addition, North Korea has to grapple with the question of regime legitimacy: it needs to improve the welfare of its people, and interact with other nations according to international norms and good business practice.

Contrary to popular perception, in the last few years North Korea has been moving towards opening its doors and establishing economic reform – slowly and gradually. Reform is a difficult process – especially for a country like North Korea. In the short run, it can be disruptive and create major social problems. North Korea faces the added challenge of anti-reform pressure from the older generation of revolutionary leaders who remain powerful. Having lost a million or more citizens to starvation and related disease, North Korea also has no margin of error. So, the economic restructuring North Korea has adopted is not of the big bang variety, but creeping reform, so gradual that some people do not notice it. Within the past two years, North Korea's changing attitudes towards economic opening and reform have become much more noticeable. This should come as no surprise, however, for reform and opening up to the world are the only choices for the North Korean economy.

The August 2001 conference on "North Korea in the World Economy," co-hosted by the Korea-America Economic Association and the William Davidson Institute of the University of Michigan Business School, assessed some of these developments. The conference took place at a highly appropriate time. North Korea was coming out into the world, albeit hesitantly. In June 2000, we witnessed the first inter-Korean summit. In November of the same year, North Korean leader Kim Jong Il hosted a visit from Secretary of State, Madeline Albright. In January 2001, Chairman Kim toured the Shanghai industrial and financial districts. In May, a high-level European Union (EU) delegation visited Pyongyang. By then North Korea had normalized relations with most members of the European Union. Shortly before our conference, Kim Jong Il made a train journey to Russia lasting twenty-four days – retracing a route once taken by his father – where he had several discussions with a visit from President Vladimir Putin. During the conference, Kim hosted President Jiang Zemin in Pyongyang.

The August 2001 conference assembled a diverse group of academics, researchers, diplomats, and government officials from the United States, South Korea, Germany, China, Japan, Canada, Sweden, Hong Kong, and Russia to assess these developments. It was held in Washington only two months after the completion of the Bush administration's review of policy toward North Korea. The conference served as a forum to share perspectives and better understand the changes in the North Korean economy. Based on the conference, this volume weighs the potential for economic reform, and considers what the international community can do to help the process, as well as where it might lead. As the ninteenth-century British statesman Benjamin Disraeli said, ignorance never settles a question. It takes information, understanding, and open-mindedness. That spirit ran through the conference and hopefully is captured in this volume.

E. Kwan Choi
E. Han Kim
Yesook Merrill
July 2002

Acknowledgements

The editors gratefully acknowledge the Korea-America Economic Association and the William Davidson Institute of the University of Michigan Business School for co-hosting the conference on "North Korea in the World Economy" on which this volume is based. We also thank the co-sponsors, the Korea Economic Institute and the Atlantic Council, for their financial and staff support. We express our sincere appreciation to the Korea Development Institute, Korea Energy Economics Institute, Korea Institute for Industrial Economics and Trade, Korea Institute of Public Finance, Korea Research Institute for Human Settlements, Korea Techno-Venture Foundation, Mitsui Life, and Samsung for providing generous financial contributions to the conference. Special thanks are due to the Knowledge Vision Forum and the LG Group for their generosity in helping support the publication of this volume.

Introduction

E. Kwan Choi

It is difficult for a small country to enjoy a high standard of living in this century unless it is part of a free trade area. North and South Korea do not belong to any free trade area. Large countries like China, the United States and Japan can act independently without relying heavily on other countries. However, even China acceded to becoming part of the World Trade Organization (WTO) in 2001.

The United States encouraged the European Countries to form the European Community after the Marshall Plan aid was wound up in 1948. However, due to the EC's great success and gradual exclusion of North America, Americans belatedly launched the North American Free Trade Agreement (NAFTA) in the early 1990s. Because opening the European market has become so difficult, President George W. Bush is trying to organize the Free Trade Area of the Americas (FTAA). Even South Korea is now engaging in an effort to achieve a free trade agreement with Japan. Unless North Korea joins a major free trade area, its future is incertain, even if the famine problem is alleviated.

The long-term future for North Korea's survival lies in becoming a member of a free trade area in Asia. However, in the Far East, China has little incentive to join because of its recent accession to the WTO. Japan's economy does not need North Korea as much as North Korea needs Japan's assistance.

In the short run, the most sensible solution is to integrate the two Korean economies, using the capital of South Korea and the low-wage labor of North Korea. The two Koreas can then export their finished products to Europe and the Americas, and import raw materials from other Asian countries. Many steps remain to be taken to reach this stage, and the experts explore and exchange ideas about the future of North Korea in this volume.

1 Progress on the Korean Peninsula

What are the prospects?

Kenneth Lieberthal

This is a broad overview of likely progress on reuniting the two countries on the Korean Peninsula. My basic thesis is that the key factors that produced forward movement over the past 18 months are no longer in evidence. I am therefore not very optimistic about progress in the next few years.

The final year of the Clinton administration saw considerable movement on the Korean Peninsula. It is worth considering the underlying forces at work: Kim Dae Jung possessed considerable political momentum and boldly moved to install a peace process that would prove irreversible. His Berlin speech played a major role, and the visit to Pyongyang was hugely important. His support for Hyundai's initiatives provided concrete benefits to North Korea. His willingness to provide North Korea with direct assistance demonstrated goodwill. President Kim based these actions on the premise that the Republic of Korea (ROK) could afford to take the lead and be generous in order to change Kim Jong Il's perceptions. But that in turn required that Kim Dae Jung maintain a strong political position in the South.

Former Defense Secretary William Perry, at the request of President Clinton, carried out a review of US policy toward North Korea and submitted a report with important recommendations. The Perry report offered the clear message to North Korea that relations with the United States could either improve sharply or become considerably worse. This process held out the prospect for real progress on dropping US sanctions, removing North Korea from our terrorism list, normalizing relations with North Korea, and giving North Korea access to help from international financial institutions. It also made clear that the United States was prepared to increase its military resources devoted to containing the North Korean threat if North Korea decided to move in the wrong direction. Perry made absolutely clear that a "steady state" was not tenable.

The Perry process also produced the Tripartite Coordination and Observation Group (TCOG), which produced unprecedented coordination of US, ROK, and Japanese approaches to dealing with North Korea. North Korea had in the past manipulated the differences among the US, ROK, and Japan to expand its own influence. The TCOG considerably reduced the room for North Korea to maneuver here. Unprecedented levels of ROK–Japanese amity in their broader relationship also contributed to the success of TCOG (and vice versa).

Despite these developments, there were some serious difficulties. For example, North Korea waited far too long before fulfilling its promise to send a high-level visitor to the United States. Presumably, Kim Jong Il did not adequately understand the politics in Washington. By the time he sent Cho, it was no longer possible for President Clinton to put together a visit to Pyongyang. Thus, even with the positive atmosphere that had been created – producing substantial changes in North Korean behavior and a major burst of optimism by all the players (including China) – the potentially crucial presidential trip to North Korea did not take place. With the advent of the George W. Bush administration in Washington, momentum has been lost and arguably the negatives now loom larger than the positives.

North Korea still clearly sees the US relationship as key, and is very reluctant to move forward significantly with South Korea until the North Korea–US relationship also is on track. The US–North Korea relationship, however, has stalled.

The five-month long post-election policy review by the new US administration brought everything to a halt. During the policy review, President Bush made harsh comments about not being able to trust the North Koreans and Kim Jong Il reacted negatively. This protracted review period cost Kim Dae Jung precious time, as the stated US position seemed to undercut his "sunshine policy".

The policy review indicated US willingness to reengage, but it stipulated terms that Kim Jong Il may well find unpalatable. These include:

- early nuclear inspections;
- troop reductions;
- no payment for electricity that would have been produced had the light-water reactors (LWRs) come on line on time;
- potential pressure on the refugee issue.

Because the United States had already signed the Agreed Framework, it is not clear how much incentive these terms provide to move forward. To date, North Korea has shown no evidence that it will accept the US agenda outlined by the policy review.

The situation in the ROK also has become less favorable. Kim Dae Jung cannot run for election again and increasingly is becoming a lame duck. North Korea's failure to follow through on the Kim Jong Il return visit has sapped Kim Dae Jung's momentum on the North–South issue. Criticism of his "sunshine policy" promises is increasing as the election draws closer. A weak economy in South Korea also is making the idea of generosity towards the North less popular. And the ROK economy may well fare badly in 2002.

It seems unlikely that anything less than a major turnaround by North Korea could rekindle significant enthusiasm for the sunshine policy, and time is working against Kim Dae Jung here. North Korea, though, may well be making the same mistake it made last year with regard to the USA. It may be assuming it can wait until late in Kim Dae Jung's administration and then try to deliver an electoral boost by offering the Kim Jong Il return visit. But by then it will likely be too late for this to produce real momentum in the ROK.

Note that a Kim Jong Il visit to Seoul holds major risks for Kim Jong Il, including the potential for large-scale demonstrations and loss of prestige. Kim Jong Il can, of course, use the visit to bargain for more aid and other benefits, but even here he is likely to gain more by holding off until closer to the ROK election.

The TCOG process also has lost considerable momentum. The ROK has expressed considerable chagrin over the way the US policy review was handled and now largely blames the United States both for crucial delays and for setting the bar too high for renewal of real engagement with the North. ROK relations with Japan have grown increasingly tense, especially over Japanese nationalist issues such as the distortion of history in textbooks and Prime Minister Junichiro Koizumi's visit to the Yasakuni shrine. The TCOG has had one preparatory meeting, one full meeting, and another full meeting planned for in September 2001. But it has not regained the energy and momentum it had under the Clinton administration, and North Korea is undoubtedly well aware of this.

Finally, the steam seems to have gone out of Japan's efforts to develop a better relationship with North Korea. This reflects, in part, the Japanese preoccupation with major domestic political developments, along with their recognition that the US–North Korea and ROK–North Korea relationships are now less dynamic. From a Japanese perspective, therefore, there now is very little pressure to improve ties with North Korea. Also, Japan recognizes that rapprochement with North Korea will hasten the day when Japan will have to lay out considerable sums in effective war reparations – hardly a positive incentive to support reunion.

Where does all of this leave us? While the future obviously is uncertain, we can anticipate the following:

- US talks with North Korea may resume but will not make rapid progress.
- Kim Dae Jung will not be able to make dramatic moves (such as the Berlin speech and his follow-up initiatives) until Kim Jong Il himself takes some significant steps to further North–South relations.
- But Kim Jong Il is likely to wait well into 2002 before making a dramatic gesture, and that could well be too late to produce the kind of reaction he seeks in the ROK.
- In this context, the new president of the ROK, who will assume office on 25 February 2003, will likely initially seek to pursue a policy toward North Korea that differs clearly from that of Kim Dae Jung for six months or more.
- Therefore, significant forward movement on reunification of the Korean Peninsula may well prove too difficult to achieve before late 2003, if then.

Note, finally, that living conditions in North Korea show no sign of improving. Drought early in 2001 and later flooding mean that the food crisis will likely grow worse. There is no reason to anticipate improvement in the urban economy in the absence of major international assistance. The energy supply situation will remain critical because North Korea lacks both generating facilities and a distribution infrastructure. Therefore, all the dangers inherent in a potential North Korean collapse will remain on the horizon. I do not anticipate such a collapse, but North Korea is indeed in disastrous condition.

Everyone agrees that the best alternative to a North Korean collapse is gradual reunification. That is what makes the more recent developments so disturbing. They seem to have effectively stalled progress toward gradual reunification for at least several more years.

Part I

Recent developments on the Korean Peninsula

2 The Korean Peninsula

Recent developments from an EU perspective[1]

Borje Ljunggren

Why did the EU get involved and what did we achieve?

In May 2001, the Swedish Prime Minister, Göran Persson, visited North and South Koreas. He did so in his capacity as chairman of the European Council and was accompanied by Dr Xavier Solana, the High Representative of the Council, and Chris Patten, European Commissioner for External Relations. Sending such a high-level delegation to North Korea clearly exceeded the established practice of the common security and foreign policy (CSFP) of the EU. Bosnia, Kosovo, Macedonia and the Middle East were areas where the EU was expected to play a role, and failure to do so would in fact be seen as a serious sign of inner weakness. But the Korean Peninsula – and North Korea – were something quite different. It was not that the EU had not been involved on the peninsula. Actually, the EU had opened up a political dialogue with North Korea as early as 1998, but that was at the level of Asia Directors (my level of responsibility). A personal visit by the President of the European Council had not been considered an option. So, why were we getting involved?

I would like to point to three main reasons, each very different in nature:

1 The security situation on the Korean Peninsula, and in particular North Korea's nuclear development program, missile launch, and export of missile technology. The fact that the EU in 1997 decided to contribute to Korean Peninsula Energy Development Organization (KEDO) was a clear sign of the EU's concern.
2 The humanitarian situation in North Korea. Ever since the severe floods of 1995, the European Commission as well as individual EU member countries have been supplying food aid to North Korea in an effort to alleviate the serious deprivations facing the North Korean people. The fact that the situation is chronic and is as much due to structural conditions as to weather conditions has led to an increasingly deep involvement by the European Union in efforts to increase the productivity of North Korean agriculture.
3 The desire of the European Union to contribute to peace and reconciliation on the peninsula in the light of President Kim Dae Jung's "sunshine policy", the impressive US–North Korean process initiated by the work of William

Perry and, of course, the historic June 2000 inter-Korean summit that caught the world by surprise.

In addition, several other factors help explain why the European Union decided to give priority to the question of the Korean Peninsula during the Swedish presidency of the EU. It is worth noting the rather special position that Sweden has on the Korean Peninsula. Sweden is, in fact, represented through three separate missions: an embassy in Seoul, an embassy in Pyongyang and a delegation in Panmunjom at the 38th parallel, the latter because since 1953 Sweden has been a member of the Neutral Nations Supervisory Commission, a body that was established when the ceasefire agreement came into being. Today no less than thirteen EU countries (all except France and Ireland), as well as the European Commission, have established diplomatic relations with North Korea. As late as the fall of 2000, only five EU countries had done so, and among them only Sweden had an embassy in Pyongyang.

One particular event also must be discussed. In December 2000, President Kim Dae Jung visited Stockholm after having received the Nobel Peace Prize in Oslo. During his meeting with Prime Minister Göran Persson, President Kim discussed his visit to Pyongyang and his talks with Chairman Kim Jong Il, stressing the importance of engagement and, in particular, of talking directly with Kim Jong Il, who clearly was in command in North Korea. During his visit to Pyongyang, President Kim had found that a meaningful exchange of views was possible. The Swedish Prime Minister was, according to the President, particularly well placed to pursue such a dialogue with the North Korean leader. A visit to Pyongyang while Sweden was in the presidency of the Union would be a significant event. No commitment was made at the meeting, but during the following months Prime Minister Persson explored the possibilities in consultations with colleagues within the EU, and in early March a preparatory mission was dispatched to Pyongyang and Seoul. The leader of that mission, State Secretary Hans Dahlgren of the Swedish Foreign Ministry, informed the North Koreans that a visit by the Swedish Prime Minister as President of the European Union might be possible provided that four assurances could be given:

1. Could North Korea confirm its commitment to the Joint Declaration signed by the two Korean leaders at the Pyongyang summit?
2. Could the North Korean leader reconfirm his intention to hold a second summit with his South Korean colleague President Kim?
3. Could the North Korean side assure that comprehensive and direct talks would be held between the EU delegation and Chairman Kim Jong Il personally?
4. Could the North Korean side assure that no subject would be excluded *a priori* from the agenda for the talk?

In addition, it was noted that if such an EU delegation were to visit North Korea, it would be accompanied by a large number of journalists.

A few weeks later a special emissary arrived in Stockholm to deliver a message from Chairman Kim to Prime Minister Persson. The message was that the Swedish Prime Minister was welcome to travel to Pyongyang under the conditions requested by the Swedish side. Shortly afterwards, a European Union summit took place in Stockholm. The idea of a high level visit to Pyongyang and Seoul was endorsed by the European leaders.

Meanwhile, the USA had elected a new administration which announced that it would undertake a policy review before any further decisions were made regarding US–North Korean relations. This move meant that an EU initiative would take place under a more complex set of circumstances. Additionally, the inter-Korean dialogue was suspended in March. After President Kim's premature visit to Washington earlier that month, the North Korean side declared that in the light of the new US position and South Korea's dependence on the USA, further inter-Korean meetings would not be meaningful for the time being. In the space of just a few months, the momentum of the inter-Korean summit of June 2000 had faded away. Under such circumstances, it became even more important than before for the EU to proceed in close consultation with Seoul and Washington, which is what happened. It was made perfectly clear that the EU did not have any ambition whatsoever to replace the USA in its strategic dialogue with North Korea. Still, the EU saw a role for itself that was no less important given the change in climate that occurred in the first few months of 2001.

The outcome of the EU visit

A high-level visit to North Korea is no routine affair, and this trip by the EU troika proved to be no exception. When the delegation arrived in Pyongyang on 2 May, no acceptable program had been presented to the preparatory team, probably primarily due to North Korea's obsession with the security of its leader. As it turned out, the EU delegation had five hours of direct talks with Chairman Kim Jong Il, during which the EU side raised all the questions that it had planned to present. Furthermore, each issue was discussed in a way that makes it reasonable to talk about a dialogue in the same way as President Kim had done when he visited Stockholm five months earlier. The talks were meaningful and a number of concrete results were produced.

Chairman Kim reconfirmed North Korea's commitment to the Joint Declaration of June 2000. Furthermore, Chairman Kim explicitly stated that he intended to hold a second summit with President Kim. In fact, he asked the Swedish Prime Minister to "tell his friend Kim Dae Jung" when meeting him in Seoul the following day that Kim Jong Il was looking forward to seeing the President. He said this in a way that suggested that he was looking forward not just to seeing a South Korean president but to engaging with Kim Dae Jung, with whom he had held fruitful talks the previous year. At the same time, it was clear that the talks would not take place any time soon. The Chairman stressed that they had to take place at the right time and had to be well prepared. It still remains to be seen whether the two Kims will meet for a second summit. My guess is that not even Kim Jong Il knows. However, I do believe that the possibility still exists, provided that the US–North Korea dialogue can recommence. The link between the resumption of the US–North Korean dialogue and a second summit was the central theme in Chairman Kim's analysis. So too, it should be added, was the Chairman's message that North Korea did not want to be an enemy of the USA.

A broad range of security issues was discussed during the meeting. Chairman Kim reconfirmed North Korea's commitment to the Agreed Framework Agreement entered into in 1994 between North Korea and the USA. He stressed that North Korea had been "prepared to go all the way" if a visit by President Clinton had materialized. It was impossible to determine the validity of that statement, but it was clear that North Korea felt very uncertain about where the USA was heading with its policy review. The fact that the review would continue for months and that it would not necessarily lead to a resumption of talks was clearly a cause of great frustration. Assertions that a policy review was not necessarily the same as a policy reversal did not sound convincing to the North Korean side.

The most significant outcome of the discussion on security was Chairman Kim's unprompted statement that North Korea would maintain its moratorium on missile testing until 2003, though the moratorium could be reviewed in the light of future developments. The latter was clearly made with reference to the ongoing policy review. The Chairman's reply to questions regarding his country's export of missile technology was considerably less comforting. According to the Chairman, North Korea had no choice but to continue exporting missile technology since it was in dire need of foreign currency. It would, however, be prepared to cease exporting if compensated for the loss of foreign exchange income. A wide range of other issues related to the international security regime was covered, such as the importance of North Korea's signing of the Comprehensive Test Ban Treaty and its full cooperation with the International Atomic Energy Agency.

Economic matters constituted another major subject for discussion. The Chairman recognized that a Soviet-style, centrally planned economy had serious weaknesses and noted that some form of free market economic elements might be required. No one in North Korea had any knowledge of how a market economy functioned. In response to this, the Swedish Prime Minister invited a North Korean delegation to visit Europe to learn how market economies function. In early 2002, such a delegation will visit five European countries.

Prior to the meeting with Chairman Kim, at a meeting with Acting President Kim Jong Nam, Chairman of the Standing Committee of Supreme People's Assembly, the question of human rights was raised and the North Koreans stated that they would be prepared to enter into a dialogue with the European Union on human rights. Such a dialogue could commence as soon as the relationship between the EU and North Korea had become a relationship between equals, through the establishment of diplomatic relations with all EU members as well as the Commission. The agreement to commence a dialogue on human rights was confirmed at the meeting with the Chairman. In fact, the next month a preparatory meeting was held in Brussels between an EU troika and a North Korean delegation. A major part of the meeting was devoted to the UN human rights regime, including North Korea's position *vis-à-vis* key UN covenants on human rights. In connection with the meeting, the delegation visited the Raoul Wallenberg Institute at Lund University in Sweden for a workshop on human rights. Another round of discussions on human rights was held in late October 2001 when an EU troika visited Pyongyang.

No fewer than seventy-five journalists and eight TV crews accompanied the delegation. President Kim, whom the EU delegation met with in Seoul the following day, considered this to be a significant outcome.

The visit constituted the start of a process which promises to be very difficult at times. Still, a worthwhile beginning was made. The North Korean leader showed, no doubt, an interest in breaking North Korea out of its isolation. Still, nothing would be considered second to state security, a stand that makes sustained confidence-building critical to further progress. In essence, the visit was a confidence-building exercise.

Impressions from dealing with North Korea

I have visited Pyongyang on four occasions during the past two years [1999, 2000]. Allow me to share just a few of my impressions.

The foremost objective of the regime is certainly to preserve itself. It would, however, be a mistake not to recognize that the regime genuinely considers the country to be encircled by more or less hostile forces. The pervasiveness of this notion, no doubt continuously fuelled by the regime itself, naturally creates an atmosphere of suspicion. They believe that the outside world wants to undermine the *juche* state. Given this climate, there is naturally a tremendous need to build trust. Doing so is a precondition for progress in any endeavor involving the North Koreans. Based on my experiences I dare say that a certain level of trust can be achieved over time, provided a persistent effort is made.

When North Korean leaders analyse their global situation, there is a strong focus on the United States. The symbol of US predominance is, of course, the presence of US troops in South Korea. However, hatred is not the operating motive. The attitude of the leadership towards the USA appears to be much more complex and clearly there is a strong desire to return to the talks that looked so promising in fall 2000. For a moment a major breakthrough seemed to be within reach. If only that moment could be recreated.

The Joint Declaration of June 2000 is seen as a major event by the leadership. A radically improved situation resulted and the process that was begun is as a rule described as "irreversible." Still, the opportunity for progress in the inter-Korea dialogue is limited as long as the strategic dialogue between North Korea and the United States is halted, and especially when South Korea is considered to have proved to be too dependent on Washington. As a consequence, possibilities to move forward that seem obvious to observers are not taken.

One of the main objectives of the North Korean leadership, with Kim Jong Il in a dominant role, is to break out of its present isolation. The outside world has experience and knowledge that would benefit North Korea. There is a growing interest not only in establishing diplomatic relations with an increasing number of countries but also in sending people abroad to receive training, e.g., in market economics, and to seek such knowledge from Australia, the United Kingdom, Sweden and other "ideologically misguided" countries.

Why is this so? Even though it has never been explicitly acknowledged by the leadership, there appears to be a growing recognition of the fact that the country is facing an economic crisis that not only causes enormous human hardship but also weakens the state at its very core, its capacity to develop and maintain its military apparatus. At the same time there is as yet no real analysis of the deepest causes of the crisis and of what would be needed to recover from it. The severe energy shortage from which the country is suffering is often referred to as *the* reason. Structural reasons, such as the absence of real markets and incentive systems, still are not part of the approved analysis. Hence, even though the nature of the economy has changed dramatically as a consequence of the crisis, no real reforms have occurred. Farmers' markets, which are of undeniable importance in today's North Korea, are allowed to exist but by default rather than as a consequence of explicit policy. What is new is an interest in matters related to reforms. Concepts such as profitability and accounting have become part of the official language, reflecting a search for new approaches. Hence, study tours to Shanghai and North Korean students studying at Australian and European universities. In Sweden, we have witnessed a growing interest in sending people on training missions, an interest to which we have responded positively.

Why is more not happening? A major reason, I believe, is that security comes first, and that bolder steps would potentially require an improved security environment. Chairman Kim is making frequent "on-the-spot inspections" in different parts of the country in an effort to improve the efficiency of the economy, but lacks a macro-reform on which to build those efforts.

How deep is the impasse and who can break it?

The situation today looks much less promising than during the period immediately after the inter-Korean summit. Basically, there is still a stalemate in the two key processes, the one between North Korea and the United States and the one between North Korea and South Korea, even though the latter has been unsuccessfully resumed a couple of times with ministerial meetings held last autumn and the South Korean President's Special Envoy visiting North Korea in April 2002. The consequences of September 11 did not in themselves appear to create a situation in which progress could not have been made.

North Korea made efforts to distance itself from terrorism by announcing that it would sign the UN convention against the financing of terrorism. Further measures along those lines were expected, because the North Korean leadership was probably fully aware of the importance of such measures in the world post-September 11. However, President Bush's labelling of North Korea as part of an axis of evil in the State of the Union Address earlier this year, carried with it an implicit military threat. Apart from its harsh language about the North Korean leadership, the perceived real military threat must have raised the North's already obsessive security concerns to unprecedented levels.

Even though President Bush during his visit to Seoul a couple of months ago reassured Koreans that the United States had no intention of attacking the North militarily, North Korea's paranoid feelings must have been awakened again among the North Korean leadership. Despite all this, there almost certainly still exists an interest in Pyongyang in getting back to the dialogue. Underneath its rhetoric, North Korea knows that continued islolation means continued crisis-management without any possibility of beginning to catch up. During his meetings with President Jiang Zemin and President Putin, as well as on several other occasions, Chairman Kim has been advised to resume the US–North Korean as well as the inter-Korean dialogues. Only the necessary formula for getting back to the negotiating table is missing.

North Korea cannot accept the broadened US agenda, which now includes North Korean ground forces, and a number of unfortunate statements have further complicated the situation. Hopefully, the North Korean leader will analyse the situation anew and decide to test the will of the Bush administration at meetings rather than through exchanging statements that widen the gap, and hopefully Washington will seek to facilitate such a process. In the meantime the EU will continue its efforts to build trust, knowing that real progress will depend on whether the two main processes, the one between the US and North Korea and the one between the two Koreas, can move forward.

Based on my own experiences I would say that it is meaningful to engage and that there really is no other alternative. The current impasse is not, and should not be, the end of the story. Soon, it will be fifty years since the Korean War ended. It is high time to move on.

Note

1 The intervention was updated at the beginning of November 2001. Significant developments that had taken place in the meantime, such as the resumption in September 2001 of the inter-Korean dialogue, have been included in the analysis.

3 Establishment of diplomatic relations between Germany and North Korea

Wolfgang Röhr

Germany takes a special interest in the security situation on the Korean Peninsula. This is not simply because the Declaration that arguably started the recent developments on the Peninsula – a statement which quickly became known as the "Berlin Declaration" – was made by President Kim Dae Jung in Berlin on 9 March 2000. Germany takes a special interest in Korean affairs because it has itself experienced – and is still experiencing – the rewards as well as the problems of reuniting two states with different social systems. We are, of course, aware that the differences between North and South Korea are in many respects – political system, economy, social structure, way of life, access of the population to information about the outside world – much greater than the respective differences between the Federal Republic of Germany and the German Democratic Republic. Last but not least, the German Interest Section in Pyongyang had for many years, along with the Swedish Embassy, been one of only two European Union (EU) member states represented in North Korea.

For several years the foremost aim of Germany's policy with respect to the Korean Peninsula was to promote a lessening of tensions and a gradual improvement of relations between North and South Korea. In particular, we had consistently urged North Korea to start a meaningful dialogue with the South; also to cease any development, production, and proliferation of missile technology and of weapons of mass destruction, and to improve the human rights situation. North Korea had answered by pointing out that these issues could best be discussed after the establishment of diplomatic relations.

During recent years, humanitarian aid from Germany to North Korea has been stepped up. Trade had fallen in the late 1990s; however, trade figures have recently increased dramatically, albeit starting from a fairly low level.

High-level contacts between Germany and North Korea began in spring 2000 when Foreign Minister Paek Nam Sun met State Minister Dr Volmer at the Auswärtiges Amt in Berlin. Dr Volmer then paid a visit to Pyongyang in September 2000. Federal Chancellor Schröder, after meeting South Korean President Kim Dae Jung in Seoul at the Asia-Europe Meeting (ASEM) Summit in October, announced that Germany was ready to establish diplomatic relations with North Korea.

After three days of sometimes difficult negotiations in February 2001, Germany and North Korea established diplomatic relations on 1 March 2001 through an exchange of notes in Berlin. The German Interest Section of the Swedish Embassy in Pyongyang became an Embassy on the same day. Similarly, the North Korean Interest Section of the People's Republic of China's Embassy in Berlin became the North Korean Embassy.

With the exchange of notes, Germany and North Korea jointly agreed on a Protocol which contained improved regulations for the freedom of movement of diplomats, the access of aid organizations to their projects, and the working conditions for German journalists in North Korea and North Korean journalists in Germany. Both sides agreed to hold talks on peace, security, and stability in Europe and North-East Asia as well as on questions of nuclear disarmament and arms control, the non-proliferation of weapons of mass destruction and missile technology. Both sides also agreed to begin a dialogue on human rights questions.

It was the firm intention of the Federal Government to achieve more than just the establishment of diplomatic relations. This made the Federal Republic of Germany one of the EU member states that established relations with North Korea rather later than sooner. We feel vindicated by the success of our negotiations on the Protocol, which in our view led to quite substantial results. Unlike the other EU member states that established relations with North Korea between January 2000 and February 2001, Germany was the only one which already had its interest section in Pyongyang in place: so, for us, there was no need to rush.

As always, the proof of the pudding is in the eating: so far, implementation of the Protocol has for the most part been quite satisfactory. But much more remains to be done, and implementation will have to be improved continually.

Among other things, we are looking at the possibilities of enhanced cooperation with North Korean universities and, in particular, an increase in the number of North Korean students studying in Germany. We also are actively promoting improved cultural exchanges. Humanitarian aid from Germany is set to continue. This year [2001], delivery of several thousand tons of beef from Germany to North Korea is planned.

We will, in close contact with our EU partners, South Korea, Japan and the United States, continue to seek meaningful talks with North Korea on the above questions. We hope that such talks will contribute to an early resumption of a substantial dialogue between North and South Korea and also between North Korea, on the one hand, and Japan and the United States, on the other. In the regular contacts that we have in Pyongyang and Berlin, we continuously urge North Korea to improve its relations with its neighbouring states. We also stand ready to help North Korea to introduce urgently needed reforms in the country itself, if and when Pyongyang is ready to accept such aid. We believe that this approach is best suited to lead to an early integration of North Korea into the international community, stability, and security on the Korean Peninsula, enhanced living conditions for the people in the North, and an improvement in the condition of human rights.

4 Significance of Chinese economic success to North Korea

Myong Chol Kim

Introduction

It is often claimed that the Democratic People's Republic of Korea (DPRK) has yet to open up to the outside world. That is a mistaken view. North Korea has already opened up, but the United States has refused to open up to North Korea. The Americans continue to try to keep North Korea out of the world economy. America's interest is obviously not in helping North Korea open up but in stifling its development.

Some people allege that the *juche* idea eschews interaction with the world economy and identifies with socialism. This also is a mistaken view. *Juche* neither identifies with any given socio-political economic system nor does it reject market-economy practices. *Juche* is an open-ended, flexible, philosophical thought that favors doing whatever is good for human beings and dismissing whatever is bad. *Juche* totally supports accepting the positive aspects of capitalism and market-economy practices.

Lessons from the Chinese experience

This conference is seeking ways to assist the DPRK in further economic interaction with the world economy. The North Koreans are committed to adopting positive aspects of market-economy practices and making them part of what they call "Korean-style socialism." There are two market-economy experimental models, from which North Korea could learn a great deal: the Russian and Chinese models. The two offer key lessons. The Chinese economic reform has been successful enough to elevate China to the position of the world's factory. China has replaced Japan as the foremost trading partner of the United States.

Despite all the North Korean rhetoric, the successful Chinese model carries three important messages for North Korea as it grapples with its economy. First, normalized relations with the United States are essential for successful economic reform involving the introduction of market-economy practices. Experience shows beyond a doubt that the bid to introduce market-economy practices is doomed unless there is a cessation of the American policy of hostility toward North Korea.

The Chinese embarked on a capitalist-oriented path in July 1979 after full diplomatic relations were established between China and the United States. Embassies were set up in their capitals in March 1979. China was granted most-favored-nation status, which entitled the Chinese to full access to the American market.

Second, strong leadership displayed by the ruling party and the government is critical for the effective introduction and operation of market-economy practices. The economic reform launched by the previous Russian government was an utter fiasco because it lacked strong leadership. Political and economic anarchy prevailed, attributable to the disbanding of the once-powerful Soviet Communist Party as the ruling party. The government created in its wake was so weak and discredited that it was unable to keep things in line.

China is totally different. The Chinese Communist Party and the Chinese government remained fully in power. Their leadership was strengthened so that they could effectively guide the expanding market-economy practices to take root and grow. They were able to maintain discipline, law and order, while keeping the expanding market-economy practices on the right track.

Third, the European role is important when American businesses stay away because of pressure from Washington. This is the case particularly with the Chinese. The otherwise effective European role has been rendered ineffective by political chaos in Russia. Europe also is in a position to serve as a source of technological know-how, expertise, training, equipment and funding, which both the United States and Japan refuse to provide.

What matters most is that the ruling authorities of the country concerned should be firmly in charge. The ruling authorities, the ruling party and the government must be strong enough to dictate the economic reform and manage the introduction and operation of market-economy practices in a fashion suited to the local conditions.

Necessary conditions for market experiment in North Korea

To sum up, a successful North Korean experiment with market-economy practices calls for three prerequisites to be satisfied:

1 ending hostile relations and establishing full diplomatic relations between Pyongyang and Washington;
2 encouraging increased European involvement in the North Korean economy;
3 strengthening the leadership of the ruling Workers Party of Korea and the DPRK government.

Of these conditions, the second and third have already been met. In particular the strong leadership of the Workers Party of Korea and the DPRK government ensures that there will be no Russian-style chaos or economic reform failure in Pyongyang. What is most important for a successful North Korean economic reform is to satisfy the first requirement.

A serious bid was made to emulate the Chinese example, but the DPRK put the cart before the horse. While still in a state of war with the United States, the North Koreans began to introduce capitalistic practices in September 1984, hoping that this would attract foreign investors.

Common sense suggested that the Americans would welcome the North Korean experiment and encourage American, European and Japanese corporations to invest in North Korea. However, the North Koreans were wrong. The Americans preferred the Cold War to capitalism in this case. The Americans departed significantly from their fundamental policy of helping spread market-economy practices and discouraged the rest of the world from getting involved in the North Korean experiment.

Active American endorsement might have produced the desired results of making the Rajin-Sonbong economic zone a success and inducing the DPRK authorities to establish similar zones in other regions of the country. However, the Cold War animosity toward North Korea shaped the American foreign policy.

The United States still refuses to end more than fifty years of hostile relations between the two countries and sign a peace treaty. The US government still imposes economic sanctions on the DPRK and keeps its name on the list of those countries that allegedly sponsor terrorism. This means that it is not Pyongyang but Washington that is blocking the introduction of market-economy practices in North Korea, thus refusing to allow improved relations between the two countries, and enhanced peace and security on the Korean Peninsula.

The US sanctions on North Korean exports

Today the US officials say that they have lifted some major economic sanctions imposed on North Korea but allege that lifting sanctions is of little benefit to the North Koreans because the DPRK has nothing to sell to the American market. This is not really the case.

A typical example in point is magnesia clinker, a key material used for fireproofing purposes. North Korea is a major exporter of magnesia clinker, which sells at 78 dollars per ton, while the Chinese product is priced at 80 dollars. American buyers prefer the North Korean product to the Chinese, but end up choosing the duty-free Chinese product because the US authorities levy a 17 percent duty on the North Korean export, making it much less competitive in the American market.

Textiles offer another example. Today the DPRK dominates the inexpensive business suit division of the Japanese market with a market share of approximately 70 percent. For instance, the suit I am wearing was made in the DPRK. I paid 50 dollars for it in Tokyo, a very reasonable price for high quality. The US tariff for North Korean-made business suits ranges from a minimum 50 percent to a maximum 300 percent, completely shutting them out of the American market.

The most scandalous thing about the American sanctions is that the North Korean businessmen are denied dollar-denominated transactions with foreign countries, especially for those transfers involving American banks. Any dollar amount sent abroad by a North Korean company is subject to confiscation by the American authorities before it reaches the foreign recipient, if its transfer involves an American bank along the way. In most deals with foreign trade partners, the North Korean companies have had to convert their dollars to non-American currencies, such as the German mark the French franc, or the British pound, and from now on euros. Each conversion is a money-losing operation for the North Koreans.

A hard fact of life is that these continuing American sanctions keep the willing North Koreans from tasting the honey of capitalism, the market-economy system. Once you know a taste of this sweet, you will never forget it and will likely try to taste it again. The North Koreans are entitled to equal economic opportunity and should never be handicapped in experimenting with market-economy practices.

North Korea is a tiny island in the seas of capitalism. The North Koreans not only have to learn how to swim but also how to fish in the capitalist seas. But the United States is doing all it can to deny the North Koreans access to expertise about swimming and fishing as well as the latest fishing gear and fishing boats. The United States, in the eyes of North Korea, appears to be determined to drown the North Koreans.

As a sign of its market economy-oriented ambition, North Korea has had as many as 500 young people trained abroad, including in Australia. Economic institutions and universities, including the highly prestigious Kim Il Sung University, have created centers or courses for training students in business administration, international business law, and other market-economy topics. Kim Il Sung University educates visiting scholars from Choson University in Tokyo which is operated by a pro-North Korean organization. The DPRK plans to educate an increasing number of technocrats versed in capitalist business operations.

European countries are now encouraging their major corporations to establish business relations with North Korean entities, including investment in North Korea and technical training. A number of major European corporations have opened offices in Pyongyang, including the German firm, Siemens, and the Swiss ABB. The United Kingdom and other European countries have agreed to offer scholarships to students from North Korea. A plan is under consideration to provide funds and facilities for the training of North Korean electronics engineers. The North Koreans have had a positive reaction to the proposed program.

A key program in Kim Jong Il's economic plan is establishing a "Silicon Valley" in North Korea. This involves developing a powerful, indigenous electronics industry capable of vaulting his country to the status of an economic power at minimum cost. Special senior high schools for future scientists and computer engineers, established in every province, enroll the brightest and best students. Their graduates are exempted from military service in order to be admitted to science and technological departments of universities. Most graduates from senior high schools join the armed forces or work with factories before they are allowed into universities.

These efforts have already resulted in the emergence of North Korea as one of the leading computer software creators. National and local software competitions are held periodically. Some products are generating a strong demand in the Japanese market. A Japanese Internet software house has commissioned a North Korean company to develop a trilingual browser with simultaneous translations of Korean, Japanese, and English into any of the three. Samsung Electronics operates a joint venture with North Korea in Beijing in the hope of developing new computer software with engineers from Pyongyang. A major electronics park is being developed in the suburbs of Pyongyang as a joint venture with South Korea. A Korean-Chinese institute of technology in Yanji, China, plans to establish a postgraduate school for computer science in Pyongyang in 2002 with undergraduate courses scheduled to begin two years later.

North Korean companies assemble TV sets and other home electronic appliances for export to the South Korean market. North Korean companies also are producing electronic components for Japanese companies. There is a strong likelihood that some of the Japanese computers you are using at the office or in the home may have parts made in the DPRK.

Benefits from improving US–North Korean relations

These are a mere foreshadow of what the DPRK will look like in the wake of its eventual full partnership in the world economy. But this will come only after the first of the previously described three prerequisites for successful economic reform is satisfied. In other words, the North Korean economy will stand to benefit most from the termination of more than fifty years of hostile relations between the two enemies, the DPRK and the United States. There are three major benefits that deserve attention.

In the first place, at long last the North Korean population will be liberated from the xenophobic, fortress mentality that has shaped the North Korean mindset. Spiritual freedom from many years of frustration will drive the North Korean population to a dramatic new quest for economic prosperity.

Second, the economy will be emancipated from several decades of war financing. Manpower, billions of military dollars, and all other resources will be released for economic reconstruction. Creating a vital infrastructure for economic modernization will be the primary task, with outdated plants being retooled and new ones built.

The third benefit will be the availability of dollar-denominated transactions in trade with other countries, an infusion of a huge amount of foreign funds in loans and investment, technology transfer, and access to the American market. This will revitalize the DPRK's relationship with the world economy and increase the foreign currency holdings North Korea greatly needs.

A key question here is when the first requirement will be met. The answer is "by 2003." It is widely known that the United States is obliged to complete and transfer to North Korea two light-water nuclear reactors for power generation. The United States will not be able to ignore this obligation, unless it is prepared to go to the extraordinary length of waging war against North Korea or letting the North Koreans emerge as a declared nuclear power with intercontinental ballistic missile (ICBM) capability.

With these nightmarish scenarios discounted, the most palatable option for the Bush administration is to settle for a package solution with North Korea: acceptance of the long-standing North Korean demands to end the hostile relations, signing a peace treaty, establishing full diplomatic relations, removing North Korea from the list of those countries that allegedly sponsor terrorism, and granting it most-favored-nation status.

5 Recent developments on the Korean Peninsula

William J. Taylor

Of course, the world is a somewhat different place than it was when I gave my brief presentation on 27 August 2001 about recent changes on the Korean Peninsula. In one way or another, governments, organizations, and peoples have been shocked by America's tragedy at the hands of terrorists and have turned their attention to the new "War on Terrorism."

However, what I had to say then remains basically the same, i.e., that there have been few significant changes from the chill in North–South Korean relations and United States–Democratic People's Republic of Korea (DPRK) relations that settled in during the first three months of 2001. Conservatives in Seoul and Washington were successful in undermining the progress of the "sunshine policy" of the Kim Dae Jung Administration and the policy of constructive engagement of North Korea under the Clinton administration. Notably, they have done so without offering safe or sane alternative policies. Generally, they have called for greater reciprocity and transparency from Pyongyang which is neither a policy nor a strategy.

Safe? Sane? We can no longer afford to return to the old "carrot and stick" diplomacy "demanding" greater, faster reciprocity, and transparency – risking a return to times of high North–South tensions. It is at such times of high tension that wars historically have begun by accident or miscalculation. We can no longer risk the kinds of crises along the demilitarized zone (DMZ) that have been all too common over the years. Why? Times have changed, beginning with the 1993 No-dong 1 test in the Sea of Japan through the Taepo-1 test over Japan in 1998. These DPRK missile capabilities, combined with what we know about their conventional forces and weapons of mass destruction, should make a North–South war well nigh unthinkable. Although the United States–Republic of Korea (ROK) Combined Forces Command would quickly and utterly devastate North Korea, it would be a "Pyrrhic" victory, given the hundreds of thousands of casualties that would be sustained by South Koreans, Americans, and Japanese.

The "sunshine policy," behind the larger objective of North–South reconciliation and much longer-range goal of unification, is essentially a patient diplomatic process. Here regular North–South communications can produce rapprochement aimed at crisis prevention or management while proceeding toward such tangible accomplishments as the Kumgangsan project, the Kyungi rail link-up, an industrial park at Kaesong, and much more. "We" (Seoul, Washington and Tokyo) had a head of steam until the late winter/early spring of 2001. What went wrong and why?

There is seldom a single explanation for any major international event. Let us examine two major reasons for the Korean decline. The first is that the Bush administration went adrift many months ago in its strategy toward the Korean Peninsula. In February 2001 Secretary of State Colin Powell stated that our policy toward North Korea basically would be to pick up where the Clinton administration left off in its policy of "constructive engagement," working in harmony with Seoul and Tokyo. That policy had built up a head of steam signaled by Secretary Madeline Albright's trip to Seoul and a return visit to Washington by Vice-Marshall Cho. President Bush promptly pulled the rug out from under Secretary of State, Powell, announcing that he did not trust the North's leadership to keep its commitments and that our policy toward North Korea would undergo a thorough policy review.

That was not the end of the problems. In mid-summer 2001, the Bush administration communicated to Pyongyang via Ambassador Pritchard and the DPRK UN Mission what the United States was prepared to discuss in renewed talks, adding arms reduction along the DMZ to the Clinton agenda. That move reflected a stunning lack of awareness by the Bush administration regarding the leadership in Pyongyang. The tenure of North Korea's government depends fundamentally on military capability until major political, economic, and psychological changes are well under way. Those changes had been moving along slowly even in North-South military confidence-building relations near the DMZ, or so my close friends in the ROK military were telling me. The complex sets of issues surrounding arms reductions should not have been placed squarely on the agenda by the Bush administration, but should have been eased onto the agenda later by the government in Seoul. The adverse reaction from Pyongyang was predictable.

A second explanation advanced by some of my respected, conservative Korean friends is that Pyongyang began backing off from the "sunshine policy" before the June summit. Evidence? Kim Jong Il's two trips to Beijing in May 2000 and January 2001. His strategy was to join a growing People's Republic of China (PRC)–Russian Federation (RF) coalition against the United States and take advantage of their political and military support while conceding little and getting everything from Seoul, Washington, and Tokyo.

How about an explanation that concludes there is some validity to both scenarios? Of course, Pyongyang is playing hardball and trying to leverage everything it can to keep the present leadership in power. The country must gather all the economic and humanitarian assistance it can to alleviate its desperate situation before conceding what it considers too much in the name of North–South "reconciliation." Of course, for Seoul, its allies and friends, high monetary and psychological costs are involved to prevent war and move toward reconciliation through spending for a strong defense, providing aid, funding family repatriations, and negotiating low-profit business agreements. But, do the conservatives have a saner or safer alternative? If so, let's see it in a comprehensive study with clear recommendations, not partisan political speeches.

There is hope. After months of policy paralysis, the Bush administration finally got back on the right track generally with Colin Powell's statements that the United States is ready to resume talks without preconditions, strongly supports the sunshine policy and urges Chairman Kim to hold a return summit in Seoul before the end of 2001. Hopefully, the message has been sent very quietly to Pyongyang that we did not intend to assign conventional arms reductions the same priority as talks about missiles/missile proliferation and nuclear verification.

Pyongyang has begun to respond again very cautiously in a direction favorable for the sunshine policy. That direction will be influenced by America's recent tragedy. They cannot overlook Russian and Chinese pledges to cooperate in one way or another with America in a "War against Terrorism." Pyongyang has expressed its own disdain for international terrorism. What did they mean by that? My interpretation is that Pyongyang realized that any instigation of or cooperation with terrorist acts brings them bad results. They want to be removed from the US "list of terrorist states." While working to secure the understanding and support of our Japanese ally, Washington should remove North Korea from the list and, in the evolving context of a totally new kind of war, strongly support Seoul's lead on the "sunshine policy." Partisan politics on major international security issues has just disappeared in America – and the same should occur in South Korea, the coming presidential election notwithstanding.

6 Progress and prospects of economic cooperation between South and North Korea

In Je Rhee

Today the world is undergoing rapid change. With the explosive development of communication and information networks, the globalization process has accelerated at an even greater speed. Now more than ever, the world has become a borderless global village. No country can stand alone in this new world, and every country must operate in a spirit of cooperation and fair competition with the others. Changes in one country spill across geopolitical borders, affecting not only regional neighbors but also the entire global community.

In light of this process towards globalization, the political situation in Noth-East Asia takes on unprecedented importance. The political environment in this region has greatly changed in the past fifty years. As you are all aware, there has been a truce between South and North Korea since the end of the Korean War. However, relations have improved greatly, with the historic South–North summit held in June 2000 acting as the turning point in rapprochement and dialogue. Since that summit, relations between the two have made rapid progress, particularly in the economic and interpersonal arenas. As a result, though inter-Korea relations are currently at a standstill for many reasons, we are confident that exchanges will continue to progress and improve in the long term.

At this point, however, it seems that North Korea's policy orientation towards South Korea has not fundamentally changed. From our viewpoint, North Korea continues to focus on increasing its military strength. Therefore, South Korea should maintain its military readiness so it can respond to any armed provocation by the North. On the other hand, we also see that the North is interested in engaging in economic cooperation with the South. North Korea will be able to escape from its poverty and develop its economy when it receives the financial support it needs from the South and the international community. However, North Korea should know that this kind of support will come only if outsiders see it sincerely seeking peace. In particular, reducing weapons of mass destruction and cutting back on conventional weapons that are deployed in forward positions close to Seoul are important elements of the détente.

While the North has not accepted the major proposals suggested by South Korea to foster peace on the Korean Peninsula and promote rapprochement and cooperation between the two Koreas, this attitude may change somewhat in the future. There are a number of promising signs. First, the North Korean leader

Kim Jong Il visited both China and Russia. We see these visits as evidence that North Korea is hoping to make the transition to become a state where the economy becomes more open while the governmental system remains intact. Second, with a US administration under President George W. Bush, there is the possibility that the North will try to improve its cooperation and relations with the international community. Third, there are signs, as seen through various meetings and agreements, that the North is rapidly moving to prepare for the reform and opening of their country, both of which are necessary in reviving its economy. We believe that this would be similar to China's approach, as that country has been slowly opening up to the global community over the years.

Change and reform by the North will be essential in bringing an era of peace and prosperity on the Korean Peninsula. The peaceful unification of the divided Korean Peninsula is the ardent desire not only of 70 million Koreans, but of the entire international community. To achieve this, we are urging North Korea to actively participate in the cooperation program as suggested by the South.

Now is the critical time for the world community to support peace-building on the Korean Peninsula. Improvements in the US–North Korean dialogues will play a key role in encouraging the North to participate in and adapt to the changing world environment. Along with the hoped-for improvement in US–North Korean relations, the signing of a peace treaty between South and North Korea would contribute greatly to peace and stability in Noth-East Asia. For these reasons, the South Korean government must continue to promote mutual cooperation between South Korea, the United States, China, Japan and Russia.

Economic cooperation between the South and North began in 1989 as simple trade, which developed into commissioned manufacturing trade in 1992. In 2000, the volume of trade between South and North Korea exceeded US$400 million, evidence that economic cooperation between the South and North has moved well beyond those first steps. As a result, we anticipate that the types of goods being traded will gradually expand beyond the agricultural and marine products and textiles manufacturing which currently account for the bulk of two-way trade. Further goods for trade would include high value-added industries such as electricity, electronics and automobiles.

Beyond this, we now urge North Korea to follow through on projects that were agreed upon with the South. These include the initiation of construction work on an industrial complex in Gaesung and restoration of the Kyungui railroad line. We also would like to see the firm establishment of the Kumkang Mountains overland tourism project and implementation of the four major issues, including the investment guarantee agreement, that were signed in 2000. Therefore, to build on the momentum of these agreements, we once again would like to urge North Korea to sincerely and wholeheartedly engage in these four endeavors that have been agreed upon by both parties.

We also see great potential for future economic cooperation in the information technology and software industries. Recently, the South Korean economy successfully overcame the Asian crisis of 1997 through painful restructuring and reform. Currently, we are facing economic difficulty due to the deterioration of the global economy. However, I strongly believe that we will be able to restore solid economic growth with the recovery of the global economy, including those of the United States and Japan. As a result, I anticipate that trade between South and North Korea will expand significantly within the next few years.

In order to assist North Korea's economy, the international community, as well as South Korea, should engage in economic cooperation with the North. Support from neighboring countries, such as the United States, China, Japan and Russia, is absolutely essential. We also see the participation and assistance of non-governmental, international organizations as playing an important and necessary role. Organizations such as the International Monetary Fund (IMF), the World Bank, and the Asian Development Bank can help to induce reform in North Korea as well as defray unification expenses on the Korean Peninsula. However, North Korea should be aware that assistance from and membership in these organizations are contingent upon resolution of nuclear missile issues with the South and the United States. North Korea is encouraged to increase transparency and allow in-depth assessments of its own economy.

In 1995, North Korea formally requested humanitarian assistance from the United Nations after severe flooding. Since then, the UN has continuously provided aid to the North. Currently, economic assistance to North Korea remains primarily in the form of food assistance due to a lack of support for other projects. Therefore, to prevent another food crisis and to resolve fundamental economic problems in the North, the establishment of an international cooperative system is essential. The system should be established on trust from the international community and a promise from North Korea for responsibility and transparency.

I believe that the transformation of international assistance (now seen mostly as an avenue of providing food aid) into an international cooperative system will be a positive step towards renewing the North Korean economy. If the North is willing to accept and abide by the rules and regulations set by the international community, to increase transparency of its own economic system, and to construct a sound institutional environment in which foreign companies can freely invest, then opportunities will only continue to grow. This would allow the international community to focus on expanding the infrastructure of the North through the construction of railways, roads, and communication networks. The end result would be to improve the quality of life of the North Koreans through economic development.

The advent of a unified Korea is consistent with the US policy of achieving stability and peace in Noth-East Asia. Both South Korea and the United States are well aware how important it is to achieve peaceful unification in the future. We also are well aware that, considering the current security structure on the peninsula, policies toward the North may not succeed without mutual cooperation between South Korea and the United States. If there are any differing viewpoints or perspectives, both countries should make ongoing efforts to reconcile those views.

There is a great deal of hope for the new millennium with regard to the Korean Peninsula, as well as concern over the continuing development of inter-Korean relations. I strongly believe that in continuing their economic cooperation and strengthening their alliance, South Korea and the United States can meet head-on the challenge of opening up the North Korean economy.

Let me close by saying that I strongly urge the international community to actively support efforts made by the South Korean government to lay the foundation for a peaceful unification based on strong national security. Just as readily, I also would like to urge countries to help increase rapprochement and cooperation between the South and the North. Finally, I urge and expect North Korea to actively and positively cooperate with the South's endeavors. With these factors in place, we all come that much closer to a vision of that borderless global village, firmly established on the principles of peace and prosperity.

Part II

The North Korean economy

7 The potential future role for the multilateral development banks on the Korean Peninsula

Bradley O. Babson

Introduction

North Korea is not a member of the World Bank nor the Asian Development Bank (ADB). If North Korea joins these institutions in the future, it would become eligible for both non-lending and lending services provided by these organizations to developing country members. There also has been a growing debate in recent years about the proper future role for the multilateral development banks (MDBs) in an era of spreading globalization and intransigent poverty. Against this backdrop, it is timely to ask what role the MDBs might usefully play in the future on the Korean Peninsula to support the emergence of North Korea into the international economic system after decades of isolation and to facilitate the gradual integration of the economies of the two Koreas as they pursue reconciliation and eventual unification. In answering this question, it is important to take into account both the special features of the Korean situation and the changing shareholder expectations of MDB policies and activities. Shaping an effective role for the MDBs will be a significant challenge for these institutions, the two Koreas, and the international community, and I hope that this chapter can make a contribution to the process.[1]

At the outset, I would like to stress that while lending resources from the World Bank and the ADB could have a significant long-term impact on the North Korean economy and regional integration, the non-lending services that they offer should prove even more helpful. The ability of the development banks to provide policy advice, technical assistance, and knowledge services, and also to convene international meetings for discussion, would most likely be called upon before they began their own lending. These services could become an important ongoing part of their activities in assisting North Korea and in supporting inter-Korean initiatives.

The special conditions on the Korean Peninsula

Developments in the past two years have led to a situation where it is conceivable to imagine the Korean Peninsula absorbed by the tasks of reconciliation and integration of North Korea into the international community. An important step was the inter-Korean summit of June 2000 where the objectives of peaceful reconciliation and gradual deepening of inter-Korean ties were affirmed by the leaders of the two Koreas. Along with this thaw in Korean relations, there has been a lessening of North Korea's isolation in the international community through normalization of relations with most of Europe and Asia and advances in dialogue with the United States and Japan on issues of regional security and weapons of mass destruction. While the change in the US government in early 2001 caused a recalibration and delay in dialogue on these security issues, the momentum for fundamental change is firmly in place and is unlikely to revert to the pre-summit status quo. While progress in defining a new peace structure will dominate the process of change on the Korean Peninsula, economic engagement will become increasingly critical for advancing reconciliation and forming a foundation for durable stability and prosperity for the Korean people.

Two basic challenges face the two Koreas as they move forward. One is to address the enormous size difference between the two economies. The initial strategy must be to help North Korea stabilize its economic contraction and then to set the economy on a path of long-term sustainable growth with the objective of narrowing the gap over time. To meet this challenge, North Korea must make changes in its internal economic policies and management in order to make best use of resources for development and to expand economic relations with other countries, including not only South Korea, but also China, Japan, Russia, and countries outside Noth-East Asia. The second challenge facing the two Koreas is to begin a gradual integration of the economies of two countries with very different economic systems. Administrative mechanisms for working on inter-Korean economic issues have already been established, an initial agenda has been set, and some tangible successes have been achieved. The pause in recent months induced by the US policy review and delay in resumption of US–North Korean dialogue should not obscure these significant accomplishments.

The ability of the two Koreas to meet these challenges depends in the first instance on the maintenance of a political environment supportive of inter-Korean reconciliation. This requires not only sustained political will within the leadership of the two countries and domestic popular support, but also satisfaction of the concerns of major powers on conditions for regional stability and security beyond the Korean Peninsula. Beyond these basic political requirements, the two Koreas face a number of obstacles before they can successfully meet the economic challenges:

- *Resource constraints.* North Korea does not have the resources necessary for capital investment in public infrastructure, especially to cover the rebuilding of the electric power system and the transport network. South Korea does not have the economic might to provide these resources on its own. Thus the two Koreas will require financial support from the international community.
- *Knowledge constraints.* North Korea does not have the knowledge of market economics nor the international experience needed to shape and manage the economic policies that will address its basic difficulties. North Korea also has little understanding of the workings of the international economic and

financial system and thus must develop trust in the fairness of the system and also in the intentions and advice of foreign economic partners.

- *Ongoing economic reforms.* South Korea still faces significant challenges in corporate restructuring and strengthening of its financial sector. Problems in the South Korean economy and delayed reform efforts can have a direct impact on the North's progress in overcoming its own problems as the two economies become more inter-linked. Looking ahead, both Koreas will have to work on economic policy and management reforms while trying to bring their economies more closely together. Information exchange and joint decision-making mechanisms will be needed and must be linked to sound political reforms and institution building.
- *Concerns of foreign investors.* Foreign investors will not provide significant financing for industrial or commercial ventures in North Korea without more transparency in economic and financial information, a legal code that respects foreign interests and is enforced, a financial system that can accommodate the needs of foreign partners, and behavior that conforms to normal business practice in negotiating and implementing international business agreements. Country and political risk factors will also deeply affect the attitude of investors. This is true for South Korean investors and for foreign investors in general. While there may be some temptation to make politically motivated investments in North Korea, and some risk that the South Korean government might grant subsidies or guarantees to encourage investment, ultimately private investment will need to be commercially and economically viable if it is going to be sustainable.
- *Concerns of donors.* Donor countries are not going to be willing to shift current North Korean financial support from humanitarian aid to significant amounts of development assistance without certain assurances. They will expect that North Korea will use these resources to attend to the basic needs of the people and to improve the commercial economy and will not divert resources into maintaining a high military profile and expenditures that exceed reasonable self-defense requirements. This is a domestic political issue in South Korea and it is a foreign policy issue for countries that have normalized relations with North Korea but wish to support a reduction in tensions, not a rearming of North Korea.

To support the two Koreas in a long-term process of overcoming these difficulties and achieving the desired objectives, the international community is faced with challenges unlike situations faced in other parts of the world. Other states divided by war in the past century – notably Germany and Vietnam – achieved political unification before attempting economic integration. To embark on a process that is both gradual and fueled by progress on the economic front is fraught with uncertainties for which there are no obvious historical guides. Experiences of other countries in coping with transitions of various kinds will be helpful, but offer no prescriptions for management of the Korean situation.

Given the complex interactions of economic and political factors, it is likely that the reconciliation process will be marked by deliberation and experimentation, or what the Chinese call "crossing the river by feeling the stones." Debates about policy and strategy, both on the Korean Peninsula and more widely within the international community, will need to be thoughtful, modest, and adaptable. After decades of military stand-off and mutual suspicion, shifting to respectful dialogue and shaping shared strategies for managing change pose a great challenge for both the Koreans and the international community. But this challenge must be met if a gradualist process is going to be successful.

Traditional role of the MDBs and the reform agenda

Historically, the core competencies of the MDBs have been to provide advice on economic policies, technical assistance for institution building, and finance for long-term economic development projects. Rehabilitation of the infrastructure is probably the oldest competency and many of the MDB business processes were defined by the requirements of large infrastructure projects, mainly in power and transport. Over the years the mandate of the MDBs has expanded to include social development, environmental protection, private sector development, poverty alleviation, structural adjustment, debt workouts, transition from centrally planned to market economies, and strengthening of institutions needed for good governance – including public administration, legal systems, and financial systems. Most recently, attention is being given to knowledge management, the digital divide, and efforts to integrate the country's complex development agenda under the concept of a comprehensive development framework.

Also, the MDB methods of working and decision-making have increasingly stressed the importance of transparency and good governance in both the public and private sectors, reflecting growing demands for accountability by shareholders and international civil society. In addition to requiring more rigorous standards for ensuring transparent competitive bidding for procurement of goods and services under contracts financed by MDB projects, social and environmental protection safeguards have been elaborated in recent years, all of which place considerable demands on borrowing countries. Broadened responsibilities for aid coordination and building of partnerships in the donor community for individual country programs and regional initiatives have accompanied the expansion of these mandates in order to promote coordinated policy dialogue, build consensus for assistance strategies, and manage more efficiently the complexities of the development assistance business.

Much of the current debate about MDB reform hinges on their effectiveness in reducing poverty and responding to financial and humanitarian crises that have accompanied the growing globalization and local conflicts that have erupted in the aftermath of the Cold War. New approaches at the forefront of the global agenda include debt forgiveness, creation of global funds, such as the one recently announced to combat HIV/AIDS, and growing appreciation of the linkages of economic development to the issues of human security. Also under discussion are questions about MDB priorities and inconsistencies and overlaps among the MDBs themselves. The reality is that the development agenda has continuously become more complex and demanding in response to global and regional developments. Ongoing MDB reform must adapt to shifting perceptions of global priorities and issues of greatest concern to vocal stakeholders while designing responses to the diverse conditions that confront different countries and regions of the world. The challenge in Korea is how best to draw upon the knowledge and competencies of the MDBs to support the unusual challenges facing the peninsula. Yet, at the same time, expectations must be relaxed so that the perfect does not become the enemy of the good in a situation where North Korea will need some time to adjust to present global standards.

Shaping a role for the future

The potential role for the MDBs on the Korean Peninsula is multifaceted. The overarching objective should be to support the long-term interests of both Koreas and contribute to building a positive environment for managing economic and social change. MDBs can be most helpful by demonstrating broad multilateral commitment to helping implement a Korean-led process and by bringing objectivity and fair-mindedness to the tasks of analyzing issues, building consensus for strategies and actions, and solving practical problems. This will ensure the overall process of inter-Korean reconciliation is advanced and a stable framework is maintained for economic development and integration. Because taking political considerations into account in the actions of MDBs is prohibited by their Articles of Agreement, the political context for inter-Korean reconciliation and reunification must be guided through other means. But the MDB's mandates should be consistent with and supportive of political developments on the peninsula, and the means used to monitor and adapt MDB programs to these political developments should be designed so that the MDB support is appropriately determined. Mechanisms and processes for coordinating political and economic decision-making will be needed, and will likely require the creation of new structures for political cooperation by the two Koreas and the international community. This would be an important topic to discuss in future inter-Korean meetings and with their dialogue partners.

The MDBs are likely to focus their future role and activities in the following areas:

- economic assessment and development strategy;
- education and training;
- mobilization of capital;
- social adjustment;
- environmental management;
- governance;
- harmonizing and integrating the two Korean systems.

A necessary aspect of any future MDB activity with North Korea will be the creation of counterpart groups within the North Korean policy-making and bureaucratic apparatus. The development of working relations will require familiarization activities and informal contacts beyond the current limited exposure of the MDBs to the North Korean government.

Economic assessment and development strategy

The MDBs together with the International Monetary Fund (IMF) will want to begin with economic assessment activities in North Korea. This foundation work is necessary to establish effective working relations, engage in substantive policy dialogue, determine priorities for future assistance, and build confidence in the MDBs in the minds of the North Korean leadership, South Korea, and the international community.

If there is one central lesson gained from more than fifty years of economic development experience since the Bretton Woods Institutions were created, it is that putting money into countries that have poor macro-economic policies and management skills does not yield good economic development. Money is wasted and countries end up with unsustainable debt service obligations. In the case of North Korea, this represents a great danger. North Korea's pattern of behavior in recent years seems to reflect a strategy of seeking external resources while resisting internal economic reform or openness. This strategy will not produce the kind of economic development that North Korea needs.

The cornerstone of the relationship of the IMF and MDBs with their client countries is the monitoring of macro-economic performance and engaging in policy dialogue and technical assistance to help countries shape sound policies and improve their management capacities. A stable macro-economic environment is crucial for attracting foreign investment, maintaining access to international financial markets, and lowering the cost of external borrowing. The regular Article IV Consultations that the IMF conducts with all of its members are a primary vehicle for monitoring and discussing how to improve macro-economic stability. The World Bank and the ADB both frequently participate in the IMF Consultations and would expect to do so in the North Korean situation. Both the World Bank and the ADB supplement this by preparing economic and sector reports that put longer-term development issues and strategies in the context of prudent macro-economic management. These reports form the basis for dialogue on overall development strategy and sector development strategies that leads to adoption of new policies, institutional development, and investment planning. Beginning a series of such studies and initiating research and technical assistance to improve information needed for good policy and program planning will likely be an early priority for the MDBs in North Korea. Establishing a baseline through a living standards measurement survey or similar instrument on which to evaluate progress over time will also be a useful contribution.

North Korea certainly will need to debate and adopt a new development strategy for the future. A major task for the MDBs and the IMF in the initial stage of their relations will be to help shape this debate in ways that will be seen to be objective and constructive without triggering resistance to open-minded discussion of issues and options. It is likely that the more outward orientation of the North Korean economy will be a central issue and this will require participation of North Korea's future economic partners. The debate on strategy will evolve as more information and analysis become available and as initial efforts to introduce changes are evaluated.

Education and training

Perhaps the greatest drawback to North Korea's ability to design and manage new economic policies and programs is the lack of knowledge of basic economics, finance, and commercial practices among policy-makers, technocrats, and enterprise managers. Also, while North Korea has a well-educated labor force and highly skilled technicians in some fields, lack of access to global knowledge and best practices inhibits the potential of the North Korean people to improve their lives and modernize their society and economy. Helping North Koreans gain access to global knowledge and experience will be one of the most valuable contributions for the MDBs.

Educational programs

The World Bank Institute (WBI) provides a rich array of learning services, including designing and delivering courses and seminars, promoting knowledge networks and communities of practice, and providing policy and technical advice. The IMF Institute also provides similar programs focusing on macro-economic and financial system policy, monitoring, and management. Similarly, the ADB Institute, based in Tokyo, promotes research on development models and organizes policy discussions and learning opportunities for member country officials. Organizing learning programs and policy workshops tailored to North Korea's needs will be a high priority for the MDBs. Such activities will contribute to the capacity building needed for a growing agenda of collaborative activities.

Working relationships: on-the-job training

The most effective mechanism for imparting practical technical and managerial knowledge is through the working relationships that are built between MDB task teams and their counterparts in producing economic assessments and preparing and implementing development projects. As MDB programs grow and diversify, these informal on-the-job learning processes become the backbone of the operational relationship between the MDB and the country and contribute significantly to building competencies in the counterpart organizations.

The Global Development Network

Inexpensive global telecommunications are transforming the use of learning technology as a tool of economic and social development. Both on the job and in the classroom, global knowledge on demand is becoming a reality for people in a growing number of countries. This is supported by the growing use of Internet-based learning tools and telecommunications investments that are sponsored by the MDBs and other development partners, using tools such as the Global Development Network and the Global Gateway. These links are already being built in South Korea, and could become a valuable tool to support North Korea's future learning needs.

Financing education and training under MDB projects

Whenever the MDBs are able to initiate normal lending programs for North Korea, education and training are likely to be major elements of their overall lending strategy. Education recently has been emphasized by the G-8 leaders in their efforts to strengthen the contribution of the MDBs in promoting productivity growth and poverty reduction.

Mobilization of capital

Mobilizing capital to finance North Korea's future economic development strategy will be a major task for MDBs, especially given the existing financial conditions in North Korea. This involves not only the resources that the MDBs can allocate through their lending and grant assistance programs, but also the contribution that MDBs can make effectively to mobilize and use domestic capital and foreign private investment. These areas likely will be more important for North Korea than MDB lending programs, and will be given priority in policy dialogue.

Raising domestic capital for investment

The most important source of capital for long-term economic development is domestic finances. North Korea needs to find ways to increase domestic savings, both in public savings through taxes and in private savings through the development of the domestic financial system. Translating these savings into productive investments through good public and private investment decision-making also is critically important. East Asia countries have achieved high savings and domestic investment rates, and this is a major reason for the region's economic success. China in 1998 had a domestic investment rate above 38 percent of the gross domestic product (GDP). Vietnam has increased its rate from 13 percent in 1990 to more than 28 percent in 1998. For a country that believes in *juche*, aiming to increase self-reliance in this way should be at the center of future economic development strategy.

The MDBs and the IMF are important sources of advice and technical assistance on mobilizing domestic capital for investment. This is their normal role in most countries, and also is often at the center of structural adjustment programs that they help design and support with policy-based lending. What is needed first is a thorough understanding of the public finance system: how North Korea's budget and tax systems are organized and how they could evolve. A review of tax policies and administration would focus on resource mobilization strategies. A public expenditure review would center on finding ways to reallocate resources so they would have a more beneficial economic impact. It is obvious that military expenditures could not be ignored in a discussion of mobilization and allocation of domestic resources, and this is likely to be a highly sensitive but necessary part of the future role of the multilateral banks. Their job will be to explain clearly the trade-off that North Korea makes between using scarce resources to maintain a large military establishment and using those resources to build a better overall economy. The independence and objectivity of the analysis will be essential if it is to make an impact on North Korea's view of this extremely sensitive political issue. But this is an issue that cannot be avoided.

An assessment of the financial system also will be a high priority. This analysis would identify ways to increase mobilization of private savings (both from firms and households), integrate them in the formal economy, and to improve the economically efficient use of such resources. It also would identify ways that the financial system needs to develop to support growing external trade and links to international financial services. Longer-term strategies for capital market development, including the establishment of a stock market, could be discussed, as they have in other former centrally planned countries such as China and Vietnam.

Foreign investment

Foreign private investment will be more important than official development assistance (ODA) in the long-term process of economic development of North Korea. The MDBs can play a critical role in supporting the mobilization of foreign private capital. This will help the North Korean government to build the policies and institutions required to attract foreign investment and reduce the perceived risk of investing in North Korea. Both the World Bank and the ADB have units that provide technical assistance in reviewing policies and institutional arrangements for private sector development, capital markets development, and foreign investment. Similarly, guidance can be provided for building financial and legal institutions needed to attract foreign private capital, and for specific industry and corporate level issues as well. Both MDBs also provide project finance and guarantees[2] that reduce risks faced by foreign investors and contribute to the mobilization of equity and loan finance for specific investments. The role of the MDB as an "honest broker" and "neutral partner" is likely to be especially important in attracting foreign investment to North Korea.

Multilateral lending

Both the World Bank and the ADB were established primarily to provide development financing to governments through lending, offering a variety of financial instruments to achieve different objectives.[3] It is possible that North Korea may use the full range of lending instruments in addressing different aspects of its future development strategy.

It is likely that the initial focus of MDB lending for North Korea will be directed toward removing policy and infrastructure obstacles to domestic and foreign investment, coupled with efforts to rehabilitate agricultural production and respond to pressing social needs in health and education. The priorities and balance of the initial lending activities will be determined based on the economic assessment discussed above and also on the plans and priorities of other donors. However, it is clear that the energy and transport sectors will likely form the core of infrastructure assistance along with agricultural rehabilitation. Support for a new industrial development strategy will form the core of the policy agenda.

Role of MDB grants

While they are primarily lending organizations, both the World Bank and the ADB have limited grant-making abilities that could be very helpful to North Korea in the early stage of their relations.[4] Typically grants are provided to finance technical assistance, training, and studies that support capacity building, and to establish the foundation for MDB policy dialogue and lending programs. While small in relation to the overall resource mobilization requirements, these grants provide leverage by removing bottlenecks and creating the building blocks of policies, institutional capacity, and pre-investment planning needed for large-scale projects.

Official development assistance mobilization and partnerships

As international assistance to North Korea shifts from humanitarian aid to economic development support, new issues will arise in North Korea's relations with those countries and organizations that are involved in providing official development assistance (ODA). Aid mobilization and coordination will become increasingly important issues, both for the donors and for the government. The efforts to integrate the economies of the two Koreas will make this an even more daunting task.

For many countries, the World Bank chairs a Consultative Group of donors that meets on a regular basis. From 1966 to 1984, the World Bank chaired such an international Consultative Group for South Korea. While this group met intermittently, it still performed a valuable role in mobilizing financial resources for South Korea's economic development at critical moments and provided an opportunity for policy dialogue between donors and the South Korean authorities. South Korean officials have suggested that a similar arrangement might be appropriate for North Korea in the future. This could be contemplated only after the questions of membership of the international financial institutions (IFIs) have been addressed. Nevertheless, a formal Consultative Group could well be a useful mechanism to coordinate international economic cooperation with North Korea in the future, especially given the very challenging tasks facing the country and its needs for resource transfers. The positive experience in the dialogue segments of the United Nations Development Programme-sponsored (UNDP) roundtable meetings in 1998 and June 2000 suggest that this type of collective policy dialogue could be successfully introduced in North Korea when conditions are suitable.

Partnerships among donors also are important at the level of mobilizing and coordinating resources to address specific needs. Recently, the World Bank has promoted the concept of a comprehensive development framework approach to aid coordination. The framework helps recipient countries and their donors to better harmonize their policy dialogue, technical assistance, and funding arrangements. Leadership is shared in this process, but the World Bank and the ADB play a major role because of their multilateral character.

Social adjustment

The isolation of North Korean society from the international community represents a huge obstacle if the country is going to open up to market-economy principles and have significantly expanded relations with foreigners, especially if North Korea is going to be the recipient of large-scale foreign investment and official development assistance. The perception gap that exists between the realities of life within North Korea and the realities outside constitutes both political challenges for the regime in Pyongyang and practical challenges in helping the North Korean population adjust to new self-perceptions and opportunities. At the heart of these challenges is the social control system within North Korea that places strict limits on individual freedoms and emphasizes almost deified reverence for the "Dear Leader." It is hard to imagine a society more vulnerable to social change and potential disruption than North Korea, although some may argue that the country already has experienced wholesale disruption stemming from severe economic contraction and food shortages. In any case, the task will be to stabilize and improve the present distressed social conditions.

How would MDBs help North Korea manage inevitable social adjustment? The MDBs would focus on moderating the downside risks of disruption, putting in place new forms of social safety nets to replace the state distribution system that already has largely broken down, and establishing policies that would promote poverty alleviation among the poorest segments of society. The vulnerability of urban households, particularly those outside favored areas such as Pyongyang, will need to be given priority along with areas of the country that have a low economic base. One element will be activities that support the growth of the informal markets that have emerged as the only viable alternative to the state distribution system in meeting the basic consumption needs of urban households. Other actions will be to find ways to rebuild the basic health care system and to adapt the education system to support the gradual integration of North Korean society with international society. Given the political sensitivities involved in managing social change of the scale required in North Korea, the objectivity and international comparative perspectives of the MDBs can make a valuable contribution to the analysis of issues and evaluation of alternative courses of action.

Environmental management

North Korea faces severe environmental dilemmas as well as social challenges. Deforestation and industrial pollution have already taken a heavy toll on the North's landscape and resources. Environmentally sustainable strategies for agricultural rehabilitation and future industrial development must receive high priority when designing a comprehensive development model for North Korea. Also, North Korea's environmental difficulties are linked with those of neighboring countries. Water and air quality are cross-border issues for the two Koreas, and North Korea is vulnerable to air pollution from China, as are South Korea and Japan.

The MDBs can assist North Korea to adopt environmentally friendly policies and investment strategies in agricultural rehabilitation, energy sector rehabilitation, and industrial development. Through the environmental safeguards that are required to accompany MDB-financed development projects, the MDBs also can help demonstrate and institutionalize good environmental planning and management practices. Also, MDBs can help integrate North Korea within existing regional initiatives to manage cross-border issues and support the development of inter-Korean environmental policy and planning mechanisms as part of the broader framework for deepening integration of the two countries in the medium and longer term. An important step in this area is to develop an environmental protection strategy for the demilitarized zone (DMZ), which contains large tracts of natural forests and harbors biodiversity resources that should be preserved as a positive legacy for future generations of Koreans.

Governance

Transparency, clear delegation of authority, rule by law, democratic processes, public accountability, and a free press are not part of the North Korean system of governance, but are the mainstream expectations of the international community in the pursuit of healthy development and human security in the twenty-first century. As North Korea opens up and more resources begin to flow into the North Korean economy, corruption and competition within the North Korean bureaucracy for control over resources can be expected to become increasingly difficult problems, as has been the case in China and Vietnam. There will be a critical need to introduce new management techniques and accountability mechanisms at the enterprise and cooperative farm level.

The MDBs should be expected to help North Korea introduce reforms that will promote economic and administrative efficiency and good governance as well as work towards meeting international norms. This is likely to take some time and encounter resistance from entrenched interests within the North Korean government. Meeting these internal norms for good governance will require far-reaching reforms of the North Korean economic and administrative systems. This challenging agenda should be addressed in partnership with other multilateral agencies such as the UNDP and the European Commission and with bilateral donors. A broad-based and sustained multilateral effort will be needed. An important part of the process will be the MDB-funded project requirements regarding competitive bidding for procurement of goods and services; accounting and auditing of project expenditures; action plans to deal with social effects such as relocation; and ex-post evaluation of projects to determine their success in meeting and sustaining their objectives. These "bread and butter" requirements of MDB projects and the technical assistance that can be provided to help North Korea meet them can make a major contribution to strengthening public institutions and accountability and bringing North Korea closer to international norms in governance.

Harmonizing and integrating the two Korean systems

What is most unusual about the Korean Peninsula situation is the potential for the two Koreas to pursue a deliberate and orderly long-term process of deepening economic integration with the aim of eventual political unification of the two countries. Following the summit of June 2000, the two Koreas moved quickly to establish an administrative structure to coordinate planning and decision-making. Agreements were reached on four treaties governing commercial economic relations and on opening a rail link between the two countries across the demilitarized zone. While these agreements represent only the beginning of a complex and long-term process, and the pause of recent months underlines the vulnerability of this process to the overarching political context, they do provide a starting point for assisting the two Koreas in achieving their economic integration goals.

There are a number of ways in which the MDBs could be enlisted to support the inter-Korean economic agenda:

- *Studies on specific integration issues.* While the MDBs in most countries carry out a program of economic and sector studies to support national development planning, it also would be feasible to conduct similar studies commissioned jointly by the two Koreas to examine issues concerning economic integration. This could include analysis of economic, technical, and institutional issues with the intention of creating strategies to address the challenges of harmonizing two very different systems over time. Infrastructure, financial, and legal system issues would be a high priority in the short run, with environmental, labor market, and social policy issues taking on more importance in the medium term.

- *Technical workshops.* As the two Koreas shape their own agenda, MDBs and others from the international community can support them by participating in technical workshops to bring global knowledge and expert opinions to the teams working on specific topics or projects. One example is the proposed Kaesong Industrial Park. There are many lessons to be learned from the experiences of other countries in how to overcome problems and make these initiatives successful. If the international community could find ways to help the two Koreas make Kaesong a success story, it would be a major contribution to the reconciliation process and trust-building for North Korea's growing participation in the international economy.
- *Projects to support infrastructure linkages.* Power, transport, telecommunications, and water basin management are four areas suitable for inter-Korean infrastructure projects in the medium term. Infrastructure to support joint tourism and industrial development initiatives such as the Mt Kumgang project and proposed Kaesong project will be given short-term priority. But the agenda will expand over the medium term to include a diversified infrastructure that will support increased investment and trade between the two Koreas. Regional projects such as linking to the trans-Siberian railroad and laying a gas pipeline across the Korean peninsula also would be possible candidates for MDB support in planning and financing.
- *Projects to support institutional harmonization.* If gradual integration of the Korean economies is going to be successful in the long run, there also will need to be movement towards institutional harmonization. This may start with legal and financial institutions, but over time will require addressing more sensitive social institutions, such as labor markets, education, and social security. Projects could be designed with MDB financing and technical assistance to support institutional adjustment and capacity building.
- *Financing inter-Korean private investments.* The International Finance Corporation, the Multilateral Guarantee Agency of the World Bank, and their equivalents at the ADB could be enlisted to promote inter-Korean investment. This could include both investments by South Korean firms in the north and North Korean firms in the south. A special program could be designed to support this objective.
- *Bridging the digital divide.* Both Koreas are keenly interested in the potential of the new information economy. New information technologies should be applied creatively to the Korean integration process, and the MDBs could pursue a dual country strategy to extend knowledge management services, such as the Global Development Network and the Global Gateway initiatives. MDBs also could promote the use of information technology to further the social integration process by reconnecting divided families and exploiting new opportunities for social interaction among Koreans sharing common interests.
- *Donor coordination.* Not only the MDBs but the broader international community want to support Korean integration, and it will become increasingly important to coordinate assistance activities and discussions on

policies and experiences. Some mechanisms to promote such coordination and dialogue covering political as well as economic aspects will likely be needed. The MDBs can make a contribution to the coordination efforts by preparing background reports and making contributions to sessions on economic issues.

Conclusion

There is an unprecedented potential role for the MDBs on the Korean Peninsula in the future. It could involve new activities and relationships for the Koreas and the international community, as well as embodying many of the traditional activities of MDBs in other countries. Whether the MDBs are invited to participate and are able to realize their potential remains to be seen. Their involvement will need the approval of both Koreas and the support of the international community. Above all, it calls for a peace process that will cause a shift from the issues of non-proliferation of weapons of mass destruction and regional security to the challenges of designing a new security architecture based on economic and political cooperation and increasing interdependence. Only then will the two Koreas realize a shared vision for a stable and prosperous future.

Appendix

Lending policies and instruments of the multilateral development banks

Both the World Bank and the ADB were established primarily to provide development finance to governments through lending instruments.[5] Mobilization of capital to provide this finance is accomplished in a number of ways, including paid-in capital subscriptions of member countries, issuance of bonds on the global capital markets, and contributions of member governments to replenish soft loan window facilities. Reserves from repayments of past loans also are now a significant source of funds for new lending. Loans offered on commercial terms with fifteen to twenty-five-year repayment periods are provided by the International Bank for Reconstruction and Development (IBRD) from the World Bank Group and by the ordinary capital resources (OCR) of the ADB. Concessional lending with a grant element of about 70 percent is provided with thirty to forty-year repayment periods by the International Development Association (IDA) of the World Bank Group and the Asian Development Fund (ADF) of the ADB.

Access to the IBRD and OCR resources is determined by country creditworthiness considerations and policies adopted by the boards of the multilateral development banks on appropriate use of such resources. Resource mobilization through bond issuance by both the IBRD and the ADB is geared to estimates of demand among borrowing countries. Costs of borrowing are reflected in lending rates.

Access to the IDA and ADF resources is based on economic development levels and the eligibility of borrowing countries, creditworthiness, and priorities set by the donor countries for allocation, as well as performance criteria for access. Allocations for individual countries are constrained by the amount of funds available from the tri-annual replenishments and repayments from past lending, as well as the number of countries eligible that are competing for funds.

Both the World Bank and the ADB offer many lending instruments to achieve different objectives. The IBRD and the IDA, for example, have two main types of lending instruments, known as investment lending and adjustment lending. They also offer guarantee instruments which are designed to help countries attract private sector involvement by underwriting government contractual commitments and by making longer-term private sector lending more accessible.

Investment lending includes the following:

- *Specific investment loans* (SILs), which are the most common instruments, support the creation, rehabilitation, and maintenance of economic, social, and institutional infrastructure.
- *Sector investment and maintenance loans* (SIMs) focus on public expenditure programs in particular sectors, aiming to create an appropriate balance among new capital investments, rehabilitation, reconstruction, and maintenance.
- *Adaptable program loans* (APLs) provide phased support for long-term development programs, involving agreement, relevant sector policies, and priorities for sector investments and recurrent expenditures.
- *Learning and innovation loans* (LILs) support small pilot-type investment and capacity-building projects that, if successful, could lead to larger projects that would build upon the learning and results of the LIL.
- *Technical assistance loans* (TALs) are used to build institutional capacity in the borrower country.
- *Financial intermediary loans* (FILs) provide long-term resources that allow local financial institutions to finance real sector investment needs.
- *Emergency recovery loans* (ERLs) support the restoration of assets and production levels immediately after an extraordinary event such as war, civil disturbance, or natural disaster.

Adjustment lending also may finance physical investments, but is justified by, and specifically linked to, broader programs of economic reform. Similar to investment lending, it includes a number of differing loans:

- *Structural adjustment loans* (SALs) support reforms in trade policy, resource mobilization, public sector management, private sector development, and social safety nets that promote growth, efficient use of resources, and sustainable balance of payments in the medium and long term.
- *Sector adjustment loans* (SECALs) support policy changes and institutional reforms in a specific sector, focusing on major sector issues such as incentive

and regulatory frameworks for private sector development, institutional capability, and sector expenditure programs.

- *Programmatic structural adjustment loans* (PSALs) are provided as part of a multi-year framework of phased support for a medium-term government program of policy reforms and institution building.
- *Special structural adjustment loans* (SSALs) support structural and social reforms by creditworthy borrowers who are approaching a possible crisis, or are already in crisis, and have exceptional external financing needs. An IMF program must be in place.
- *Rehabilitation loans* (RILs) support government policy reform programs creating an environment conducive to private sector investment. They are aimed at where foreign exchange is required for urgent rehabilitation of key infrastructure and productive facilities.
- *Debt reduction loans* (DRLs) help highly indebted, eligible countries reduce commercial debt and debt service to a manageable level as part of a medium-term financing plan in support of sustainable growth.

A wide range of lending instruments is available to match the differing needs of countries. In virtually all cases, however, they are designed to ensure that physical investment is undertaken in a fiscally sustainable way and that funds are used only for the purposes intended. Disbursement of investment loans is made against physical progress of the project, while disbursement of adjustment loans is made in line with performance in meeting conditions specified in the loan.

Issues needing to be addressed for North Korea to gain access to MDB resources

There are political and legal issues relating to membership that must be resolved before North Korea can gain access to the resources of the MDBs. In addition, there are a number of other factors that will determine the extent to which these banks can mobilize resources for lending to North Korea:

- *IDA/ADF eligibility*. The MDBs must determine whether North Korea will be eligible for their concessional lending windows. This will be based primarily on the estimate of the GDP per capita and how it fits with the IDA eligibility criteria in force at that time. The advantage for North Korea would be the low cost of such funds. The disadvantage is that IDA/ADF funds are limited and North Korea would be competing with Africa, Central America, South Asia, Cambodia, Vietnam, and even Indonesia for a share of the funding available. Any increment for North Korea in the future also will have to be proposed by the IDA Deputies and appropriated by the legislatures of the donor governments. Given the large infrastructure investment requirements in North Korea, it is unlikely that IDA/ADF funds alone could be anywhere near sufficient to meet the requirements. Some countries, such as Indonesia and India, receive blend programs that include both IDA/ADF and IBRD/OCR lending. Typically the IBRD/OCR loans go towards infrastructure projects, while the concessional lending supports social and environmentally oriented projects. The potential for a North Korean blend program should be explored, if it is determined to be IDA-eligible.

- *Creditworthiness.* The amount of lending any bank will provide to North Korea – whether it is from MDBs or commercial banks – will be strongly influenced by assessments of North Korea's ability to repay the loans. Any future program of lending by the World Bank and ADB will need to be based on such an assessment, which in turn requires that there be an acceptable macro-economic context for determining the amount of borrowing that North Korea can prudently afford.
- *Economic policy performance and institutional capacity.* All loans provided by the MDBs have to be approved by their Boards of Executive Directors. These Boards will require some evidence that North Korea is making genuine efforts to improve its economic policies and strengthen economic management capacities. The timing and amount of lending will be affected by the government's own priorities and level of effort in these areas. At the initial stages of a future lending program, meeting the expectations of the Boards will likely be a significant challenge for North Korea.
- *Country assistance strategy* (CAS). The amount as well as the composition of lending will be shaped primarily by country assistance strategies that are prepared by the staff of the MDBs in close consultation with the government as well as other partners. These strategies provide the context and rationale for the program of both lending and non-lending services to be provided during a multi-year (usually three-year) programming cycle. All relevant considerations are included in the CAS documents which are discussed by the Board of Executive Directors and provide the foundation for management decisions on country programs and budgets.
- *Safeguard policies.* Environmental and social protection is taken very seriously by the MDBs, and specific lending operations must be designed to mitigate any detrimental environmental or social effects. In these cases, detailed environmental action plans and resettlement action plans must be prepared and approved before loans are approved. North Korea's willingness and ability to address these concerns will have a bearing on future MDB lending.

Grant instruments available to the multilateral development banks

While the World Bank and the ADB are primarily loan-financing institutions, both also administer grant programs and mobilize grant resources through trust funds that complement their lending activities. In the case of North Korea, the ability of the MDBs to provide such grant assistance in the early phase of their programs is likely to be especially important.

Grants mobilized by the MDBs generally come in three forms. One is grants made to member countries and executed by them, normally for technical assistance, studies, and training. Small amounts of equipment may be purchased in conjunction with funds for technical assistance or studies. Some of these grants are funded by the multilateral bank out of its own resources. For example, the Institutional Development Fund of the World Bank provides for capacity building that cannot be accomplished through other means. Most grants, however, are provided by bilateral donors and administered by the multilateral bank for specified purposes under trust fund agreements. Two of the largest grants at the World Bank are funded by the Japanese government, mainly for project preparation (PHRD) and poverty alleviation (Social Development Fund) activities. The ADB also has a significant grant program of this type for studies and project preparation. Some programs, such as the Global Environment Fund (GEF), involve significant sums and also decision processes that involve other partners.

In special situations, grant funds have been established at the country level, such as for East Timor, Bosnia and Herzegovina, and the West Bank and Gaza. These country funds require specific approval by the Board of Executive Directors before their establishment. In the case of North Korea, it may be possible to consider creating a trust fund of this type that is funded by one or more donor countries. The fund could support an early program of studies, technical assistance, and training needed to build the foundation for a normal program of lending later on. To do so would require broad-based support among the Bank's Board of Executive Directors and their agreement on strategy for use of the fund.

A second type of grant is executed by the MDB to provide services to member countries or to finance consultants to participate in bank-led work activities. Typically, these are funded through the bilateral trust funds set up by individual donor countries with the banks.

The third form is grants mobilized to complement MDB lending through co-financing. This is an effective way for donor countries to leverage their limited grant resources available for official development assistance with the larger capital mobilization capacity of the multilateral development banks on loan terms. The complementarity of the grant-funded activities with the procurements supported by the bank loans is an important form of partnership in development finance.

Guarantee programs

The Multilateral Investment Guarantee Agency (MIGA) is a member of the World Bank Group that provides investment guarantees against certain non-commercial risks to foreign investors in developing member countries. MIGA provides long-term (up to fifteen and sometimes twenty years) coverage for political risks of transfer restriction, expropriation, breach of contract, and war or civil disturbance. MIGA can insure new cross-border investments originating in any MIGA member country that are destined for any developing member country. New investment contributions associated with the expansion or modernization, or financial restructuring of existing projects also are eligible, as are acquisitions that involve privatization of state-owned enterprises. Types of foreign investment that can be covered include equity, shareholder loans, and shareholder loan guarantees, as long as the loans run for more than three years.

The World Bank also offers a guarantee instrument that addresses the need to provide political risk mitigation products to commercial lenders contemplating financial investment in the infrastructure sectors of developing countries. The Bank's objective in offering guarantees is to mobilize private capital for such projects on a "lender of last resort" basis. Three types of guarantees are offered:

- Partial credit guarantees cover debt service defaults on a specified portion of a loan or bond. The guarantees allow public sector projects to extend maturities and lower interest rate spreads.
- Partial risk guarantees cover debt service defaults on a loan to a private sector project caused by a government's failure to meet its contractual obligations related to a private project.
- Policy-based guarantees cover a portion of debt service on a borrowing by an eligible member country from private foreign creditors in support of agreed structural, institutional, and social policies and reforms.

While these guarantee facilities were designed for countries that are eligible to borrow from the International Bank for Reconstruction and Development (IBRD), there is provision to provide enclave guarantees to countries that receive only International Development Association (IDA) Credits, and partial risk guarantees are available to IDA borrowers. The guarantee program could be useful to North Korea, although there are many technical considerations that would require investigation at both the country and project level. The ADB also has a guarantee program.

Notes

1 The views expressed in this chapter are solely those of the author and do not necessarily represent those of the World Bank or the Asian Development Bank, their Executive Directors, or the countries they represent.

2 The International Finance Corporation (IFC) is the primary organization within the World Bank Group that provides project finance and advisory services, and the ADB has a similar capability. The Multilateral Investment Guarantee Agency (MIGA) provides investment guarantees against non-commercial risks, and the International Bank for Reconstruction and Development and ADB also have limited guarantee facilities that are available for certain situations. The Appendix provides details on the MDB guarantee programs.

3 The Appendix provides a description of MDB lending policies and instruments and also a discussion of issues to be addressed before North Korea can gain access to these resources.

4 The Appendix provides a description of grant instruments currently available to the MDBs, although future grant policy is presently being debated among MDB.

5 While the IMF is not primarily a lending institution for development purposes, among its financial support instruments available for the poorest member countries is the Poverty Reduction Growth Facility (PRGF). Loans are disbursed over three years at an annual rate of 0.5 percent with a 5½ year grace period and a ten-year repayment period. Access to these resources is tied to a country's quota share and disbursement is made in accordance with strict adherence to conditions specified for the loan.

8 Prospects and problems for Korean economic integration

A long-term view

Joachim Ahrens

Introduction

There is increasing evidence that the future political and economic prospects on the Korean Peninsula may be brighter than imagined some years ago. But at the same time, the expected change brings considerable uncertainties, risks, and costs. On the one hand, North and South Korea seemingly have embarked on a consultative and cooperative process aimed at national reconciliation. This is partly because both countries have new leaderships. While pursuing his so-called "sunshine policy," Kim Dae Jung has called for the peaceful coexistence of the two nations, held out the prospect of aid and bilateral economic cooperation to North Korea, and offered a long-term unification proposal. In addition, Kim Jong Il appears to have consolidated his power and gained acceptance by the political elites as well as the citizenry. Denunciations of capitalist countries have decreased in both Kim Jong Il's statements and North Korean media reports. The government now seems to realize the constraints of its autarkic development strategy. It has begun to normalize its relations with other nations and seems to be willing to consider the model of "one country, two systems" (similar to the model of China and Hong Kong) as a feasible long-term development option (Noland 2000a).

On the other hand, competing ideologies in the two Koreas as well as old animosities still impede genuine progress toward integration. The North's nuclear threat potential, its reliance on the export of military goods for hard currency revenues, and its resistance to market-oriented reform present further obstacles. Moreover, South Korea still faces its own problems in overcoming economic and political deficiencies, which have contributed to the recent financial and economic crisis. Until these problems are resolved, the South Korean political elites and citizenry may not find it in their best interest to support any high-speed economic integration or even unification in the short term. Despite these impediments to reform in North Korea and peninsular integration, the two Koreas appear ready to embark on the long process of redefining their relations and establishing new forms of cooperation.

Although the direction of the expected fundamental shift in inter-Korean dynamics is far from clear, a "muddling-though" scenario seems to be most likely according to most observers.[1] However, a "muddling-through" strategy will not be viable indefinitely. Regime-preserving reforms will inevitably foster further economic decline. This eventually will force the North Korean leadership to choose whether to allow the economy to collapse and consequently to risk their political survival or to seek to maintain power through genuine, though gradual, economic reforms.

The realization of this latter option presupposes the willingness and ability of the leadership to adequately change, adjust or reinterpret the predominant *juche* ideology. Nevertheless, it does not seem to be a highly unrealistic medium- and long-term scenario, at least where external *economic* cooperation is concerned. This scenario may not be preferable from the perspective of pure economic theory (Wolf 1998) but it appears to be more feasible for these political reasons: (1) strengthening economic cooperation between the two Koreas may be one of the least politically sensitive areas of reform (at least in the early stages of cooperation); (2) a more gradual opening could help the North Korean leadership to maintain control over economic development; (3) gradual reforms might allow the North Korean leadership to slowly adjust its ideological label that may be attached to the reform process. In this context, it would be conceivable to expect a gradual shift in political articulation and action toward a "socialist market-based economy, North-Korean style;" and (4) gradualism also may be favored by the South Korean government and citizenry. Even if the cumulative economic costs would be greater than under a "big bang-cum-rapid unification" scenario, these costs could be distributed over a much longer period of time, making integration more affordable for the South Korean economy.

Therefore, this chapter seeks to elaborate on an appropriate institutional design for a *staggered economic integration process* and to identify the reform requirements relating to the North Korean economy. It will be argued that such a strategy requires a protracted and negotiated process of integration involving both Koreas as equal partners. The outcome may be national reconciliation through a multi-stage process from normalization of inter-Korean relations and bilateral consultation to economic cooperation and integration to a confederation (that is, a one nation–two systems model). On the long route to reform and integration, the dynamics of the development process may (at some point) open up a window of opportunity that makes unification a viable choice.

Governing economic integration

Recently, the North Korean leadership has started to downplay its earlier rhetoric describing an external opening as a "Trojan horse tasked with destabilizing socialism."[2] Thus, Noland (2001: 6) reasons that the North Koreans are looking "for a face-saving way to introduce [new ideas with respect to economic opening] into domestic discourse." In fact, there is an increasing number of signals that could be interpreted as reflecting a new kind of thinking: North and South Korea agreed to strengthen mutual trust through cooperative activities in business transactions, cooperation and exchanges in the areas of cultural, athletic, health, environmental, and social affairs as well as through resolving humanitarian issues. Furthermore, following the North–South summit in 2000, North Korea actually signed four treaties with South Korea relating to investment guarantees, financial transactions, settling trade disputes, a legal framework for foreign direct investment, and taxation. Moreover, given the greater flexibility in South Korean policy-making *vis-à-vis* the North, several *chaebols* started to engage in further economic cooperation with the North, which may generate new hard currency infusions into North Korean economic projects.[3]

So far, activities have emphasized inter-Korean consultation and one-off projects, that is unique investment projects which are usually not repeated and do not generate significant spillover effects. Since the latter help earn foreign exchange and do not pose a threat to the systemic organizational characteristics of the planned economy, such projects are highly desirable for the political leadership. But this also means that such *ad hoc* opening measures cannot directly contribute to a sustainable path of economic development. With respect to further opening up its economy, which also requires complementary market-based reforms in the domestic economy, the political elites face substantial risks. This not only relates to significantly increasing exposure to international competition through enhanced trade and foreign investment, but also to potential changes in output composition, which would necessarily cause major structural adjustment processes and large-scale redeployment of millions of workers. Ultimately, these risks may seriously threaten the survival of the Kim Jong Il regime. Therefore, an economic integration strategy is to be identified that maps the way from cooperation to deeper stages of economic integration, that accounts for conditions on the political side and seeks to minimize the economic and political costs of opening up the borders.

Basically, the degree of economic cooperation and collaboration achieved so far in non-political areas and (above all) the political thaw that appears to have started with the historical summit, may provide a useful point of departure to promote economic integration in the long term. From an institutional and political-economy point of view, economic integration needs to be undertaken step by step in order to take advantage of an international and particularly an inter-Korean division of labor and to enhance both the allocative and the dynamic efficiency of spatially growing markets. Perhaps even more important, a gradual and staggered integration process is to be preferred to a (at least theoretically conceivable) rapid integration, because this would avoid excessive (and unrealistic) demands on the political capabilities, the economic capacity, and the ideological receptivity of the North Korean system, as well as the financial capacity of South Korea that is needed to support and manage the integration process.

In principle, gradual economic integration includes increasingly deeper stages of consultation, cooperation, and coordination as shown in Table 8.1. The various stages of the road from project-style cooperation to establishing a free trade area to ever deeper forms of integration that may ultimately entail the

Table 8.1 Stages of economic integration

Forms	*Free trade*	*Common tariff*	*Mobility of factors of production*	*Harmonization of economic policies*	*Standardization of economic policies*
Free-trade area	•				
Customs union	•	•			
Common market	•	•	•		
Economic union	•	•	•	•	
Full economic union	•	•	•	•	•

Source: Beckmann *et al.* (2000: 4)

realization of a full economic union are associated with different phases of market and policy integration as well as varying political costs. Economic integration is defined as a dynamic process in which economic barriers between goods and factor markets of (initially) relatively independent economies are reduced in graduated steps (deregulation or market integration), in order to increase the overall welfare of the integrating countries. In addition, new institutions and organizations (such as a common central bank or anti-trust agencies) governing the integration area are gradually created. Distorted market signals are corrected through cooperation and coordination of the economic policies conducted by the integration parties (policy integration) (Beckmann *et al.* 2000). Typically, market integration dominates the first stages of the process, whereas policy (and institutional) integration becomes increasingly important at later stages of collaboration. This shift in emphasis also implies a shift in potential political costs, because increasing policy and institutional integration presupposes a growing loss of sovereignty in economic policy-making. This, in turn, will not only limit the number of policy instruments that are available to national policy-makers, but will also undermine political control abilities with respect to structural adjustment and economic development priorities.

There is no automatic mechanism ensuring that each of these stages of integration is realized. In theory, it is conceivable that one or more stages may be skipped during the integration process if the countries involved mutually agree to do so (Molle 1997). However, with respect to inter-Korean relations, such an accelerated integration hardly seems to be feasible, except for the scenarios which assume a collapse of the North Korean economy and instantaneous absorption into South Korea. Due to the highly politicized nature of a potential reconciliation process, an approach involving protracted stages appears to be the only feasible option. Accordingly, an idealized model, on which a gradual integration of the two Korean economies could be based, is portrayed in Figure 8.1.

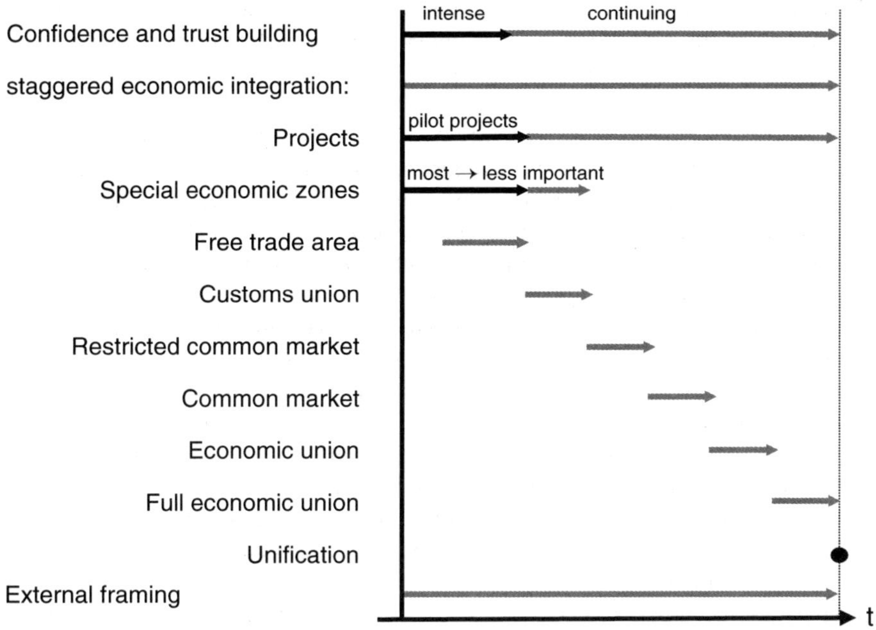

Figure 8.1 An idealized model of economic integration

Three factors stand out in Figure 8.1: (1) confidence and trust building measures (CTBM); (2) the staggered economic integration process; and (3) the external framing of economic integration. The unalterable foundation of any progress in integration would be the continuation and intensification of government-led CTBM. These would have to be complemented by creating an institutional and legal framework for inter-Korean economic exchange and gradually increasing CTBM through non-official channels (e.g., family reunions, study trips, external training programs for North Korean bureaucrats, engineers, etc., and partnerships between towns, clubs, and associations).

The staggered integration strategy would be at the center of the process. Economic cooperation already achieved and business contracts approved by the North Korean leadership may serve as suitable starting points. Even if one-off projects such as the Mt Kumgang tourism project, possible concessions for South Korean or other foreign investors to extract natural resources, or Special Economic Zones (SEZs) in remote areas do not yield major spillover effects on structural change and economic reform in North Korea, they still serve the purpose of strengthening mutual trust. In that sense, one-off projects offer learning processes for the North Korean government and bureaucracy as well as foreign investors enabling all parties to find more effective ways for collaboration. Gradually, such pilot projects could be complemented by projects that offer prospects for (limited) spillovers into the broader economy, e.g., industrial parks and preferential investment zones in urban areas.

From the perspective of economic theory, free trade and investment would be the most efficient means due to their demonstration and educational effects, the improvement of allocative efficiency, and the potential competitive pressure on regional and local authorities to attract investment. However, a rapid move towards a free-trade (and investment) area will not be politically feasible in the short term. First of all, subnational jurisdictions do not enjoy any significant autonomy in today's North Korea, so an inter-jurisdictional competition could not evolve. Second, a sudden exposure to competition from abroad and hence the introduction of world market prices could accelerate the potential collapse of the domestic economy, if the external opening is not accompanied by internal reforms and safeguarded by international (financial) assistance. And, finally, a rapid transition towards a free-trade area, and hence the (at least) implicit acceptance of capitalist norms and rules, would not be possible for ideological and political reasons.

Note in this context that even if an ideological shift towards a more market-based economic system similar to the Chinese or Vietnamese models were possible, such a change on the ground could not occur overnight. Moreover, North Korea would not have access to external financial assistance, because it has at present neither access to international capital markets nor is it a member of international organizations such as the International Monetary Fund (IMF), the World Bank, or the Asian Development Bank (ADB). Most important, however, since a free-trade area between a market economy and a centrally planned economy would not work, even the first stage of integration listed in Table 8.1 would require some basic market-oriented reforms in the North. This is hardly to be expected in the short or medium run.

In the Korean case, an economic integration process would be highly politicized from the very beginning. The degree of politicization would increase further as more policy integration became necessary in order to accomplish deeper integration. Since the North Korean leadership is at present neither willing nor able to credibly commit to internal reforms, the establishment of SEZs appears to be an economically useful and politically feasible strategy that should be adopted before any serious discussion of building a free-trade area can take place.

Officially, the North Korean regime laid the groundwork for foreign investment in 1984 by adopting the Foreign Joint Venture Law. At the beginning of the 1990s, further business laws were enacted (nominally) offering generous provisions for foreign investment and the Rajin-Sonbong Economic and Trade Zone was established. Moreover, the country participated in the Tuman River Project that aimed to create a joint industrial venture with China and Russia. However, the results of these undertakings have been disappointing. The projects failed because of unfavorable decisions concerning the geographical locations of the SEZs, the lack of logistical and transportation infrastructure, and overly protectionist policy measures of the North Korean government (Kim 2001: Lee 2001). Even more important has been the inability of the North Korean leadership to credibly commit to secure foreign investment.

A government that operates with no limits, constitutional or otherwise, is too powerful. If there are no safeguards to deter policy-makers from altering rights, laws, and regulations at will or from undertaking confiscatory policies, transactions which involve the government as a contracting party are not reliable. When political leaders are more concerned with retaining power than with efficiency reasoning, they will simply ignore the importance of credible commitments for private investment, thereby causing substantial political uncertainty. Mikhail Gorbachev's request to foreign companies in 1990 to make investments in the USSR illustrates the point: "Those [companies] who are with us now have good prospects of participating in our great country ... [whereas those who wait] will remain observers for years to come – *we will see to it.*"[4] This kind of carrot-and-stick approach towards international investors and the open willingness to exercise bureaucratic discretion creates a substantial contractual hazard. It not only threatens those companies that have already undertaken investments but also increases the value of waiting for potential future investors. As Williamson (1995) argues, the lesson to be learned here is that rules which provide relatively few degrees of freedom can have crucial advantages over political discretion which allows for more degrees of freedom.

In this context, Litwack and Qian (1998) persuasively argue that the establishment of SEZs could be used as an effective catalyst for international economic integration and transition even in socialist economies which do not opt in favor of a bold economic transformation program. The creation of SEZs may reduce the political risk faced by foreign investors, because it alleviates the credible commitment problem. SEZs usually enjoy preferential tax regulations and considerable local autonomy in economic affairs and receive comparatively high levels of public resources. Such projects are second-best choices from the viewpoint of economic theory due to a relatively inefficient allocation of resources and rising regional inequality. However, SEZs have the advantages that they can absorb foreign investment without affecting the domestic economy, they can support learning processes, and would allow time to build up strategic economic relations with South Korea, China, or Russia without the need to immediately engage in a major economic reform program. A critical point is that the North Korean government would in principle be able to increase its political credibility if it undertook major public infrastructure and logistical investment in SEZs. This would credibly signal its commitment due to the irreversible nature (that is, the sunk costs) of such investments. Preferential tax treatment of economic activities in SEZs may additionally support but not substitute for the public investment policy. Finally, if the SEZs perform well over time, they may gradually yield increasing tax revenues which the government could use to finance social programs in the domestic economy.

Even if the overall commitment to economic reform is extremely low in North Korea, the establishment of SEZs may represent an opportunity for the political regime to accept reduced diminished freedom in policy-making in exchange for attracting foreign investment and hence increasing public revenues. In order to be capable of financing public investment in SEZs, the North Korean regime needs to avoid "white-elephant projects" in the domestic economy and be willing to accept bilateral external assistance.

If single projects, and especially SEZs, succeed over time and if relations with South Korea further improve, the North Korean leadership eventually may be willing to start gradual economic reforms in the domestic economy. This would allow for the creation of a free trade area and subsequently a customs union with the South. Such integration milestones would yield considerable efficiency gains in economic exchange, but would require some policy coordination mainly relating to (foreign) trade and competition policies.

The creation of a common market that ensures the free mobility of goods, services, capital, and labour would be conceivable in the long run, if the North Korean economy were prepared to compete with South Korean companies. But since a common market also requires the harmonization of technical, environmental, and social standards for specific products as well as free movement of labor, the two Koreas would be well advised to agree initially on a "restricted" common market, which offers temporary protection to the North Korean economy. Due to the substantial development gap between North and South Korea, the former can hardly be expected to successfully compete in a common market if it has to adjust its production processes to South Korean standards. Similarly, as long as a huge inter-Korean income gap and a (partially) politically controlled North Korean economy exists, free movement of labor may generate a mass migration on the peninsula. This would sorely tax the absorption capacity of the South and make the North suffer from a substantial brain drain.

Finally, a (full) economic union would require harmonization (and standardization) of the economic policies of the two Koreas. This relates particularly to the introduction of a single currency and the adoption of common labor market, fiscal, and welfare policies. Such a union would eventually conclude the integration process in the very long term.

The idealized integration model, portrayed in Figure 8.1, shows, however, yet another factor affecting the process of integration: the external framing of peninsula integration is necessary not only for North Korea to gain access to financial and technical assistance from abroad, but also in order to externally safeguard the integration process from a geopolitical and security perspective. Difficulties of integration as well as the specific concerns of third states could be more easily overcome by employing a "two-plus-x formula" in an external flanking of the integration process (Pfennig 2001). In particular, those countries which have a stake in North-East Asian development such as China, Japan, Russia, the United States, and possibly the European Union should be involved. In this context, it is of utmost importance that the external structure could not be interpreted by the North Korean regime as an attempt to undermine its political sovereignty. Therefore, external safeguards and support have to go hand-in-hand with confidence-building measures, including the provision of adequate assurances (especially, security guarantees).

A staggered approach to integration is a highly complex and politically sensitive process, even if it is restricted to the economic realm. Effective economic integration and underlying policy reform require credible commitments, that political promises will actually be delivered, as well as the adequate administrative capacity of state institutions and the technical and political capability of policy-makers to implement new policies and enforce the new rules of the game. In this regard, the *governance structure* underlying the integration process is of utmost importance. A governance structure affects the incentives of regime leaders, bureaucrats, and economic agents and determines the terms of exchange between them. Thus, the capacity of a governance structure plays a critical role with respect to the formation, implementation, and sustainability of integration policies. In this regard, the *political institutions* guiding market and policy integration play a dominant role, because they determine how different actors are involved in political processes, what kinds of economic reforms are politically feasible, and how the behavior of individual actors is shaped (North 1990: Ahrens 2002).

Rules, which ought to enhance the quality of policy-making during the integration process, need to demonstrate distinct characteristics: (1) they must be clearly defined over a sufficiently large domain of possible events, and political as well as economic agents must be confident that they are properly enforced; (2) all actors must know and understand the rules and be able to recognize whether or not they are followed; (3) the set of rules must be sufficiently flexible to allow for institutional change if preferences or specific societal needs evolve over time. This also presupposes the existence of various channels through which both Korean governments can equally initiate and contribute to institutional reform proposals; and (4) institutional safeguards must be in place that deter powerful political and economic actors who might arbitrarily circumvent or change existing rules at the expense of Korean society as a whole.

These four characteristics can be subsumed under four dimensions of governance: *predictability*, *transparency*, *participation*, and *accountability*. All these key principles are required for the sound management of public resources, for the creation of an enabling environment for cross-country market transactions, and most importantly for elaborating a consensual strategy of economic integration on the Korean Peninsula. Governance provides the overall perspective from which these principles are derived. A governance structure is effective if it ensures that public policies are properly implemented, that (private) businesses can thrive within a given legal and regulatory framework, which is not subject to arbitrary political interference, and eventually that the adaptive efficiency (in the Northian sense) of both the polity and the economy is enhanced. Therefore, the Korean conciliation and rapprochement process must be adequately governed by formal and informal institutions, in order to make economic integration a viable and stable policy choice (see Figure 8.2).

If the long-term integration process is perceived as being divided into four phases from normalization to market integration to policy coordination to eventual unification, one may be able to assign the establishment of different institutions and organizations to these phases. These inter-governmental or supranational political institutions serve to internally and externally monitor and

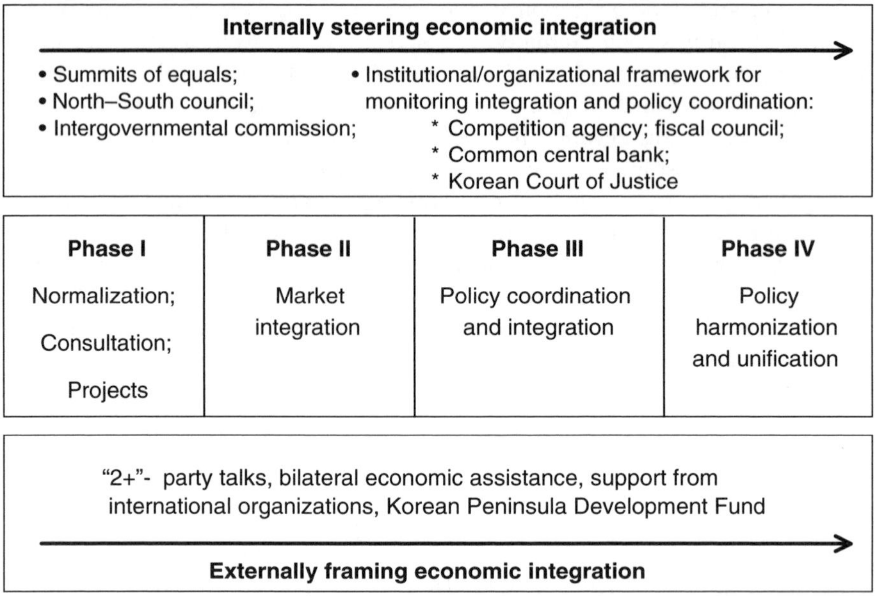

Figure 8.2 Governing economic integration

safeguard the integration process. Since the design of a concrete strategy of institution building will be contingent on specific future developments, Figure 8.2 sketches only a few key components of such a strategy.

Gradually increasing inter-Korean consultation and cooperation in the economic realm as well as in areas that do not relate to core political controversies represents a suitable starting point for the normalization of North–South relations, because such activities may serve the interests of both parties. In the normalization phase, when the formal institutionalization of inter-Korean cooperation will not yet have taken place, joint projects, policies, and strategic planning should be conducted by bringing together the heads of state at informal "summits of equals." Formal institution building becomes necessary at the stages of market and policy integration, in order to steer economic cooperation and coordination. Thus, the activities in Phases II and III need to be governed by an intergovernmental commission with equal representation from the North and South Korean governments. This commission would be responsible for policy implementation and have to make unanimous decisions. Its work could be guided and supervised by a North–South council, that is, meetings of the heads of state as well as of ministerial councils at regular intervals.

If policy integration should become increasingly important, more institutions and organizations need to be created, ranging from a competition agency policing the common market to a fiscal council coordinating public finances and eventually a common central bank. In addition, a Korean Court of Justice would be helpful in resolving economic disputes that may occur more frequently as integration deepens. Furthermore, the integration process could be promoted from the very beginning by strengthening the Korean Peninsula Energy Development Organization (KEDO) and establishing complementary organizations and institutional arrangements such as a Korean Agency for Training and Public Administration to modernize the economic bureaucracies in both Koreas, a Korean Environmental Agency, or a Joint Commission for Historical and Cultural Research. The latter may be an especially effective instrument for building confidence and trust. North–South projects in cultural and historical research may facilitate the identification of common ground and roots in non-political areas and should benefit both parties (Pfennig 2001). Finally, the external support of the integration process through bilateral and multilateral forums may be facilitated by the creation of a Korean Peninsula Development Fund that pools resources for public and private investment.

Transforming the North Korean economy: gain without pain?

Economic integration of the two Koreas cannot take place without market-oriented reforms of the North Korean economy. Much research has been done on the systemic transformation from centrally planned to market economies in Central and Eastern Europe (CEE) as well as in Asia. This research has yielded a substantial set of well-founded and empirically supported policy recommendations, especially with respect to the policy components of economic transformation, the sequencing, pacing, and timing problems of transition, and political-economy problems relating to the implementation and sustainability of reform policies.[5] It is beyond the scope of this chapter to review that research and to elaborate a transition strategy for North Korea. In fact, such an endeavor would be misleading, because most of the findings in the literature cannot be directly related to the North Korean case. The main reason is that (in contrast to other transition economies in CEE and Asia) North Korea has a centrally planned economy embedded in a highly centralized unitary state, the political leadership of which is neither willing nor able to make credible political commitments to a comprehensive transition strategy. Therefore, the following considerations focus on some key problems of domestic transition that are critical to a gradual economic integration process with South Korea. In this context, it is important to discuss how the incentive compatibility of North Korean economic policy-making and North–South integration might be enhanced, so that gradual reform and integration could become a viable future strategy choice for the Kim Jong Il regime.

Transition, North Korean style?

Figure 8.3 lists the main components of an economic transformation strategy and suggests an idealized model of sequencing and timing for the required transformation steps. Virtually all reforms or at least the preparations for them need to be initiated quickly, even if it takes decades for implementation. However, this idealized model has not been realized in any of the transition

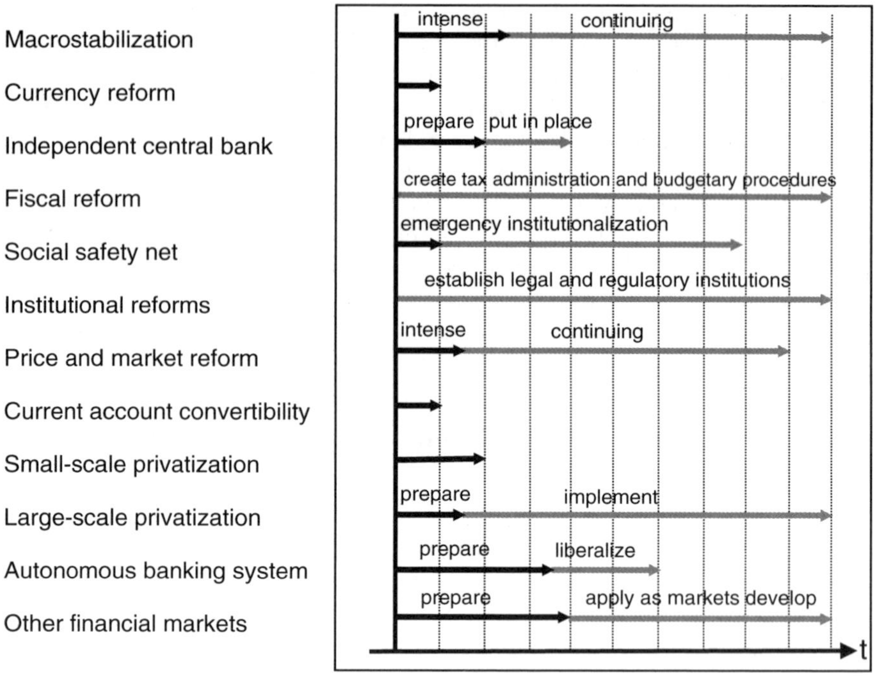

Figure 8.3 An idealized model of sequencing and timing

Source: Gros and Steinherr (1995: 102)

economies in CEE or East Asia. Due to differences in initial conditions, institutional and political structures, and inevitable setbacks which occur in any transformation program, transition policies and outcomes have differed widely across countries.

The differences have been most striking between the successful reformers in CEE and in East Asia. While the former by and large pursued a quick transition to a market system ('shock therapy'), the latter chose a gradual approach. Although a big-bang strategy may be most efficient from the viewpoint of orthodox economic theory, expected outcomes can materialize only if country-specific circumstances are conducive to bold reforms. In this context, the existence of a societal consensus, credible commitment of the political leadership (including appropriate state capacity and capability to implement reforms), and possibly an external anchor of transformation play critical roles. These preconditions were fulfilled in the most advanced transition economies of CEE where the reform policies have been reinforced by these countries' prospective membership in the European Union. In contrast, neither China nor Vietnam (the most successful reformers in East Asia) met these requirements at the beginning of their transition and neither does North Korea. Does this imply theoretically that North Korea should opt for a gradual approach rather than a big-bang approach? Not necessarily. Note that the North Korean economy differs greatly from the Chinese and Vietnamese economies, especially in structural terms. The latter's gradual approach was greatly facilitated by the fact that the agricultural sector had absorbed more than 70 percent of the labor force at the beginning of the reform processes, compared to roughly 33 percent in North Korea. Hence, North Korea could not follow the lead of China and Vietnam in liberalizing the agricultural sector and releasing surplus labor into a potentially emerging light manufacturing sector (Noland 2000b). But ultimately, the starting conditions for agricultural reform in North Korea do not appear to be a major obstacle to restructuring. A greater impediment is the current heavy-industry bias.

Another argument against a gradual approach is that the North Korean leadership lacks the necessary legitimacy to institute gradual reforms, that there is no trust in the ability of its untested technocratic apparatus to implement reform, and that reforms would undermine the ideological justification for the North Korean regime. But this argument would apply equally for rejecting a big-bang approach. In fact, the key Korean question does not relate to the shock therapy versus gradualism debate, but rather to what kinds of reforms are politically feasible.

Pollack and Lee (1999) argue that, without economic reforms and a subsequent economic recovery, the longer-term survival prospects of the North Korea regime will become increasingly grim. They predict a progressive decline taking the form of a descending spiral from economic and political atrophy to economic breakdown to political instability. This in turn will lead to regime breakdown, regime or state collapse, and eventually to conflict or absorption into South Korea. The regime's chances for survival shrink from stage to stage. If the decay process is accelerated, there will be no alternative to a big-bang transformation and absorption into the South Korean economy. The only remaining question will be just when the shock treatment of the North's economy will start.

At present, North Korea is in the midst of gradual decay, that is, between economic and political atrophy and economic breakdown. In this situation, most observers agree that a big-bang transformation of the economy (although it theoretically may generate the largest welfare gains[6]) would invoke the highest political risks and therefore is neither politically nor ideologically feasible. Bold and radical market-oriented reforms come with prohibitive political costs and ultimately threaten the regime's survival. What about gradual reforms? Pollack and Lee (1999: xiii) argue that, from a normative perspective and for (geo)political, security, and social reasons, "It would no doubt be vastly preferable if a transformation in the North unfolded gradually and free of major violence or internal upheaval, enabling a step-by-step process of peninsula integration and diminished levels of military confrontation."

Genuine economic reforms installed on a gradual basis seem to be a remote possibility today. However, recent developments in North Korea seem to suggest that Kim Jong Il has consolidated his power and managed to streamline the government bureaucracy, making it more effective in managing and implementing policy changes and dealing with foreign actors. The restructuring of the bureaucracy has led to a younger and more technically oriented administration. Moreover, North Korea has changed its legal basis for governing economic management. Limits relating to private property (including the means of production) have been relaxed, rudimentary cost accounting standards have been established, and the notions of price, cost, and profit have been introduced in economic management. Furthermore, constitutional amendments emphasize the economic goal of "growth and prosperity of the Fatherland." That differs strikingly from the earlier prescription aiming at the "country's independent development." According to Babson (2001), these changes may presage a new policy direction which could turn out to be more market-friendly as well as more outward-oriented than the country's former constitution. These developments also appear to be consistent with other steps taken by the North Korean leadership such as the cautious economic opening resulting in one-off projects, plans to promote international joint ventures, and considerable growth in inter-Korean trade. Thus, North Korea may be regarded as a country beginning to move cautiously toward a hybrid economic system.

But does the regime have the ability to undertake further economic reform? A binding condition for further change is that economic reform measures will be politically feasible only if the political power of the North Korean elites is not undermined. Specifically, this implies that reform and integration must not question the sovereignty of the North Korean state, they must be designed in a way that they can be justified by decent ideological shifts, they have to be in the interest of the North Korean leadership, and they should create no losers. In addition, North Korea must be receptive to external advice and support, and North Koreans need to be treated as equal partners in potential integration projects conducted jointly with South Korea or other countries.

At first glance, the fulfillment of these preconditions seems to be unlikely. However, if one takes a long-term perspective, accounts for recent political and economic changes in North Korea as well as the positive diplomatic signals of both North and South Korea since the historic summit, and additionally considers that a hard landing in the North would be detrimental to South Korea as well as all the other countries that have a stake in Noth-East Asian development, a more optimistic assessment of reform prospects may emerge.

Under the assumptions that (1) North Korea is willing to enact at least muddling-through types of economic reforms; (2) it is receptive to cautious and gradually increasing cooperation with South Korea and other countries; and (3) the latter will support North Korea in economic terms, the Kim Jong Il regime may find it in its interest to engage in an external opening strategy as outlined above. Even the first steps of such an effort (international projects and the establishment of SEZs) may yield considerable economic gains for North Korea, given its persistent negative growth rates throughout the 1990s. At the beginning of such an external opening, only minor adjustments would need to be made to the domestic economy. Of all the transformation tasks listed in Figure 8.3, only some non-threatening structural reforms would have to be undertaken at this stage. These would mainly relate to the modernization of the economic bureaucracy to enable it to cooperate with foreign investors and to manage the implementation of projects and SEZs.

The Chinese example

In addition, North Korea could – similarly to China – adopt a dual-track approach to further domestic reform. (This would be consistent with the opening strategy suggested above.) Moreover, such an approach requires neither complete price liberalization nor the introduction of full currency convertibility nor a large-scale privatization of state-owned enterprises. And most importantly, this approach does not presuppose major political change.

Note the following political economy puzzles relating to China: (1) market-oriented reforms have been effectively conducted without major political reforms; (2) the national government has appeared to act with substantial political discretion and to have the power to suddenly reverse the policy reforms; (3) only rudimentary attempts have been made to establish secure private property rights, and the authorities have neither developed a code of commercial law nor established an independent judiciary; and (4) reforms, so far, have succeeded without large-scale privatization and complete liberalization of markets (that is, factors emphatically stressed by mainstream economists as being crucial for economic transition) (Montinola *et al.* 1995; Qian 1999).

In fact, political reforms in China have neither opened the door for the emergence of a democratic order nor have they sought to separate the Communist Party and the state. Today's China lacks almost all of the formal characteristics of a democracy. Nevertheless, several critical changes have occurred over the past twenty years: (1) political decentralization has shifted considerable power to lower levels of government and altered the relations between the central government and sub-national jurisdictions in ways which cannot be reversed easily; (2) with the Communist Party having increasingly favored a pragmatic, market-based policy approach, a significant ideological shift in political thinking has taken place that has supported and fostered economic reforms; and (3) the government has significantly increased the degree of openness in its economy (Shirk 1993; Montinola *et al.* 1995).

The reforms realized thus far in China can be seen as a two-stage process. During the first phase (1978–93), both the economic and the political systems were reformed through a combination of conventional and unconventional measures. These included political decentralization, entry as well as expansion of private firms and particularly local government enterprises (the so-called township-and-village enterprises), a subtle dual-track strategy for market liberalization, and enhancement of financial stability by employing "financial dualism". During the second phase (since 1994), increased efforts have been made to replace the old socialist economic system with a rule-based, market-oriented economy that increasingly relies on best-practice institutions that have proved to be effective in advanced economies.

Finally, decentralization combined with a so-called dual-track approach to price liberalization allowed the government to conduct economic reforms without creating losers, thus developing a shared-growth strategy, Chinese style.[7] While decentralization-cum-gradual marketization has played a crucial role in promoting economic growth, reform-minded Chinese policy-makers could not rely solely on market mechanisms for several reasons. First, there was no initial broad-based consensus in favor of market-oriented reforms; second, in order to maintain power, it was politically impossible to dismantle the old planning system at one stroke; and third, during systemic transformation there is always a need to prevent the emergence of political coalitions that seek to reverse the transition and to compensate those who will be hurt by policy reforms. Initially, this held true for numerous bureaucrats and other government employees, workers as well as consumers who were used to receiving large implicit subsidies under the planning system. For these reasons, a dual-track approach was pursued in China. Qian (1999: 17) succinctly summarizes how the system worked:

> Under the plan track, economic agents were assigned rights to and obligations for fixed quantities of goods at fixed plan prices as specified in the pre-existing plan. In addition, a market track was introduced under which economic agents participated in the market at free market prices, provided that they fulfilled their obligations under the pre-existing plan. With this approach, real market prices and markets as a resource allocation institution were created in China in the very early stages of reform.

Although this approach was frequently criticized by neoclassical economists for being incomplete and distorting resource allocation, theoretical reasoning and the practical experiences in China showed that the dual-track liberalization can be, and in fact was, efficient *and* provided the means to compensate potential losers from market reforms.[8] While the market track provided participating economic agents with the opportunity to improve their position, the plan track implicitly provided transfers that compensated those who might suffer from marketization by delivering the previous rents, which continued to exist under the maintained plan arrangements. Eventually, the dual-track liberalization served to reduce opposition to economic reforms *ex ante* (because it temporarily protected status-quo rents) and increased the opposition to reform reversal *ex post* (because an increasing number of agents benefited from the reforms over the course of time).[9]

Adjusting the Chinese-style reform approach to North Korean circumstances may turn out to be the easiest strategy that allows the North Korean leadership to gradually shift from "system-defending reforms" to "system-adjusting reforms" without losing face. Furthermore, through a dual-track approach in combination with a gradual opening of the economy through SEZs, the leadership could further justify the maintenance of its political monopoly and yet make its potential commitment to sustained economic development more credible for its citizens and external investors. Greater credibility, in turn, would reinforce confidence-building measures and enhance trust between North Korea and other countries.

Conclusion: lessons to be learned (or ignored)

An unalterable precondition for the gradual reform and integration strategy outlined above is the willingness and the credible commitment of the North Korean leadership to avoid conflict on the Korean Peninsula and to foster economic development. As long as this precondition is not fulfilled, the outlined strategy remains an illusion. If, however, the Kim Jong Il regime recognizes the potential benefits of strengthening inter-Korean economic exchange and chooses a gradual reform strategy, collapse of the North Korean economy and polity could be avoided. Of course, a muddling-though approach or partial reforms may lead to what Noland (2001: 13) called "'apparatchik capitalism,' in which the political elites would use their control over state power to channel the lion's share of rents generated by a partially marketized and non-transparent economy to themselves." But even such a low-level reform equilibrium could be sustained only temporarily, because a greater degree of openness and a hybrid domestic economy would create new political and economic dynamics on the Korean Peninsula.

If North Korea chooses to conduct genuine, gradual external and internal reforms, it could enjoy a great advantage that no other transition economy (except the former German Democratic Republic (GDR)) has had – an international environment that is fundamentally supportive. On the one hand, this relates to the concerns of other countries, such as China, Japan, and the United States, that have vital interests in maintaining political stability on the Korean Peninsula. On the other hand, this relates to the potential role of South Korea as a benefactor.

The latter point particularly encourages scholars and policy-makers to draw lessons from the German unification. Although the big-bang style transformation of the former GDR and its rapid absorption into the Federal Republic of Germany (FRG) substantially differ from the gradual transition and integration strategy outlined above, some valuable lessons can be identified:

- A potential North Korean collapse would place a huge economic and financial burden on Seoul (as the East German breakdown did on the FRG). Hence, a gradual reform and integration approach is preferable to shock therapy for both sides: It would be less expensive for the South, and it would allow the North Korean leadership to save face.
- Due to the suddenness of the East German collapse, rapid economic and social changes forced political leaders into a reactive rather than a proactive role. There was little time to consider, formulate, and implement a coherent transformation strategy. Recent political developments in the Koreas may open the door for long-term strategic policy-making that allows politicians to assume a proactive role.

- Another lesson from German unification, but also from experiences of other transition economies in CEE, is that a basic trust in market forces is necessary but not sufficient for sustained economic development. In particular, institution building must be taken seriously. In this context, North Korea could benefit from access to an effective and market-proven system of (economic) institutions, laws, and regulations as well as highly skilled administrators who are available in the South. However, a simple transfer of institutions to a (former) controlled economy may impede the allocation of resources if the market institutions are not adapted to the needs and structural characteristics of the transition economy. Thus, institutional reform needs to proceed in a flexible way that takes path dependence of economic development into account.
- Experiences in Germany and CEE show that political leadership and good governance are of great importance in shaping the expectations of citizens and the business community. This lesson also applies to policy-making in both Koreas during the stages of economic reform and integration. This especially holds true for avoiding irrational expectations regarding the time frame envisioned for economic convergence and the costs of integration (that is, do not promise "blossoming landscapes" – a promise that proved to be a critical policy mistake in the course of German unification). Effective governance also is the key to the credibility of economic reforms. This does not necessarily presuppose democratic reforms. More important in the Korean case (as it was for the Chinese) is to enhance the capacity and the capability of the state apparatus to deliver promises made and to avoid opportunistic political behavior.
- Where privatization is concerned, valuable lessons could be drawn from German experiences that were based on individual sale options. In contrast to different approaches pursued in CEE, notably the voucher privatizations in the Czech Republic and Russia, the German solution in particular avoided problems relating to the corporate control of privatized companies. However, the sale option (although theoretically appealing) will not be feasible for North Korea because of the limited commitment of the North Korean regime to a genuine transformation of the domestic economy. Therefore, the Chinese strategy to introduce hard budget constraints and competition for state-owned enterprises and township-and-village enterprises appears to be more promising. In addition, the private sector could be gradually strengthened from below, that is through the promotion of private small and medium-sized firms in a gradually emerging non-state sector (especially in the areas of agriculture and trade).
- In contrast to the German experience, a gradual approach to transition may involve the option not to form a monetary union at the very beginning of the reform process. On the one hand, this will require maintaining controls on the movement of labor. On the other hand, this allows for maintaining the exchange rate as an instrument of economic policy-making and it also allows for continuing wage differentials in the two economies, which can reflect different levels of productivity.

- In South Korea, good governance was the key to sustained economic and social development. This especially reflects the shared-growth strategy from the 1960s to the 1980s, the meritocratic civil service, and the government–business interface that effectively tied the hands of policy-makers and prevented them from opportunistic behavior. However, since South Korea has entered an advanced stage of economic development, the government–business component of this governance structure in particular has become counterproductive and needs structural reform. During the course of potential economic integration of the two Koreas, a primary challenge is to maintain the shared-growth character of policy-making in South Korea, to transfer this approach to North Korea, and to accept also the necessity to share (temporary) losses that occur in the course of economic integration.
- Finally, the East European experience with transition reveals that the sequencing and timing of reforms are of utmost importance. In this respect, macro-economic stabilization *and* institution building need to be given the highest priority. Since institution building is a time-consuming process, a gradual transition strategy may be superior to a big-bang approach.

In conclusion, it should be emphasized once again that the success of increased economic cooperation between North and South Korea depends heavily on the intentions, capacities, and capabilities of the North Korean administration and political elites. A necessary condition for consensual economic integration would be the willingness of these elites to accept a certain degree of reform in current practices. If the Kim Jong Il regime is prepared to fulfill these preconditions, the gradual integration and reform strategy outlined above may represent a politically feasible and economically effective way to realize a soft-landing-cum-integration scenario.

Notes

1 See Noland (2000b), Pollack and Lee (1999). Regarding an in-depth discussion of various scenarios (including the collapse scenario) as well as policy implications, see ibid.
2 Joint editorial of Rodong Sinmun and Kulloja on 31 May 1999, quoted in Noland (2000b: 116).
3 See Lee (2001) and Noland (2001). Regarding the improvement of (economic) relations between the two Koreas after the inauguration of Kim Dae Jung's "sunshine policy", see Noland (2000b) and the literature referred to therein.
4 *International Herald Tribune*, 5 June 1990; quoted in Williamson (1995: 187).
5 See, e.g., Stiglitz (1999), EBRD (1999), Roland (2000), and Ahrens (2002).
6 Regarding the potential welfare gains for North and South Korea in case of successful economic reform in the North or the absorption of the North into South Korea, see Noland *et al.* (1998, 2000).
7 Note that this does not imply a reduction in income inequality. In fact, inequality across regions is reported to have increased during decentralization *inter alia* due to the failure of the central government to ensure a common market. Inequalities within regions, however, have been significantly reduced; see Montinola *et al.* (1995).

8 See, e.g., Lau *et al.* (1997 and 2000). Note that single-track or big-bang liberalization as it was essentially pursued in CEE, including Russia, can lead to efficiency but cannot avoid a transformational recession due to persisting market imperfections (Kornai 1994; Li 1999; Roland and Verdier 1999).

9 For a detailed discussion of the dual-track approach, see Lau *et al.* (2000).

References

Ahrens, Joachim (2002) *Governance and Economic Development: A Comparative Institutional Approach*, Cheltenham: Edward Elgar.

Babson, Bradley O. (2001) "North Korean Economy Today," in Chang-Ho Yoon and Lawrence J. Lau (eds), *North Korea in Transition: Prospects for Economic and Social Reform*, Cheltenham: Edward Elgar, pp. 19–28.

Beckmann, Rainer, Hebler Martin, Kösters, Wim and Neimke, Markus (2000) "Theoretische Konzepte zum Europäischen Integrationsprozeß: ein aktueller Überblick," Bochum: Institut für Europäische Wirtschaft Diskussionsbeiträge 31.

European Bank for Reconstruction and Development (1999) *Transition Report 1999: Ten Years of Transition*, London: EBRD.

Gros, Daniel and Steinherr, Alfred (1995) *Winds of Change: Economic Transition in Central and Eastern Europe*, 2nd edn, New York: Longman.

Kim, Icksoo (2001) "The Rajin-Sonbong Economic and Trade Zone (RSETZ): The Sources of Difficulties and Lessons for the Future," in Chang-Ho Yoon and Lawrence J. Lau (eds), *North Korea in Transition: Prospects for Economic and Social Reform*, Cheltenham: Edward Elgar, pp. 301–33.

Kornai, Janos (1994) "Transformational Recession: The Main Causes," *Journal of Comparative Economics*, 19(1), 39–63.

Lau, Lawrence J., Qian, Yingyi and Roland, Gérard (1997) "Pareto-Improving Economic Reforms Through Dual-Track Liberalization," *Economics Letters*, 55(2), 285–92.

Lau, Lawrence J., Qian, Yingyi and Roland, Gérard (2000) "Reform without Losers: An Interpretation of China's Dual-Track Approach to Transition," *Journal of Political Economy*, 108 (1), 120–43.

Lee, Jong-Wha (2001) "Policy Reforms and the Prospects of Economic Growth in North Korea," in Chang-Ho Yoon and Lawrence J. Lau (eds), *North Korea in Transition: Prospects for Economic and Social Reform*, Cheltenham: Edward Elgar, pp. 94–115.

Li, Wei (1999) "A Tale of Two Reforms," *RAND Journal of Economics*, 30(1), 120–36.

Litwack, John M. and Qian, Yingyi (1998) "Balanced or Unbalanced Development: Special Economic Zones as Catalysts for Transition," *Journal for Comparative Economics*, 26(1), 1–25.

Molle, Willem (1997) *The Economics of European Integration: Theory, Practice, Policy* 3rd edn, Aldershot: Ashgate.

Montinola, Gabriella, Qian, Yingyi and Weingast, Barry R. (1995) "Federalism, Chinese Style: The Political Basis for Economic Success in China," *World Politics*, 48(1), 50–81.

Noland, Marcus (2000a) "The Two Koreas: Prospects for Economic Cooperation and Integration" (East-West Center Special Reports, No. 7, December). Honolulu, Hawaii.

Noland, Marcus (2000b) *Avoiding the Apocalypse: The Future of the Two Koreas*, Washington, DC: Institute for International Economics.

Noland, Marcus (2001) "North Korea's External Economic Relations," in Samuel S. Kim and Tai Hwan Lee (eds), *North Korea and Northeast Asia: New Patterns of Conflict and Cooperation*, Lanham, MD: Rowman & Littlefield.

Noland, Marcus, Robinson, Sherman and Liu, LiGang (1998) "The Costs and Benefits of Korean Unification," *Asian Survey*, 38(8), 801–14.

Noland, Marcus, Robinson, Sherman and Wang, Tao (2000) "Modeling Korean Unification", *Journal of Comparative Economics*, 28(2), 400–21.

North, Douglass C. (1990) "A Transaction Cost Theory of Politics," *Journal of Theoretical Politics*, 2 (4), 355–67.

Pfennig, Werner (2001) "From Division through Normalization to Unification: A Comparative View on Developments in Germany and Korea," *Korea Observer*, 32(1), 13–58.

Pollack, Jonathan D. and Lee, Chung Min (1999) *Preparing for Korean Unification: Scenarios and Implications*, Santa Monica: RAND Foundation.

Qian, Yingyi (1999) "The Institutional Foundations of China's Market Transition," paper prepared for the World Bank's Annual Conference on Development Economics, Washington, DC, 28–30 April 1999.

Roland, Gérard (2000) *Transition and Economics: Politics, Markets and Firms*, Cambridge, MA: MIT Press.

Roland, Gérard and Verdier, Thierry (1999) "Transition and the Output Fall," *Economics of Transition*, 7(1), 1–28.

Shirk, Susan L. (1993) *The Political Logic of Economic Reform in China*, Berkeley, CA: University of California Press.

Stiglitz, Joseph E. (1999) "Whither Reform? Ten Years of the Transition," paper prepared for the Annual Bank Conference on Development Economics, Washington, DC, 28–30 April 1999. http://www.worldbank.org/research/abcde/washington_11/pdfs/stiglitz.pdf.

Williamson, Oliver E. (1995) "The Institutions and Governance of Economic Development and Reform," in Michael, Bruno and Boris Pleskovic (eds), *Proceedings of the World Bank Annual Conference on Development Economics 1994*, Washington, DC: World Bank, pp. 171–97.

Wolf, Holger (1998) "Korean Unification: Lessons from Germany," in Marcus, Noland (ed.), *Economic Integration of the Korean Peninsula*, Washington, DC: Institute for International Economics, pp. 165–89.

9 Managing development assistance in the DPRK

Thomas F. McCarthy

Introduction

This chapter deals with how the Democratic People's Republic of Korea (DPRK) might manage its relationships with the International Monetary Fund (IMF) and the multilateral banks. It suggests that the DPRK can handle conceptual economic policy formulation and infrastructure investment planning work much better than most observers think, but that friction with the International Financial Institutions (IFIs) could arise quickly because of institutional barriers to the actual implementation of lending programs. More importantly than the internal problems this might create for the IFIs, poor implementation – and the resulting poor economic performance – could quickly undermine the DPRK's political commitment to change. Therefore, building institutional competency is crucial.

This chapter also suggests that "development management" should be looked at from a wider perspective. Many people see the DPRK's relationships with the IFIs as driven primarily by a process of Korean economic integration. That is not an illogical assumption and it may well prove to be largely true. But it also is necessary to consider different DPRK policy priorities. The DPRK may well try to use IFI assistance to increase its range of strategic policy options, both economic and political, thus deliberately balancing its "exposure" to a US-dominated Republic of Korea (ROK) by building economic bridges to China, Russia, and the European Union. This second course is certainly likely if the DPRK continues to perceive US foreign policy as being opposed to the Korean "reconciliation" process.

Finding the right approach to "development management" will depend to a great extent on the strategic directions in which DPRK leadership decides to look – or feels compelled to look – for the country's economic future. One approach to working with the IFIs might function well if DPRK leaders opt for primarily some form of economic integration with a trusted ROK for its future growth. Quite another plan might be more appropriate if they see a strategic need to strengthen ties with non-Korean partners. The grayer world of reality will probably find the DPRK pursuing shifting priorities within the context of regional economic groupings, without opting for clear-cut choices.

The IFIs need to be both sensitive and flexible in approaching policy management and investment planning tasks in the DPRK, especially during the period when institutions and people are learning to work together. In particular, the IFIs should expect the DPRK to rely heavily on China for counsel. It will take time and patience to build confidence in other sources of advice, particularly from America. International organizations such as the United Nations Development Program (UNDP) can play important bridge building roles under such transitional circumstances if, and only if, they have adequate budgets and are able to attract their best professional staff to assignments in Pyongyang.

Creating the institutional skills needed to support an economic opening and to build effective working relationships with the IFIs could easily have begun long ago. But the United States, primarily, and Japan as well, have prevented the IMF and the banks from officially beginning even preparatory policy studies or basic technical assistance and training work. These political barriers to institutional development assistance were aggravated by the UNDP's failure to meet its explicit 1998 Geneva promises to provide substantial interim technical assistance and training support, a major breach of faith that is only now being rectified.

Work on training and institutional issues needs to begin immediately. With the lack of quick and high-quality support from the IMF/the World Bank, and other international communities, the DPRK may be unable to sustain the sorts of policy initiatives needed to spur growth, irrespective of whether those policies focus on eventual economic integration with the ROK or on a wider array of strategic economic partnerships. The easiest way to get this process moving is to give the IMF, the World Bank, and the Asian Development Bank (ADB) the same freedom to work in the DPRK as they have in other countries. Preventing them from beginning work only impedes the process of economic opening.

Embarking on IFI work

Policy efforts to remove the most fundamental barriers to growth obviously will be the first order of business for the IFIs in the DPRK. The DPRK has had ample time to contemplate and consider the results of economic change in the ROK and in China. It is much better prepared to deal with these issues than most people realize. Agreeing on the outlines of a basic policy framework for a more open economy should not pose a major conceptual challenge if the regime decides that it wants to do so.

DPRK leaders know that they have no real choice but to open up economically. And they very much want to do just that. Increasingly, DPRK efforts are achieving concrete results, with solid prospects of ROK investment in power, transport, and other infrastructure; near certain Russian-sponsored investments in rail and natural gas, and growing interest by firms from Australia, Canada, and the European Union countries. For better or worse, US foreign policy already has essentially excluded US companies from these rapidly emerging opportunities in the DPRK and probably in the larger region as well.

Obviously, some countries or firms will invest partially for political motives. But even the most politically driven economic partners are unlikely to actually make significant investments until an acceptable policy framework and reasonable institutional safeguards are in place. Those tasks must be the DPRK's next order of business.

But these "next steps" – and any real movement toward IFI-assisted change – remain in something of a "chicken or egg" limbo. DPRK leaders believe, rightly or wrongly, that as long as the United States acts to exclude the country from the IFIs and the wider world of international finance, there will be few obvious benefits from major reforms. Decision-making on economic modernization therefore remains entangled in the complex and US-dominated process of reviewing the DPRK's admission to the IFIs. As long as one does not occur, neither will the other. This offers the DPRK the nebulous benefit of being able to blame the United States for continuing to block its admission to the IFIs, but it does nothing to resolve matters. In this sense, the sooner the United States ends its opposition to the DPRK's entry into the IFIs, if only to call the country's bluff, the sooner some sort of economic change can begin with all its predictable and unpredictable consequences.

Inevitably, at some point the DPRK will be able to join the IFIs and the work of opening its economy – and its society – can begin. The banks and the IMF have ample practical experience as well as the technical skills needed to offer first-class professional help to the DPRK. The DPRK is certain to welcome such assistance as it seeks its own answers to development policy questions. The IFIs and private financial and legal advisors should be able to help identify enough attractive alternatives to embark on a process of sensible decision-making on economic modernization.

The DPRK is equally certain to seek wider counsel with regard to the delicate linkages between policy reform and political stability. That stability will always be the overriding constraint on decision-making. In this crucial area, in addition to its own resources, the DPRK will turn not only to the IMF and the World Bank but also to the Bank's largest single borrower, the DPRK's oldest friend, and the world champion of regime survival. Both the IFIs and the DPRK probably should consider themselves lucky that China is also one of the countries that have made the best use of the World Bank/IMF policy formulation and management advice and, perhaps most importantly, that China has come to trust both institutions. In the end, we can only hope that China's policy influence will be constructive as well as possibly dominant. The IFIs also need to listen when China speaks. Chinese advice may turn out to be as useful to them as to the DPRK.

This is not the moment for hypothesizing about the specifics of the DPRK's likely first steps toward policy reform. The DPRK's economic problems are profound and, in a sense, almost "crude." However, at least at the beginning, policy work clearly will not require the economic equivalent of rocket science. A long series of difficult but doable tasks needs to be addressed and completed. Authority over fiscal and monetary policy must be clarified. Prices and wages must conform closely to border levels. Interest rates must be rationalized. Basic statistical information must be gathered and analyzed. International banking ties must be established. And the population must be prepared for the disruptions and suffering that will certainly follow. And so on ... essentially the same predictable ritual followed by all of the centrally planned economies as they move toward market reform.

Infrastructure modernization

Infrastructure modernization needs to begin quickly, not as an end in itself, but as a *sine qua non* condition for attracting all sorts of commercial investment, both foreign and domestic. The DPRK needs immediate investment in power, transport, communications, and perhaps irrigation infrastructure. To some extent the banks can link lending for infrastructure to the adoption of previously agreed-upon policy measures, but success seems unlikely for two different sets of reasons. First, infrastructure has deteriorated to the point that a great deal of the necessary rehabilitation work can no longer be delayed. Even the best economic policies will not succeed with the severe infrastructure constraints now occurring in the DPRK. Second, many infrastructure development investments in the DPRK are so inherently attractive that regional investors and lenders are likely to go forward irrespective of "policy perfection." The money-making opportunities intrinsic in linking Japan and Korea to China and Europe by rail, of selling natural gas and other natural resources to Seoul, and of rebuilding colonial era regional hydropower grids are enough to lure infrastructure investment to the DPRK.

As in the case of economic policy formulation, both the ROK and China can offer many "lessons not to be learned again" for the DPRK. It is important to remember that both countries have confronted essentially the same problems that are now facing the DPRK. The DPRK can draw its own conclusions about what has gone well and what has not. It will have a strong basis for doing so because the experiences of both countries have been so extensively documented and analyzed by development economists. With regard to near-term infrastructure and investment promotion issues, it seems particularly relevant to recognize that neighboring parts of China face many of the same industrial policy and infrastructure modernization challenges as the DPRK, and that at least some of these common problems may be susceptible to cooperative solutions.

As anyone who has visited Pyongyang knows, DPRK managers and engineers are reasonably unfamiliar with the execution of traditional infrastructure projects, economically sound or otherwise. The country already has been totally rebuilt once with "foreign aid." The Soviet Union and its allies always had major industrial and infrastructure investment programs operating in all sectors of the economy. China also has long supported the DPRK and continues to be by far its largest international "donor." Its border provinces offer obvious opportunities for early economic cooperation efforts.

The DPRK has demonstrably powerful planning and management capabilities. Things get done, however inefficiently and cumbersomely. At least at the beginning, when fine-tuning will not be essential and while the "entrepreneurial spirit" is still growing, most government agencies will be able to meet their commitments to IFIs. This may not represent the currently fashionable approach to development, but we need to remember that the IFIs loved and indeed, cultivated these sorts of government capabilities just fifteen years ago.

Finally, we should remember that the DPRK once saw itself as a development aid player, with numerous assistance projects in Africa and elsewhere. Without passing judgment on the effectiveness of these endeavors, we acknowledge that they did create a substantial cadre of officials with exposure to the more basic sorts of development assistance efforts.

Managing IFI relationships

The key challenge for the IFIs here – as everywhere else – will be to help the DPRK develop a sound institutional framework for development. Work will be much more challenging than in the more open centrally planned countries. Freeing up communications and transportation to allow commerce to grow, loosening planning controls over factories and cooperatives, opening more markets, and establishing more transparent legal regimes; these are the sorts of profound institutional changes which the government must be willing to risk if policy changes and new investments are to have an impact. The DPRK's ability and willingness to pursue these sorts of adventures will depend greatly on internal political factors which donors will neither understand nor control.

The IFIs need to exercise extreme caution in proposing institutional models for development policy management. They need to remember that the current leadership of the DPRK has *never* had substantial dealings with "Western" development agencies and that its institutions are rooted in traditions that predate the Japanese invasion and the beginning of industrialization. There will be no "returning to" or resurrecting anything that is likely to be relevant to an IFI-guided economic development process. The DPRK is not East Germany or even China. No other centrally planned economy was so isolated for so long, and the IFIs will have to take great care in extrapolating from their experiences for other settings. They will have to accept things as they are at the beginning. In particular, they will need to adapt to carefully separated, "stove-piped" communications systems that require substantial time for decision-making and use quite rigid management and control systems. The extent to which potential private sector investors (who are able to put their money in any country they choose) will accept these constraints is another question entirely.

The DPRK has other unusual characteristics. Because it has had diplomatic relationships with only a few Western countries, official bilateral aid agencies as well as the IFIs have never had a presence in Pyongyang. Instead, the "development community" presence in the past five or so years, or roughly since the beginning of the "natural catastrophes" and openly recognized food shortages has consisted largely of World Food Program (WFP) staff, smaller contingents from other UN agencies, and a changing collection of resident and non-resident non-governmental organizations (NGOs). Even taken together, these official groups and NGOs provide nothing approximating meaningful economic development assistance. Even applying the most liberal estimates, the total amount of actual development investment – concrete resource transfers for productive investment does not add up to more than a few million dollars a year (especially when possible "food-for-work" development impacts are set aside). Simply put, aside from the Chinese and (more recently) ROK fertilizer support and modest International Fund for Agricultural Development (IFAD) lending in agriculture, the DPRK has not received any substantial development assistance in well over ten years.

The upshot is that the small number of DPRK officials with experience who could be useful in "development management" have instead devoted their time to food aid work, to relationships with underfunded and understaffed UN agencies, and to fire fighting to prevent NGO problems from undermining diplomatic relationships with Europe and the United States. None of their skills or efforts have been brought to bear on practical economic development work.

The DPRK has sought assistance to deal with these predictable institutional problems since at least 1998 with almost no response from the international community. Delays in building the skills needed to address these barriers to economic modernization are now regrettably inevitable. Those delays, in turn, will needlessly slow the pace of change and probably will undermine the status and influence of the technocrats who have been supporting a more open economy.

Neither the DPRK nor the donor community have much time left if these institutional tasks are to be addressed at least in part before the country has to confront the practical challenges of economic modernization. The UNDP is probably the only realistic "platform" for such an effort. But even after four years of promises, the UNDP in Pyongyang has been unable to marshal even minimal professional staff or budget resources. Nevertheless there are no obviously attractive options to UNDP assistance if the DPRK and the donor community want to be ready to support near-term IFI policy work and lending. Donors need to decide very quickly to either (i) provide adequate and immediate support for a dramatically revitalized UNDP program, or (ii) move toward other alternatives such as European Union assistance or direct, and costly, execution by the World Bank and the IMF. The longer these donors wait, the harder and riskier it will be to support DPRK efforts at modernization.

In summary, the DPRK should be able to handle initial IFI policy formulation and investment planning work quite adequately. However, institutional weaknesses will make practical implementation very difficult, and possibly will undermine political support for economic modernization. The IFIs will be better able to help the DPRK deal with the political and institutional dimensions of development by recognizing the potentially constructive role of China. The United States needs to relax its restrictions on IFI preparatory work in the DPRK if it wants an economic opening to get underway. And the donor community needs to provide speedy and significant support to the new UNDP efforts to improve its performance in the DPRK.

Part III

Prospects for economic development in North Korea

10 Prospects for developing a North–South joint venture complex

Seon Lee and Nakki Baek

Introduction

Since the announcement of the South–North Joint Declaration on June 15 during the historic inter-Korean summit, there have been remarkable changes in South–North Korean relations. Also, the scope of the interchange has been magnified and expanded to the military and cultural areas. Another noticeable change is the conspicuous progress of inter-Korean economic cooperation in the industrial sectors, especially in the information technology (IT) industry.

The advent of South–North cooperation in joint investment projects will give new impetus to South–North relations since both sides recognize that it provides mutual benefits. Even though relations have somewhat slowed after the actions of the George W. Bush government in the United States, economic cooperation continues.

In this chapter, three major issues are examined. First, the development process and some characteristics of South–North economic cooperation are reviewed in order to determine overall development strategies. Second, we also examine how the joint venture projects, which are needed by both sides, are carried out and what fields of joint venture projects are likely to be acceptable. Finally, policy implications are suggested in order to increase future cooperation in the venture business sector.

Inter-Korean economic cooperation: history and current status

History

In October 1988, the Republic of Korea (ROK) government authorized the interchanges of goods and services with the Democratic People's Republic of Korea (DPRK) and economic cooperation was begun on a private commercial basis. It developed rapidly during the early 1990s, under the "Agreement on Reconciliation, Non-aggression, and Exchanges and Cooperation between South and North Korea" that was enforced on February 1992 after their joint entry into the United Nations (UN).

However, during the mid-1990s, the growth of economic cooperation slowed down due to the large gap in economic structure and power between the two countries. In particular, the lack of progress could be attributed to North Korea's policies that limited its role to private companies, and which also avoided government-level communication with ROK.

However, the "sunshine policy" that the Kim Dae Jung government has pursued patiently has resulted in a new breakthrough in South–North relations. Finally, economic cooperation reached a turning point based on the South–North Joint Declaration on June 15. In particular, the summit meeting caused the North Korean government to accept the need for government-level talks with the ROK, and as a result, more vigorous economic cooperation is expected.

During the latter half of 2000, an institutional framework for promoting economic cooperation was established, as part of the follow-up measures of the summit meeting. It consisted of four agreements on investment protection, clearing settlement, prevention of double taxation on income, and procedure for resolving commercial disputes. More recently, however, the relationship seems to be hampered by the uncertainties in the US–DPRK relationship.

Current status

Overview of exports and imports

Total amounts of trade had increased continuously from US$100 million in 1991 to US$425 million in 2000, including imports of US$152 million and exports of US$273 million. In 2001, however, total trade volumes for the first half of the year were US$197 million, showing a 2.7 percent decrease. Imports from North Korea reached only US$63 million, and exports amounted to US$134 million.

Intra-Korean trade accounts for the major portion of the DPRK's trade. The ROK has become one of the three major trading partners of the North, and the trade surplus with the South seems to have contributed substantially to the DPRK's trade balance improvement. The total volume of inter-Korean trade from 1989 to June 2001 amounted to US$2,724 million, with US$640 million of trade surplus.

Although the trade balance changed to a surplus since 1998 (see Table 10.1), it should be pointed out that this trade balance includes non-commercial transactions such as the fertilizer aid to North Korea, transactions related to the light water reactor (LWR) project, and Mt Kumgang tourism.

Thus, the real trade balance of the DPRK, excluding non-commercial transactions, is still a surplus. In terms of real trade balance, the DPRK achieved surpluses of US$41 million and US$54 million in 1998 and 1999, respectively. In 2000, the ROK nominally achieved US$120 million of trade surplus. But, except for non-commercial transactions, North Korea still earned a surplus amounting to US$57 million.

Imports from the North include agricultural and fishery products, textiles, and steel and metal products. Major exports to the North are chemical products such as fertilizer, textiles, electric and electronic products, machinery, and transportation equipment (see Table 10.2).

Table 10.1 Exports and imports, 1989-2001, in thousand US$

Year	*Import*	*Export*	*Total*	*Trade balance*
1989	18,655	69	18,724	△18,586
1990	12,278	1,187	13,465	△11,091
1991	105,722	5,547	111,269	△100,175
1992	162,863	10,563	173,426	△152,300
1993	178,166	8,245	186,591	△169,741
1994	176,298	18,248	194,546	△158,050
1995	222,855	64,435	287,290	△158,420
1996	182,399	69,638	252,037	△112,761
1997	193,069	115,269	308,337	△77,800
1998	92,264	129,679	221,943	37,415
1999	121,604	211,832	333,437	90,228
2000	152,373	272,775	425,148	120,402
2001. 1-6	63,266	134,024	197,290	70,758

Source: Ministry of Unification (2001b)

Note: △ = Trade balance of more imports than exports.

Table 10.2 Commercial and non-commercial transactions, in thousand US$

	1999(A)	*2000(B)*	*Increase rate (B/A. %)*
Import	121,604	152,373	25.3
Commercial	121,482	150,517	23.9
Non-commercial	122	1,856	1,421.3
Export	211,832	272,775	28.8
Commercial	67,553	93,823	38.7
Non-commercial	144,279	179,052	24.1
Trade balance (total)	90,228	120,402	
Trade balance (commercial)	–53,929	–56,794	

Source: Ministry of Unification (2001b)

Specifically, agricultural and fishery products totalled 47.2 percent, accounting for the biggest portion of imports from North Korea. Textile products were 35.2 percent, steel and metal products garnered 7.7 percent, and electric and electronic products recorded 5.4 percent (see Figure 10.1).

On the other hand, exports of fertilizers constituted the biggest portion at 35 percent. The next highest export item was textiles, accounting for 15.9 percent. Machinery and transportation equipment, electronic and electric products, and non-metallic mineral products recorded 11.8 percent, 10.3 percent, and 7.5 percent, respectively (see Figure 10.2).

As overall trade has increased, the number of trading companies and commodities also has increased remarkably. The total number of trading companies was 581 in 1999 and 652 in 2000 (see Table 10.3). Of these, 151 companies were engaged in the commission-based processing business.

Meanwhile, there was also a huge increase in trading items (see Table 10.4).

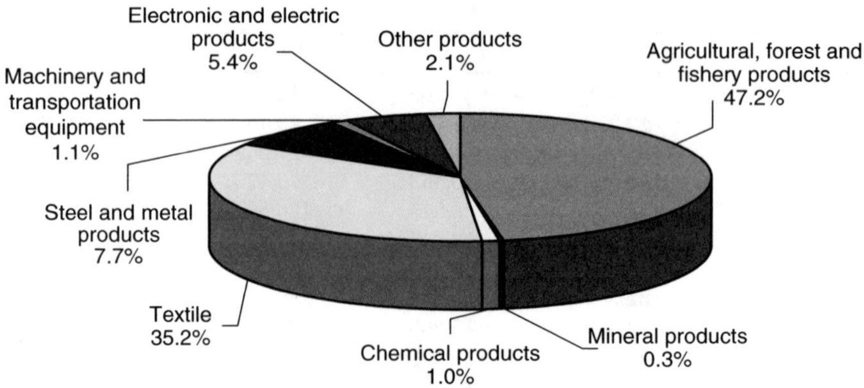

Figure 10.1 Composition of imports from the North in 2000

Source: Ministry of Unification (2000)

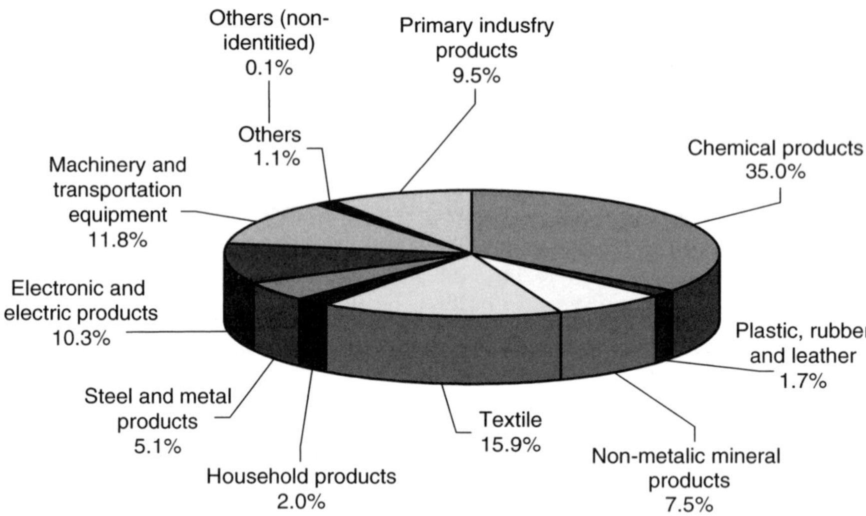

Figure 10.2 Composition of exports to the North in 2000

Source: Ministry of Unification (2000)

Table 10.3 Number of trading firms, 1989–2000

	1989	*1990*	*1991*	*1992*	*1993*	*1994*	*1995*	*1996*	*1997*	*1998*	*1999*	*2000*
Total	30	38	100	147	127	145	258	333	442	378	581	652
Processing trade	–	–	–	4	7	9	18	38	48	72	132	151

Source: Ministry of Unification (2000)

Table 10.4 Number of trading items, 1989–2000

	1989	*1990*	*1991*	*1992*	*1993*	*1994*	*1995*	*1996*	*1997*	*1998*	*1999*	*2000*
Total	26	26	61	100	101	159	263	280	385	486	525	647
Processing trade	–	–	–	9	36	65	84	113	98	144	185	257

Source: Ministry of Unification (2000)

There were 647 items in 2000, 122 items more than the previous year. In particular, 257 items were commission-based processing goods.

Commission-based processing trade

The processing-on-commission trade can be divided into two types. One is simple processing-on-commission without transferred facilities. The other is commission-based processing with transferred facilities. The processing trade is largely based on simple processing-on-commission.

This commission-based processing trade started in 1992, and since then has increased rapidly. The total volume of commission-based processing trade in 2000 was US$129 million, constituting 30.4 percent of total trade or 52.9 percent of commercial trade. Thus, the share of commission-based processing trade increased from 3.8 percent in 1993 to 30.4 percent in 2000.

In addition, the composition of processing trade items has been diversified from mainly textiles and clothes to electronic and electric products. Thus, the share of textile products in the total volume of imports in processing trade decreased continuously from 89.4 percent in 1997 to 74.3 percent in 2000.

With regard to the commission-based processing trade, it is worth noting that participation of small and venture firms in the processing-on-commission business has increased rapidly, especially since 1999 (see Table 10.5). At the same time, the locations are diversifying from the Pyongyang-Nampo area to other places such as the Shinuijoo and Najin-Sonbong areas.

Table 10.5 Commission-based processing trade, 1992–2001, in thousand US$

	Import	*Export*	*Total*	*Shares in total trade*
1992	638	200	839	0.5
1993	2,935	4,023	7,008	3.8
1994	14,231	11,343	25,563	13.2
1995	21,174	24,718	45,892	16.0
1996	36,238	38,164	74,402	29.5
1997	42,894	36,175	79,069	25.6
1998	41,371	29,617	70,988	32.0
1999	53,736	45,883	99,620	29.9
2000	71,966	57,224	129,190	30.4
2001.1–6	23,494	21,658	45,152	22.9

Source: Ministry of Unification (2001b)

Investment cooperation

The cooperation projects consist of the light-water reactor (LWR) Project, Mt Kumgang tourism project and other investment cooperation projects. The volume of transactions reached US$69 million in 2000, mainly composed of the relevant exports of US$67 million, which account for 97.3 percent of total volume of transactions.

Under the present government, investment cooperation has reached a turning point. The ROK government enacted the "Measures for Activation of Inter-Korean Economic Cooperation" on 30 April 1998. Encouraged by this policy, the visits of Southern businessmen to the North began to increase dramatically in order to promote commission-based processing or direct investment. In addition, the areas of cooperation also are diversified into areas such as the IT industry, tourism, and fishery.

Hyundai Asan embarked on the Mt Kumgang tourism project on 18 November 1998. From then to the end of June 2001, a total of 410,000 tourists visited Mt Kumgang. In particular, during 2000, Mt Kumgang tourism recorded 396 cruise tours for more than about 212,000 tourists. In 2001, however, the Mt Kumgang project faced a serious crisis, due to a reduction in the number of tourists and the excessive financial burden of tour fees paid to the North. Also, the development project involving mineral water in Mt Kumgang that was initiated by Taechang Co. is almost ready for mass production.

In addition, Samsung Electronics Co. opened the Software Development Center in Beijing jointly with Choson Computer Center of the North in March 2000. Furthermore, Hanabiz.com contracted for joint program development with Pyongyang Informatics Center in April 2000. N-Track Co. of the South proposed to construct the IT Business Town in Pyongyang with Gwangmyongsung Co. in April 2001.

As a result of these active interchanges, the number of cooperative partnerships is forty-one in the economic area and thirty in the socio-cultural area, as of June 2001 (see Table 10.6). In terms of cooperation projects, there are eighteen in the economic area and twenty-three in the socio-cultural area, totaling forty-one. The rapid increase in socio-cultural cooperation could be

Table 10.6 Number of partnerships and projects as of June 2001

	1991	*1992*	*1993*	*1994*	*1995*	*1996*	*1997*	*1998*	*1999*	*2000*	*2001.6*	*Total*
Economic area		1			6(1)	4	15(5)	10(9)	2(1)	1(2)	2	41(18)
Socio-cultural area	2(2)						1(1)	7(5)	7(5)	9(5)	4(5)	30(23)
Total	2(2)	1			6(1)	4	16(6)	17(14)	9(6)	10(7)	6(5)	71(41)

Source: Ministry of Unification (2001b)
Note: Figures in parentheses are the number of cooperation projects approved.

attributed to the "Measures for Promoting Inter-Korean Interchanges and Cooperation" enacted in 1998.

South–North cooperation in the joint venture projects

Current status

The economic cooperation of small and venture businesses has been conducted mainly through commodity transactions and processing-on-commission trade so far.

More recently, however, the cooperation areas have been diversified to include investment areas, especially in the IT sector.

The share of small and medium enterprises (SMEs) in the total trade accounts for roughly more than 90 percent of the number of firms engaged in South–North cooperation and about 50 percent in terms of trade amounts.

Commission-based processing trade

SMEs are more actively involved in the processing trade. As stated above, after 1999 the SMEs' participation in the commission-based processing trade began to expand. Thus, in 1999, SMEs comprised 83.3 percent of the firms and accounted for 62.4 percent of trade amounts (see Table 10.7).

According to the results of a survey conducted by Korea International Trade Association (KITA) in June 2000, SMEs with an average size ranging from US$100,000 to less than US$1 million accounted for about 40 percent for the previous three years. In particular, SMEs with less than US$10,000 of processing trade reached 21.8 percent (see Table 10.8).

With regard to SMEs' imports through the processing trade by industry, textiles and clothes recorded the highest total of 61.0 percent (see Table 10.9). They were followed by electronic and electric products at 12.5 percent and agricultural, forest, and fishery products at 10.9 percent.

Table 10.7 SMEs' commission-based processing trade based on imports, in thousand US$

	Cases			*Amount*		
	Total (A)	*SMEs (B)*	*Ratio (B/A, %)*	*Total (A)*	*SMEs (B)*	*Ratio (B/A, %)*
1995	18	8	44.4	21,174	536	2.5
1996	38	23	60.5	36,238	5,400	14.9
1997	48	33	68.8	42,894	10,821	25.2
1998	52	38	73.1	41,371	11,483	27.8
1999	78	65	83.3	53,736	33,544	62.4
1995–1999	234	167	71.4	195,413	61,784	31.6

Source: Small and Medium Industry Promotion Corporation (SMIPC)
Note: Figures are recalculated based on the data from the Ministry of Unification.

Table 10.8 Average size of SMEs' processing trade, 1997–2000

Size of CPT (on annul average, US$)	*Response ratio (%)*
Less than 10,000	21.8
10,000–less than 100,000	23.6
100,000–less than 1,000,000	40.0
1,000,000–less than 10,000,000	12.7
10,000,000 or more	1.8
Total	100.0

Source: Korea International Trade Association (2000)

Table 10.9 SMEs' imports through processing trade by industry

	Textiles & clothes	*Electric & electronics*	*Agricultural, forest and fishery products*	*Chemical, machinery and metals*	*Household products*	*Total*
Shares (%)	61.0	12.5	10.9	7.8	7.8	100.0

Source: Korea International Trade Association (2000)

Most SMEs appear to prefer joint business arrangements. In this area, it is worth noting the joint scheme supported by Small and Medium Industry Promotion Corporation (SMIPC). It is the first example of the cooperative processing investment by IMRI Co., Sung Nam Electronics Co. and Se Kwang Techno Electronics. They joined together to carry out commission-based processing production with facilities provided by the South. Their factories are located in the District of Daedong River, Pyongyang.

This type of joint venture with the North is considered a success. IMRI Co. has begun to import the computer monitors produced by commission-based processing efforts since 1999. At the end of June 2001, the total amount of imports exceeded US$2 million which is more than twice the total investment (see Table 10.10).

Area of investment cooperation

Of the forty-one companies considered for cooperation partnership, only eighteen cases were approved as of June 2001 (Table 10.6). Of the eighteen on-going projects, eight are conducted by small and medium enterprises. Of these, however, only a few cases seem to have successfully progressed thus far. They include the Mt Kumgang's mineral water project conducted by Taechang Co. and the automobile repairs and assembly plant project conducted by Pyonghwa Motors. On the other hand, most of the projects, which were undertaken in the Rajin-Sonbong area are in trouble. There the DPRK government began to strictly control the visits of South Korean businessmen after 1998.

Since the South–North summit meeting, many small and venture firms are pursuing business opportunities in the various fields of social overhead capital

Table 10.10 SMEs' cooperative investments, in million Korean won

Name of company	Products	Facility financing: Own capital	Facility financing: Loans from SMIPC	Facility financing: Sub-total	Working capital	Total	Imports[2] (US$ 1,000)
IMRI	Computer monitors	30	454 (208)[1]	484	500 (500)	984 (708)	2,368
Sung Nam Electronics Co. Ltd.	Audio tapes, Compact lamps	1,012	2,721 (320)	3,733	500 (500)	4,233 (820)	521
Se Kwang Techno Electronics	Electron coils		220 (–)	220	500 (400)	720 (400)	138
Total		1,042	3,395 (528)	4,437	1,500 (1,400)	5,937 (1,928)	3,027

Source: Small and Medium Industry Promotion Corporation
Notes: 1 Figures in parentheses are the amounts of loans as of 2000.
2 As of June 2001.

(SOC), Internet business, and commission-based processing of light industry products. In particular, South–North cooperation in the IT industry has been most active recently.

Prospects for joint venture projects

As stated earlier, South–North cooperation has begun to increase in the various fields since the Inter-Korean summit meeting of June 2000. There has been especially remarkable progress in the IT industry. The major ongoing projects in the IT sector are as shown in Table 10.11.

- Hanabiz.com of the South and Pyongyang Informatics Center (PIC) of the North jointly established the Hana Program Center in Dandung, China on 2 August 2000, in order to jointly develop software programs as well as to provide IT education and training for the North Korean IT personnel. Both sides jointly invested US$2 million.
- N-Track Co. of the South was to build the industrial complex for the Korea Institute for Technology Development in Pyongyang with Gwangmyong-sung Chong Co. in April of 2001. The initiative would study the joint development of animation, assembly of parts and components, network-related equipment, and various game-related products.
- Da-San Internet, the specialized producer of network equipment made an agreement with Samchonri Chong Co. of the North to equip 2Mbps level SDSL for twenty institutions and organizations in Pyongyang. The People's Network, a venture company specializing in animation, also made an agreement with 4.26 Children's Movies Production, North Korea's sole

Table 10.11 Ongoing joint venture projects

Name of company	*Business partners*	*Type of business*	*Location*	*Investment amount*
△ International Corn Foundation (R&D)	Agricultural Science Institute	Joint research for developing super corn	Pyongyang and other places	3.1→21.6 (billions of won) ('99.3.25)
△ Samsung Electronics	Choson Computer Center	South–North joint development of software	Beijing	727→1,544 (US$1,000)
Hanabiz.com	Pyongyang Informatics Center	South–North joint development of programs	Dandung	2000 (US$ 1,000)
N-Track	Kwangmyongsung Chong Co.	Construction of Korea Institute for Technology Development	Pyongyang	4,000 (US$ 1,000)

Source: Ministry of Unification (2001b)
Note: △ represents the firms which already have approval for cooperation projects.

animation producer, regarding the joint production of animation amounting to US$3 million during the next two years.

- Samsung Electronics opened the Software Joint Development Center in Beijing with Choson Computer Center of North Korea in March 2000 to develop software programs.

In the socio-cultural area, there has been a remarkable recent expansion, as shown in Table 10.12.

As explained above, there has been a conspicuous expansion in the IT sector, especially in the fields of software development, animation, information communications networks, and translation of multiple-languages. Here, it is relevant to review briefly the current status of the DPRK's IT industry in North Korea to determine the most promising fields for joint venture projects.

The North Korean government selected the IT industry as a strategic growth sector under the comprehensive "Information Technology Development Plan." According to this plan, they will focus on PC production, software development and building information communications networks. The DPRK planned to rely on advanced technology and capital from the ROK and Western nations to cultivate IT manpower education. The Program Training Bureau and the Computer Training Center were established for this purpose under the Ministry of Education in March 2000. In addition, the Computer Talents Cultivation Center also was established in the Mangyongae Palace of Students and Youth, Pyongyang Palace of Students and Youth, and Kumsung Middle Schools in April 2001.

The DPRK is at an early stage of the computer hardware development. They are not able to produce computers due to external constraints such as Coordinating Committee on Multilateral Export Controls (COCOM) and the

Table 10.12 Ongoing projects in socio-cultural areas

Name of company	*Partners*	*Type of business*	*Amount*
△ Northeast Asian Educational and Cultural Cooperation Foundation	International Economic Cooperation Committee, Administration and Economy Committee of Rajin-Sonbong	Establishment of Science and Technology University in Rajin-Sonbong	5,000 (US$ 1,000)
△ Sysgen Co. Ltd	Pan-Pacific Choson People's Association for Promotion of Economic Development	Opening of domestic mirror site on economic and industrial information of Choson Info Bank	600 (US$ 1,000)
Yami Co. Ltd.	Pan-Pacific Choson People's Association for Promotion of Economic Development	South–North joint manufacture of animations	n.a.
△ Hanaro Telecom	Samchonri Chong Co.	Joint manufacture of 3D animations	190 (US$ 1,000)
△ Northeast Asian Educational and Cultural Cooperation Foundation	Ministry of Education	Establishment and operation of Pyongyang Information Science and Technology University	40 (Billions of won)

Source: Ministry of Unification (2001b)
Note: △ represents the firms which already have approval for cooperation projects.

Wassenaar Arrangement. However, it is known that they can assemble 32-bit computers using key components imported from more advanced neighboring countries.

Nonetheless, the DPRK secures a high level of software technology and exports its products to Japan, China and African nations. Nearly ten institutions, including the Choson Computer Center, have developed more than 170 software programs. The North exports some products with fingerprint and voice recognition technologies.

In the Internet area, e-mail and data searches are possible only for certain authorized institutions which are linked to the Gwangmyong broadband communications network. But access to international networks is impossible, because there is no Internet Protocol address officially registered for the DPRK's country code. The DPRK planned to complete its nationwide networks for the Internet and e-mail for major party and government institutions in 2001.

North Korea's IT industry remains at an early stage of development due to a shortage of professional staff and a low level of computer-using citizens.

However, they have a smart software program for testing physical organizations and advanced technologies in game designing, and fingerprint and voice recognition.

Promotion strategies and policy implications

In order to promote South–North venture cooperation, it is most important to remove the existing institutional and political constraints. First of all, trade with North Korea, especially in high-tech products, is strictly constrained due to the Wassenaar Arrangement. According to the Wassenaar Arrangement, which replaced COCOM since 1994, even the Pentium level PC may not be provided to the North.

Second, political uncertainty plays a role in discouraging economic cooperation. In 2001, trade performances have decreased substantially because of the adverse political environment. Thus, political stability is a necessary condition to achieve successful economic results.

Third, red-tape deregulation by the ROK would help to promote joint venture projects. This would remove the complications involved in visiting the North, and would help to process business cooperation measures quickly. Usually it takes more than two to three months to complete the official permit to visit. It takes longer than a year to finalize business contracts with the North. One businessman complained that it is more difficult and takes more time to process business in the South than in the North.

In order to develop closer joint cooperation in venture projects, it would be highly desirable to build a joint venture complex. This could produce synergistic effects among the firms through the exchanges of relevant information, personnel, communication infrastructures, and so on.

A step-by-step approach would be the practical and efficient way to develop a joint venture complex. At the first stage, the joint complex could be located in Beijing or Dandung, China. The advantage of locating in a third country is to escape the regulations and constraints of the Wassenaar Arrangement. In addition, joint operations in a third country also can ease or remove conflicts and difficulties that could occur due to North Korea's strict control.

In the second stage, when international sanctions against North Korea such as the Wassenaar Arrangement are removed, and after the relationship between the United States and the DPRK has improved, the joint venture complex could be constructed in the DPRK. It could be built in the existing established industrial zones such as Pyongyang-Nampo, Gaesung-Haejoo, Shinuijoo, Anjoo-Sooncheon, Hamhung-Wonsan, Cheongjin-Kimchak, Najin-Sonbong, and Kanggae-Mampo.

As for the communication networks, there are three major optical cable networks in the North: the Pyongyang-Hunchun line, the Pyongyang-Shinuijoo line, and the Pyongyang-Panmunjeom line. These communication infrastructures should be considered in locating the joint venture complex. In this respect, the Pyongyang or Gaesung areas constitute the promising candidates.

Finally, in the third stage when all political constraints and uncertainties are removed, the joint venture complex could be developed in the ROK. In this stage, there would be several locational advantages such as social infrastructure, manpower, training and education, research and development, and so on.

The most important synergistic effects of the joint venture complex are tied to the funding and marketing services, which are crucial in guiding successful business in the initial stage of venture projects. There are enough venture funds and angels in the South, which has already amassed enough good experience during past three years of the venture boom. At the same time, the ROK's export companies have extensive worldwide marketing connections, which are so important to the success of venture schemes. Since venture projects are usually technology-intensive on the medium and small scale, rather than capital-intensive, they are a good starting point for both the ROK and DPRK.

References

Korea International Trade Association (2000) *Survey on Small and Medium Enterprises Joining in the Inter-Korean Processing Trade,* June. Korea: Korea International Trade Association.

Ministry of Unification, ROK (2000) *Overall Performance of Inter-Korean Exchanges and Cooperation in 2000,* December 2000. Korea: Ministry of Unification.

Ministry of Unification, ROK (2001a) *Korean Unification Bulletin,* various issues. Korea: Ministry of Unification.

Ministry of Unification, ROK (2001b) *Report on Intra-Korean Interchange and Cooperation for June 2001.* Korea: Ministry of Unification.

Presidential Commission on Small and Medium Business and KIET (2000) *Strategies for Progressing South-North Economic Cooperation of Small and Medium Enterprises,* Seoul: Korea Institute for Industrial Economics and Trade (in Korean).

Yoon, Chang-Ho and Lau, Lawrence J. (eds.) (2001) *North Korea in Transition: Prospects for Economic and Social Reform,* Cheltenham: Edward Elgar.

11 The urban dimension of the North Korean economy

A speculative analysis

Bertrand Renaud[1]

Introduction

This chapter explores the urban dimension of the North Korean economy. Few areas of economic management of centrally planned economies have met with such widespread dissatisfaction and broad popular support for reforms as housing and urban development. This dissatisfaction arises from the peculiar systemic features of the "socialist city." Since the early 1990s we have been able to study the economics of this type of city based on data from cities of the former Soviet Union, Central Europe, and also China and Vietnam. Of course, no such access to information exists today in North Korea.

As a starting point, I ask only one question: based on the body of knowledge that we have gained from other centrally planned economies (CPE), what are the systemic features of the North Korean urban economy that we expect to find? By so doing, the chapter applies to North Korean cities the method of "rigorous speculation" used earlier by Noland *et al.* (2000) on North Korean macroeconomic and trade performance. According to Noland and his colleagues, "rigorous speculation" is the incorporation of fragmentary information into a consistent analytical framework that can clarify alternative scenarios regarding current economic conditions in North Korea. The results can then suggest suitable reforms to stimulate the economy.

Using a medical analogy, the focus is how the "personal history and diagnosis" of the North Korean urban system should be conducted some day. The analysis should not be misconstrued or misused: it is *not* offered as an actual diagnosis of the North Korean urban system. Rather, using our body of knowledge of the anatomy and physiology of the "socialist city," it speculates about what we should expect to find in the Democratic People's Republic of Korea (DPRK) urban system. This "pre-diagnosis" relies on the limited yet often revealing information available on the North Korean urban system and its patterns of investment. We also can narrow the range of uncertainty about the structure of the North Korean urban system by means of international comparisons. For instance, should we expect the North Korea system of cities to have more in common with the Soviet cities of Russia than with Chinese or Vietnamese cities, both in terms of time paths of development and of institutional arrangements?

Why investigate the performance of the DPRK urban system?

Given the constant preoccupation with security issues and the progressive decline of the DPRK economy since the early 1980s, there is intrinsic merit in thinking analytically about an important economic sector that is seldom, if ever, discussed. In addition, there are macro-economic reasons for considering the impact of DPRK urban policies on the decline of national economic performance and on the reforms needed to revive growth.

Where does the urban economy fit into the North Korean CPE system? North Korea's military economy claims an unusually large share of national output by any standard. Planners of the civilian economy have predominantly focused on heavy industry. The food crisis of the 1990s has trained international attention on the dismal performance of agriculture. Yet North Korea is a substantially urban economy and the largest share of its total national output originates from its cities. North Korean urban assets are expected to form a major component of total DPRK national wealth, even if the weight of this sector is totally obscured by CPE national accounting methods. As is well known, CPE planners treat housing as a "distribution good" rather than a "commodity good" and assign a low strategic rank to the "communal services" within construction accounts.[2] But should we not expect that decades of negative returns on these large urban assets – especially on housing – are making their own perverse contribution to the very low productivity of the North Korean economy and its drift into deeper "secular" economic decline since the mid-1980s?[3]

How important are North Korean urban assets? Given the relatively high level of urbanization of the country, the housing stock can be expected to be at least 20 percent of total reproducible assets. Adding the value of urban land to buildings (which is never done in CPE national accounting) would raise further this share of housing in total national wealth. Given this share of total assets, it is expected that the housing sector and its urban infrastructure have been playing a significant yet poorly measured role in the slowdown and eventual decline of CPE economies. In a highly urbanized *market* economy such as the United States, the weight of housing is higher. For instance, the 1992 breakdown of the composition of total US fixed *tangible* wealth (i.e., excluding financial assets) showed that the residential sector represented 56 percent of total tangible wealth.[4]

In market economies the performance of the housing sector is a major component of macro-economic management. For instance, under monetary policies of inflation targeting, central bankers also are well aware of the impact of housing *assets'* performance on overall economic performance.

During fifty years of urbanization after the Korean War, the DPRK has been a prototypical CPE. The DPRK administrative-command system is one of the last – if not the last – systems to remain in force today. As in other socialist economies, we expect this administrative-command system to have turned the North Korean city, and housing in particular, into a disconcerting and disorientating environment for a market economist.[5] In market economies, when housing sector distortions do exist, they are predominantly found on the supply side. In CPE economies, however, housing is part of the total compensation provided by state enterprises and other public employers. As a result, we expect North Korean housing to suffer from significant demand-side distortions. In addition, we would likely see severe supply-side problems caused by the absence of land markets, vague property rights, unresponsive urban regulations based on administrative convenience, and inter-agency bargaining without substantive public participation.

Organization of the analysis

The analysis is organized in three sections. First, we review the stages of development of North Korean urbanization over the past fifty years to gain a clearer view of the origins of today's urban system. Then, the second section explores supply-side issues and the impact on the quality of urban investment decisions under an administrative-command system dominated by physical planners who are unrestrained by markets. The third section outlines demand-side issues and the economic distortions that should be anticipated in the North Korean economy. Conceptually, the poor performance of socialist housing systems could be said to originate in viewing housing exclusively as a social issue and in failing to manage this class of assets as a major economic sector; but the problems are deeper and multi-dimensional. After these three sections, we should be in a better position to evaluate the hypothesis that the rate of return on housing and other urban assets is likely to be negative in resource-intensive DPRK cities.

Overview of urbanization in the DPRK, 1950–2000

North Korean urbanization in international perspective

Three of the four remaining communist countries in the world are in Asia, and all three share the heritage of the great East Asian tradition. However, the level of DPRK urbanization is significantly higher than that in China and Vietnam. In their demographic analysis, Eberstadt and Bannister found that DPRK "population statistics had an unexpected degree of internal consistency and reasonableness" and that "the figures reflect reality" (1992: 11). Based on such credible demographic data, here is a picture of North Korean urbanization:

- Considerable progress has been made in the economic transformation of North Korea into an urban society. Figure 11.1 based on UN population data, shows that the DPRK level of urbanization was three times higher than in China and Vietnam until 1980. Contrary to what is sometimes too casually asserted, urban conditions and policy needs in North Korea should be expected to be structurally different from those found in the two other Asian countries.
- The pace of urbanization in North Korea was equal to or higher than that in South Korea until 1970. Aggregate data show an unusual leveling off of

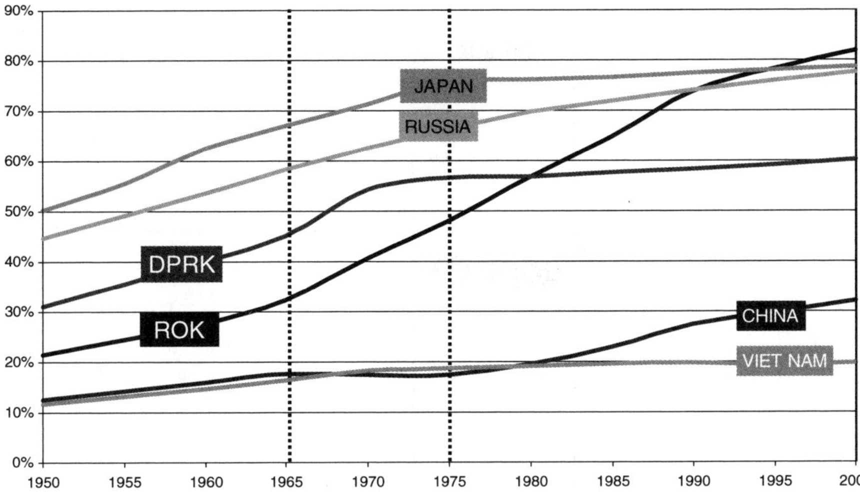

Figure 11.1 North Korea, ROK, Japan, Russia, China and Vietnam: urbanization levels, 1950–2000

Source: UN Population Division. World Urbanization Prospects 1999

DPRK urbanization after 1975 which may be linked to the downturn of the CPE system.[6]

- Given the historical North–South competition, it is worth noting that South Korea surpassed the level of North Korean urbanization in 1980.
- The information analyzed in the chapter shows that the Soviet Union was the leading external CPE influence on North Korean urban institutions and policies. In terms of specific comparators, Figure 11.2 suggests that Romania is the CPE that exhibits the urbanization path closest to that of the DPRK. A noticeable difference is the apparent acceleration in urbanization in the DPRK during the period 1965–75 for which there is no equivalent in Romania.
- The analysis of demographic data from the DPRK Central Statistics in Eberstadt and Bannister (1992) confirms that the greatest growth pressures on North Korean cities were in the 1950s and 1960s when the *tempo* of urbanization was very high (see Figure 11.3).[7] Numerically, the largest rise in the urban population was from 1965 to 1975. The core physical and spatial features of the North Korean cities as they exist today were shaped in that period.

Regional investment patterns: Pyongyang vs other North Korean cities

So great is the difference between living in North Korea's capital city and living elsewhere in the country that some feeling for Pyongyang is absolutely necessary to gain an appreciation of the privileged life in North Korea (Hunter 1999, Chapter 14).

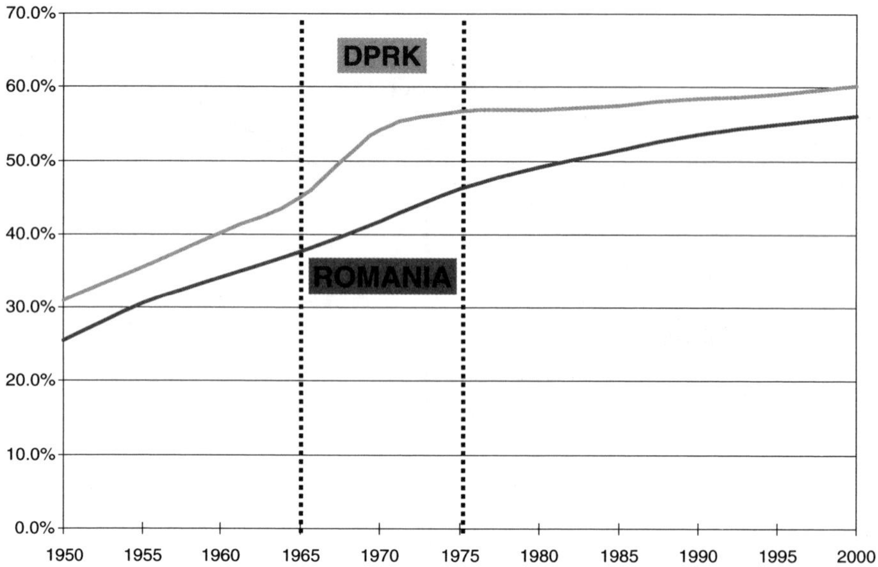

Figure 11.2 DPRK and Romania: urbanization 1950–2000

Source: UN Population Division. World Urbanization Prospects 1999

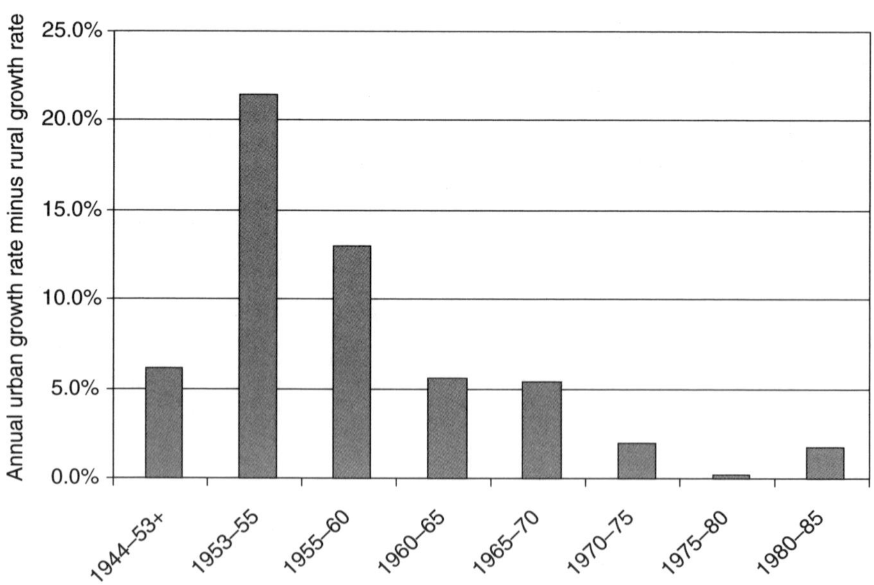

Figure 11.3 North Korea: tempo of urbanization, 1944–85

Source: UN Population Division. World Urbanization Prospects 1999

Differences in urban conditions (housing in particular) across cities under the administrative-command systems of CPEs tend to be the reverse of market systems where housing unit sizes are smaller and costs tend to be higher in very large cities. In CPEs, large cities are treated better than small cities. In the Soviet system, at equal population size, cities that were administrative centers were consistently favored by administrative processes. As a showcase, and being the city of investment decision-makers, Moscow was treated best. In CPE systems, local governments were very weak, especially compared to central ministries, and the latter had great difficulties coordinating their investments across sectors. As a result, poor housing conditions, severe physical and social infrastructure shortages in new industrial centers, and areas where natural resources needed to be exploited were often a major obstacle to manpower stability and economic development. The quality of the rural stock everywhere was much lower than that of the urban stock (Renaud 1992).

Hunter's descriptions of Pyongyang suggest a very comparable investment pattern in the DPRK. In fact, there is a strong presumption that regional investment distortions are more severe in North Korea after the Korean War because Pyongyang was rebuilt entirely as a new city. As Figure 11.4 shows, the city size distribution of North Korean cities is surprisingly skewed for a CPE system. Pyongyang towers over the entire city system; its population was 2.35 million in 1987 (Eberstadt-Bannister 1992) and 2.85 million in 1995 (UN data).

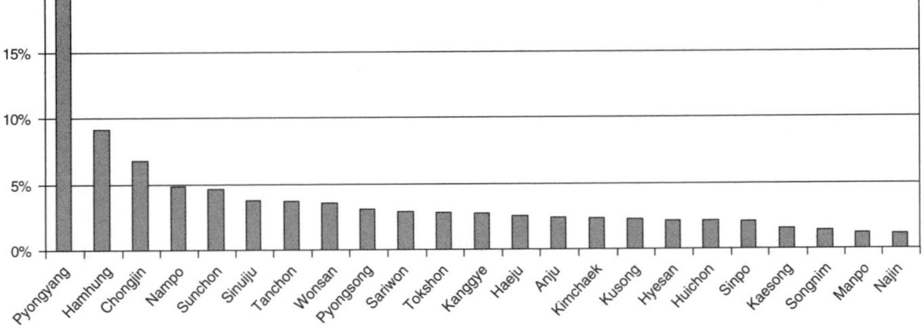

Figure 11.4 North Korea: city size distribution, 1987

Source: Eberstadt and Bannister (1992), data from DPRK Central Statistics Bureau

The supply side of North Korea's urban system

Pyongyang, or the socio-economic costs of a model socialist city

> Kim Il-song built a showcase city in Pyongyang. . . . In the natural beauty of its parks and rivers, the grandeur of its public buildings, and its wide tree-lined avenues – all sparkling clean – and the careful control of the people living there, which creates a unique impression of a spacious, uncrowded Asian city, Pyongyang strikes many observers as one of the most beautiful cities they have ever seen.
>
> (Hunter 1999: 117)

> In order to maintain its orderly, uncluttered appearance, bicycles and trucks are forbidden in certain sections of Pyongyang. Visitors are always struck by the lack of vehicular traffic in the city. Since there are no privately owned automobiles, the only cars present are those owned by the government and used to transport high-level party and government officials, university professors, distinguished artists, sports figures and entertainers. Other people travel by bus or trolley, or on the Pyongyang subway, if they cannot walk to their destination.
>
> (ibid.: 119)

A beautiful city also can be economically unsustainable, and livability for its residents may be very low. There are good reasons to believe that Pyongyang is economically and spatially quite an inefficient city. Because one-third of the total North Korean *urban* population lives there, the hidden costs to the national economy in terms of operating costs and low productivity are expected to be large. Why is that?

In studies of Soviet urbanization carried out in the early 1990s, we learned what happens when urban development takes place after land has been nationalized. The effects will be negative, large and lasting where land is administratively allocated by a centralized urban planning organization rather than traded in a decentralized fashion by individuals and firms through open markets (Bertaud and Renaud 1994, 1997).

The critical *spatial* difference between the *socialist city* and the *market city* is that an efficient and livable market city has negative population density and land price gradients. *Negative density and price gradients are resource-preserving* and critical to the economic well-being of cities. They also impact on the efficiency of the entire national economy: when a country such as North Korea reaches a high level of urbanization, we expect that more than 85 percent of the gross national product (GNP) originates in cities. These negative gradients reflect the fact that the market city is a city that strives to improve access to jobs and urban services for all its businesses and residents in the most economical way. These negative gradients are the unplanned result of the continual competition for land and recycling of already built land parcels into better uses; they do not happen by fiat.[8]

The market city

In a market city, developers are critical professionals who are *value*-maximizers. They compete for the same location. The winning bid will go to the activity estimated to be most valuable (i.e., profitable) at that site. Land prices exert their pressure on the whole supply of land, including the land already built. As the city expands, land prices tend to rise throughout the city. Land prices remain the highest in the most accessible locations. Land densities increase in central locations with the recycling of land through demolition and reconstruction. The consumption of land space per job or per resident decreases because more efficient land users outbid less efficient land-users who then move to peripheral locations. Figure 11.5 outlines the spontaneous land-use pattern that emerges from the bidding competition by alternative activities. This land-use pattern is not the result of master planning by a Chief Architect taking instructions from higher officials, it is the organic outcome of countless individual decisions.

The socialist city

In a supply-driven command system, the profession of developer is unknown and alien. In socialist cities such as Pyongyang, the state organizations producing housing and other buildings respond to very different incentives under the command system. Bureaucratic building organizations are *cost-minimizers,* and serious "agency" problems arise. Construction organizations have very little or no interest in final user satisfaction because future occupants of their buildings are not their clients. These construction organizations are working for other administrations, state enterprises, and, to a very limited extent, municipal governments. The performance of the socialist construction *kombinat* (or its North

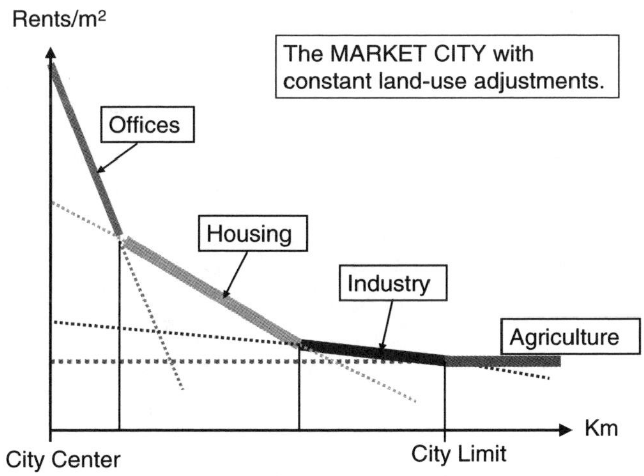

Figure 11.5 Land-use pattern in the market city

Korean equivalent) is measured bureaucratically by its ability to reduce *input costs* while meeting assigned production targets. In terms of building sites, land may be free but it must be allocated by city planners from what is available. Due to the lack of incentives for land recycling, the supply of land is thus limited to the new land areas developed at the outer fringe. If the supply of serviced land is lagging behind the floor space production target, the building density in the outer rings of the city will tend to rise. More floor space will be stacked on the more distant land. The outcome is that densities will rise at the urban periphery.

The positive density gradient of the socialist city is perverse in terms of wasted time for physical infrastructure needs, travel requirements, energy uses, and overall economic productivity. If we compare two cities with the same total land area and the same population, travel requirements usually will be sharply higher in socialist cities – especially in new cities and rapidly growing ones. To illustrate this point, Figure 11.6 compares the density gradients of Moscow and Paris. Within a radius of 14 km, we find the same population in Paris and Moscow. However, the population is 42 percent more dispersed in Moscow, implying higher trip requirements among other costs (Bertaud and Renaud 1997).

Additional "compensating" urban distortions

The structure of incentives in the socialist city does not produce a resource-preserving, efficient negative density gradient. This very large spatial distortion is made more bearable to residents of such cities only by the existence of other *non-*

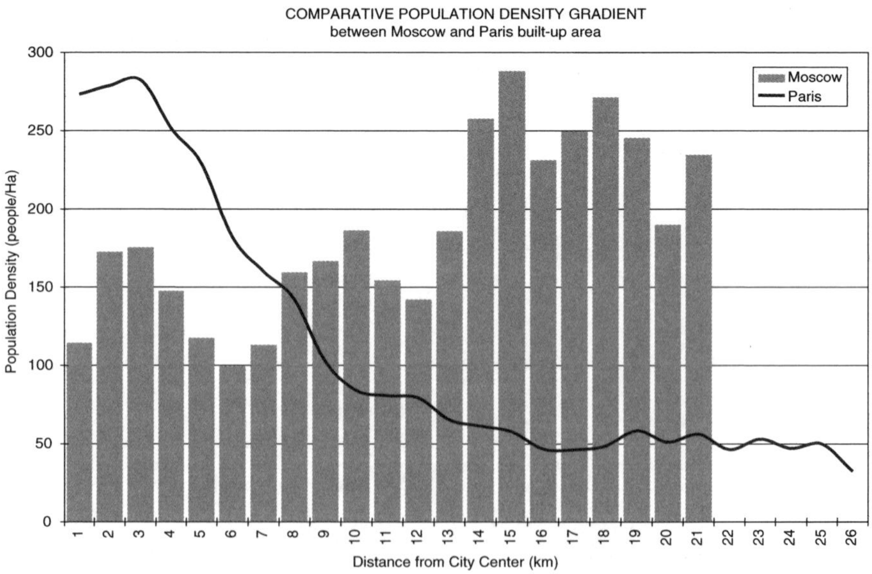

Figure 11.6 Density gradients in Paris and Moscow

Source: Bertaud and Renaud 1997

spatial (and therefore less immediately visible) economic distortions. The failure to price and trade land in these energy-intensive cities was compounded during the Soviet era by artificially low energy prices for transportation and heating. In a CPE, there are no interest charges on capital costs. Even very long-term infrastructure investments in CPEs are funded on a pay-as-you go basis. There also is no incentive toward life-cycle costing of high-rise residential buildings, because initial building capital costs and recurrent operating costs are the responsibility of totally different bureaucracies that lack effective incentives to coordinate their efforts.

Another distortion which is part of the socialist labor system makes the spatial inefficiency of a socialist city more bearable to city residents. Urban transportation studies made in market cities show that city residents behave as if they priced the value of their travel time at between one-third and one-half of their hourly wage equivalent. In socialist cities, the economic out-of-pocket and time costs of lengthy commuting will be partially masked by the artificially low value that urban residents place on their time, based on their low cash wage which we discuss below as part of the demand-side section. All these interacting distortions result in low productivity for the entire economy.

Impact of the economic contraction since the late 1980s

The impact of the abrupt end of Soviet energy subsidies in 1990 on North Korean cities, and on Pyongyang in particular, must have been quite significant as suggested by well-publicized night-time satellite photos. Living standards must have declined significantly for the vast majority of urban residents in terms of productivity on the job, journeys to work and home heating. The economic decline of the economy since the mid-1980s must also have led to a drop in new housing construction, as well as an accelerating consumption of the housing capital stock through deferred or zero maintenance of most existing buildings.

Figure 11.6 also suggests some significant distributive impacts of housing privatization once the transition to a market economy will get underway. Distant suburban residents (in the case of Moscow those between 9 km and 22 km where densities are above the market gradient line) will find themselves living in units of negative market value. Meanwhile, the privileged few who are living in the city center (where current densities fall below the market gradient line) could expect large windfalls. Such imbalances could be even more acute in Pyongyang than in Moscow because it is an entirely planned new city without a remaining pre-socialist historical center.

Impact of the monopolistic building industry on consumer choice

> Housing construction increased with each successive development plan. Some 600,000 housing units were built from 1954 to 1960, 800,000 units from 1961 to 1969, and over 1,000,000 in the 1970s. By 1976, North Korea had constructed new housing for almost three fourths of its urban and rural

> households – a notable accomplishment. ... From all reports, the people mention housing first and foremost, when they talked about how the Communists have improved their lives. ... The paradox is that while North Koreans generally acknowledged the advances in housing and give the regime credit in this area, they nonetheless cite cramped housing as one of their major complaints. Crowded housing conditions usually head any list of common grievances.
>
> (Hunter 1999: 187, 190)

> Kim's answer to the postwar housing crisis lay in building multistoried apartment complexes of prefabricated construction. ... Much of the prefabricated construction of the 1960s and early 1970s was of poor quality, compared to the better quality of traditional methods of brick construction done on the site. North Korean construction of the 1960s is famous for its ill-fitting windows, cracked walls and ceilings, uneven floors, leaking roofs and warped plate glass.
>
> In recent years, North Korean technology in construction has improved dramatically. Many of the newer apartment buildings are over twenty stories high, compared to the typical five- or six-story apartment houses of the 1960s and the ten to twelve story buildings of the 1970s. ... The newer apartments are an improvement in their more modern conveniences, such as central heating, running water, flush toilets, and elevators that work. ... Pyongyang is way ahead of the rest of the country in this respect. ... The standardization of North Korea's prefabricated housing is such that one can talk about the average urban apartment with a reasonable degree of confidence. There are three or four basic designs for individual apartments that are used over and over again.
>
> (ibid.: 191–3)

Hunter's study of North Korea was published in 1999 but it was actually completed in the late 1970s. Her work coincided with the time when North Korea's urbanization was leveling off, suggesting that the national economy itself was beginning to stall (see Figure 11.1). She appears to have captured the socio-economic features of the North Korean CPE at its zenith. Her analyses based on interviews with defectors create a picture of the evolution and quality of the housing stock in North Korea during the period 1955 to 1975 that closely parallels the experience of Soviet Russia, one or two central plans ahead of North Korea. In the late 1950s, under Nikita Krushchev, the Soviet Union embarked upon the greatest program of mass production of industrial housing that probably will ever be attempted in world history. Unfortunately, as in North Korea, the resulting housing stock from that very large experiment is of such poor quality that it now goes by the derisive of "*Krushcheby*," a Russian word play on Krushchev's name and the word "slum."

The Russian experience with housing is well analyzed in the lucid and compassionate study edited by Brumfield and Ruble (1993) in cooperation with their Russian colleagues. In particular, in his chapter entitled "From Krushcheby to Korobki" ("From slums to superblock") Ruble reports how in order to meet production quotas and schedules, state construction organizations raised the "optimal" height from five stories during the Krushchev period, to nine stories, then sixteen stories and finally thirty-seven stories in the mid-1980s. Under the cover of "modern planning theory," federal architects even attempted to lower the number of alternative designs to eight standard apartments to serve the huge USSR urban system that ranged across eleven time zones and every possible climate! Ruble also reports that as Russian apartments grew in height in the 1960s, the size of units shrunk as construction *kombinats* were under permanent pressure to trim back "living space."[9]

Who produces new housing in North Korea today? Do state enterprises still claim almost total domination? As a point of comparison, Table 11.1 gives the housing supply breakdown in Russia in 1990 at the end of the CPE era and the fitful start of the market reforms. Table 11.2 gives the 1988 sources of housing funds in Russia. How different is the DPRK housing supply system today from Soviet Russia a decade ago?

Mismatch between changing household needs and a rigid housing stock[10]

Clearly, the lack of responsiveness to consumer preferences by state building organizations is quite costly. It also has cumulative effects over time as the urban physical stock expands. However, it would be technically difficult to assign a reliable economic value to the loss of consumer welfare resulting from the lack of

Table 11.1 Suppliers of housing in Russia, 1990

Type of housing	*Million square meters*	*(%)*
State housing	52.1	86.1
Individual housing	5.5	9.1
Cooperative housing	2.9	5.8
Total	60.5	100.0

Source: Renaud (1992), T.5

Table 11.2 Sources of housing funds, Russia, 1988

Sources of funds	*(%)*
State capital investment	62
Enterprise Social Funds	7
Kolkhozy (state farms)	7
Cooperative funds	8
Population savings	16

Source: Renaud (1992), T.6

housing choice. We suspect that the ratio between perceived value by households and the actual resource cost of housing inputs is unfavorable.[11] The magnitude of the welfare loss can be suggested graphically only by comparing housing choices in a market economy with those in a CPE.

Figure 11.7 shows the wide range of combinations of land consumption and floor space offered by Malaysia's private housing markets in 1988. A wide range of trade-offs between land consumption and housing unit space is available to meet the needs of families of all incomes, wealth and size. The practical domain of actual options is delineated by the triangular envelope.

Figure 11.8 describes options available in socialist Chinese cities prior to the major housing reforms begun in 1988. As in North Korea, the range of options was starkly poor.

Figure 11.9 superimposes the two situations in Figures 11.7 and 11.8 to suggest the extent of the loss of diversity and welfare resulting from the incentive structure of state builders in a socialist city.

In addition to the serious supply-side distortions that we should anticipate in the cities of North Korea, and in Pyongyang in particular, demand-side distortions should be expected as well. These demand-side distortions are not as visually tangible as the supply-side distortions of the socialist city.

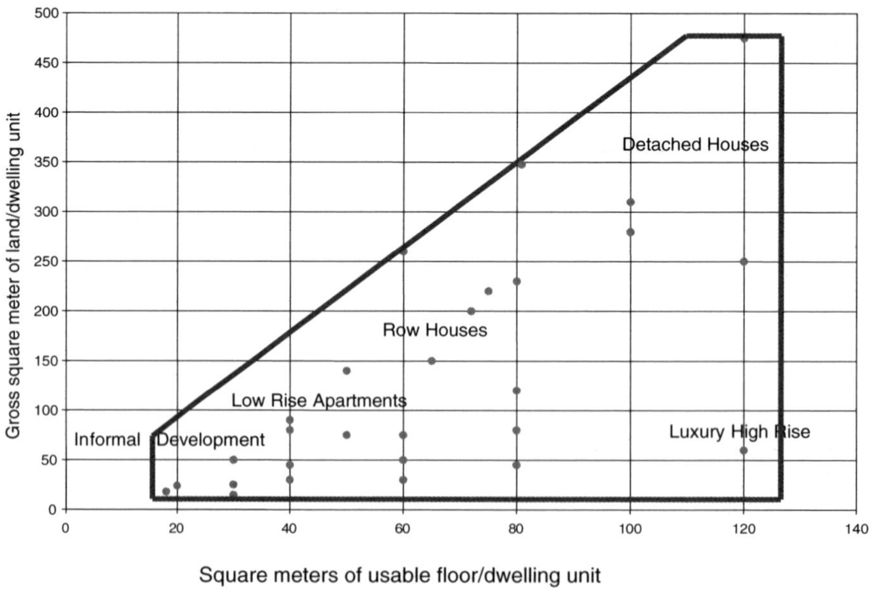

Figure 11.7 Socialist versus market cities – range of housing choices: Malaysia

Source: Bertaud (1988)

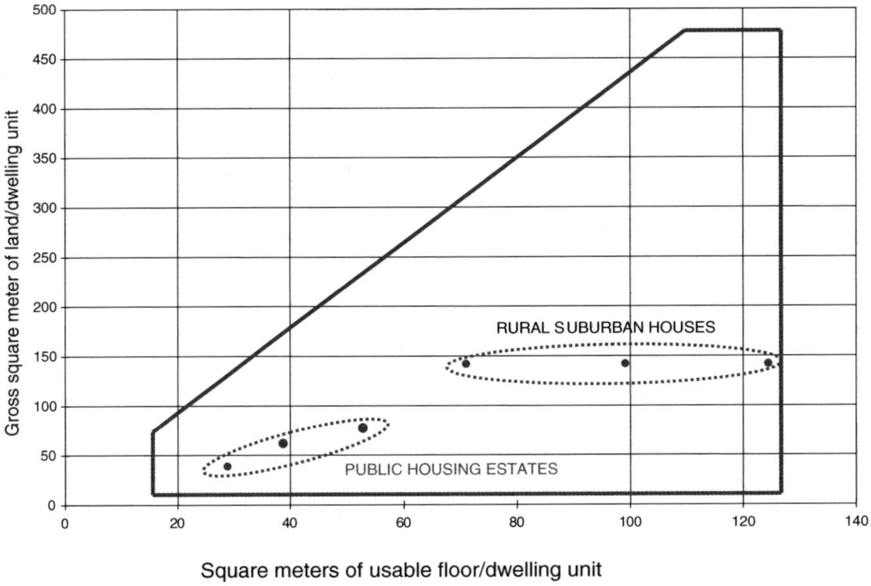

Figure 11.8 Socialist versus market cities – range of housing choices: China, 1980s

Source: Bertaud (1988)

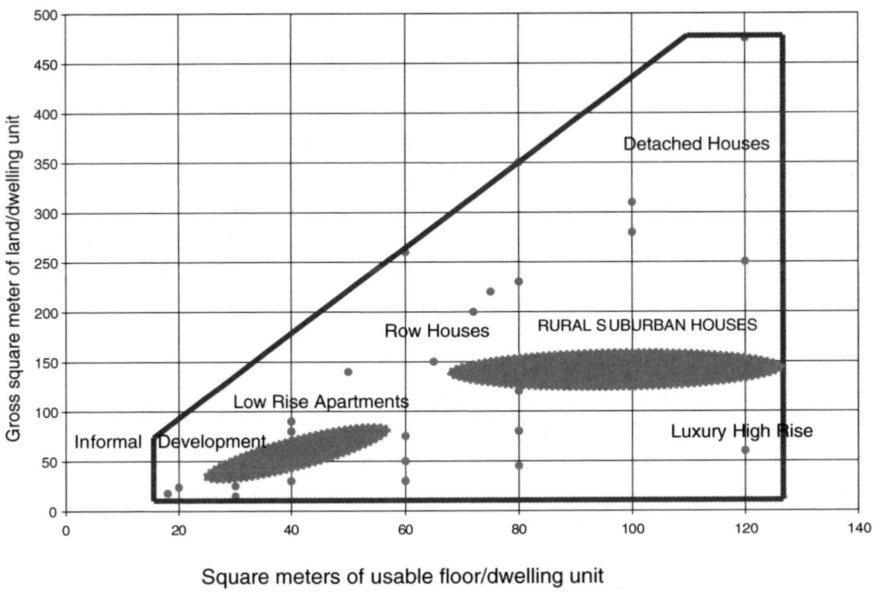

Figure 11.9 Socialist versus market cities – range of housing choices: DPRK versus Malaysia

Source: Bertaud (1988)

The demand side of North Korean housing

They are five demand-side aspects to highlight in the functioning of the socialist housing economy: (1) wage distortions and the associated regressive subsidies in kind; (2) distortion in ownership rights; (3) distortions in the pricing of housing services; (4) zero vacancy rates, waiting lists and the increasing misallocation of the housing stock over time; and (5) the tight control over labor mobility by means of residency permits in order to control the demand for urban housing and infrastructure services in favored cities.

Cash socialist wages differ from actual total labor compensation

> To judge from wages alone, there would seem to be considerable equality in North Korea. The privileged would appear to live roughly twice as well as ordinary North Korean working people and about three times as well as the lowest-paid unskilled workers. ... But the statistics are misleading because money is a poor measure of living standards in North Korea.
>
> (Hunter 1999: 142)

The lack of mechanisms for feedback between the construction organizations and the final users and the rigid "standardization of demand" that the building industry is able to impose on households are made possible (or enforced, if one prefers) by the structure of the socialist wage. This mechanism would appear to remain in full force in the DPRK.

CPE economies operate under the principle of "low cash wages" from which the state has removed the purchasing power for housing, transport, health services, education, and retirement. In essence, all the major elements (human, physical, and financial) of household asset formation are removed from the direct control of individuals. Socialist wages serve to pay for daily necessities and consumer services. Critical assets then are provided either free or heavily subsidized as "distribution goods" controlled by the state. They are channeled through the place of employment. The result is the total dependence of the individual on the work unit, a control system often popularly described before the 1979 reforms by the Chinese as the "iron rice bowl."

The standard efficiency analysis of public economics suggests that such a large implicit wage tax is highly distortionary and carries with it a heavy "deadweight loss" from which nobody gains. It is merely a hidden drain on the economy's efficiency. In a market system, economic theory suggests that the size of this deadweight loss is proportional to the square of the tax rate and that it increases with the elasticity of demand and supply. For this reason, several small taxes (with low tax rates) yielding the same aggregate resources are less distorting.[12] Of course, one might argue that the deadweight loss might not be that great in North Korea because labor elasticities are likely to be very low. The other side of the coin is minimal labor productivity.

Because of the dominant role played by income in-kind in CPE labor systems, the main social inequalities in CPEs do not come from cash wages. From the viewpoint of a market economist, implicit subsidies are linked to apartment units and not to the socio-economic characteristics of households. As a result, the larger the apartment unit, the more subsidized a family is. However, it is probably more useful to take the perspective of total labor compensation. Contrary to the equalitarian claims of CPE systems, housing is the principal source of inequality. Pensions, access to superior health services, and education are the other main channels. There is evidence of a high correlation between socio-economic status and access to housing in all CPEs. Hunter (1999) describes these CPE channels of labor compensation in the case of North Korea.

It is worth mentioning that, in spite of so many distortions, the structural parameters of housing demand estimated in the Soviet Union for the pre-reform era were found to be very similar to those of market economies (Alexeev 1987 and 1988). In other words, behavioral parameters for market households and socialist households are the same.

Public ownership structure with socialist tenant rights

The former Soviet Union had the most distorted ownership structure of all the main socialist housing systems. It had the highest rate of public ownership of the urban housing stock: more than 78 percent Union-wide compared to 67 percent in China, 56 percent in Poland, 33 percent in Romania, and 25 percent in Hungary. Western estimates at the end of the 1980s were the opposite: 2 percent in the United States, 7 percent in Germany, 17 percent in France, 30 percent in the UK, and 38 percent in Sweden; moreover, this public stock is managed quite differently. In Russia proper, cities above 100,000 people were almost entirely under public ownership. We expect close to 100 percent of public ownership in North Korean cities as well. The important qualifier is that socialist tenant rights typically carry significant (if non-tradable) elements of ownership, such as the right to transfer occupancy rights to children.

Distorted pricing structure

In terms of prices, the Soviet housing system had the most distorted socialist housing prices among CPE economies in three areas. First, rent-income ratios reflecting the price that households paid for their state-provided housing were extremely low. In fact, these rents were similar to a fee and were so named in most CPE countries. Table 11.3 shows the expenditure ratios in terms of household income that were observed at the start of market-oriented reforms (except in Hungary where the market reforms were pioneered under the "*Gulash* socialism" of Janos Kadar in the early 1980s).

According to Hunter (1999: 195), the pricing structure in North Korea in the mid-1970s was very similar to that of the USSR. Given the rigidities of CPE systems, there is a good probability that this pricing has remained essentially the

Table 11.3 Housing and utilities as percentage of income in CPEs

Country	*Year*	*Total*	*Rent Only*	*Utilities*
Bulgaria	1988	12.1	7.6	4.5
Hungary	1987	8.7	1.6	7.1
Poland	1986	4.4	2.0	2.4
Romania	1989	4.4	3.0	1.0
Yugoslavia	1988	9.3	2.8	6.5
USSR	1989	2.5	1.0	1.5
N-Korea	1970s	2.0	1.0	1.0

Source: Renaud (1992)

same. The problems with such very low rates are that they cover only a small fraction of the true economic maintenance cost of the building and of utilities. During the period of decline of the 1990s in North Korea the results must have been an accelerated depreciation of buildings and a sharp deterioration in utility services in the form of frequent interruptions and poor quality when available. In contrast to these low CPE ratios, in high income OECD countries, household expenditure ratios for housing and utilities were 24 percent each for France, the UK, Canada and Germany, and 29 percent for the USA in 1999. In a market economy of North Korea's level we would expect expenditure ratios between 15 percent and 20 percent.

Zero vacancy rates, waiting lists and misallocation of units over time

CPE urban systems are characterized by immobility. One important reason is that the institutions and incentives in these physically oriented systems have created an environment of zero vacancy rates across the existing stock of housing, offices and every other form of real estate. In a market city, vacancy rates are fundamental to the reshaping of the stock of urban assets. While buildings themselves cannot move, vacancy rates across districts and neighborhoods act as substitutes. There is a very close relationship between the dynamics of market rents and vacancy rates in adjusting building uses over time.

When prices are not used to clear markets, the only remedy to zero vacancy rates is waiting lists. Few problems have caused more tensions in CPEs than their inefficient housing allocation mechanisms. Waiting lists are a permanent feature of CPE life, almost an obsession. In Moscow, there were several waiting lists which were managed separately but not independently: municipal waiting lists, cooperative waiting lists, enterprise waiting lists, etc.[13] Inclusion on the housing waiting list was not automatic. The decision was based on needs and related to affiliation with a specific work unit. Household income was not a consideration. The most important indicator of need was the misleading indicator of "square meter of living space per capita" already mentioned. This need criterion deliberately eliminated critical aspects of housing quality such as shared facilities in communal apartment, location and neighborhood socio-economic and ecological quality. In particular, under the "living space" criterion, residents of communal apartments were seriously penalized. Manipulation of this complex bureaucratic system was frequent. Some people were much more equal than others, and the sullen resentment of the preferred treatment of the *nomenklatura* ran deep. There is no reason to expect a different situation in North Korean cities.

The drift over time toward an increasing misallocation of the housing stock is a structural feature of state-owned housing systems. In fluid market cities, households restructure their housing use over their life cycle. By contrast, as a rigid CPE housing system ages, the mismatch grows between the composition of the housing stock and the demographic structure of the population. Young families with children cannot find adequate housing, while comparatively older households have too much space. After decades of economic stagnation or decline, surveys would be needed to assess the extent of this problem in DPRK cities.

Housing stock conditions, residency permits and labor mobility

> Part of Kim's design in creating his dream city, as he called Pyongyang, was to limit the size of the city's population. According to defectors, everyone wants to live in Pyongyang. … North Koreans cannot move into or out of Pyongyang without official approval. In this regard, Kim Il-song adopted some of the controls the Soviet used in Moscow. … North Korean controls are much tighter than the Soviet controls were.
>
> (Hunter 1999: 118–19)

Residency permits are a feature of CPEs. The *propiska* of Russia and the *hukou* of China are internal passports that have been used extensively in the past as instruments of "labor discipline" and of "population distribution policy and spatial planning." They are still in use today in both countries, but now as "urban planning" instruments to deny "floating populations" the right to claim services from the cities where they have moved. This passport system is a source of inequity and economic inefficiency. There have been times when rural residents were subjected to the equivalent of socialist indenture labor by being denied a *propiska* to move to cities. As noted by Hunter, the population of highly favored cities like Moscow has been stabilized through this passport system. During days of pervasive consumer good shortages, the local *propiska* often has been required for shopping. For the convenience of city officials and permanent residents, temporary residency permits of a few months also are issued to meet short-term needs in sectors experiencing serious labor shortages, but such permits do not give the right to housing.

Even when internal passports are abolished, there will continue to be a negative employment impact on labor mobility caused by the lasting rigidity of the housing stock, and the absence of a flexible rental market. Studies of Poland after the transition by Mayo and Stein, and of Scotland (where about 50 percent of the housing stock is in public ownership) by Hughes and McCormick have demonstrated that rigidities in public housing systems raise unemployment rates significantly by preventing workers from moving to where the jobs are.

Conclusion

> Nothing is permanent except change.
>
> (Heraclites, Greek philosopher, 6th century BC)

Based on what we now understand about the dynamics of the "socialist city," we can make strong hypotheses about the likely state of the DPRK urban system today. International analyses as well as the direct North Korean evidence lead us to believe that the CPE urban system of North Korea is not sustainable in its present form. The deadweight losses and the economic inefficiencies caused by the numerous "agency" problems spread throughout the North Korean urban system must be serious indeed. The breakdown of the trade relationships with Council for Mutual Economic Assistance (CMEA) countries after 1990 must have revealed and added to prior structural weaknesses.

The current status of North Korean cities begs the question of what reforms will be necessary and in what sequence. One day, North Korea will be able to draw on the decade's accumulated experience of other CPEs. Any serious reform process requires specific (not merely plausible) answers to three successive questions. We could only present specific assumptions ("rigorous speculations") about the first question of how we should go about evaluating current urban conditions in the DPRK. The other two questions of how to *design* urban reforms in the specific North Korean context and then how to *implement* them must wait. It is hoped that the outline of the economic features and serious distortions of a socialist city presented here may reassure some readers that the "theory-to-fact" ratio of urban analysis in socialist economies has improved in the past decade. When the time comes, Korean and international analysts will be able to diagnose the specificities of North Korean cities more quickly than was possible fifteen years ago and can proceed from there.

Notes

1 The author is an advisor, Financial Sector Development Department, the World Bank, Washington, DC. This study builds upon his direct experience in transition economies in Asia, the former Soviet Union and Central and Eastern Europe after 1988. He owes a special debt to the path-breaking work of his long-time colleague Alain Bertaud. The analysis presented is strictly personal and does not represent official views of the World Bank nor any of its affiliated organizations.

2 For a side-by-side comparison of the terminology, conceptual treatment and organization principles of a CPE housing system with that of market economies, see Renaud (1991: 6–9).

3 For a comprehensive case study of the housing system, in Soviet Russia, see the World Bank (1994).

4 The complete 1992 US tangible wealth breakdown was: residential, 56 percent; equipment, 17 percent; durable goods, 12 percent; retail/commercial real estate, 5 percent; offices, 6 percent; warehousing, 4 percent.

5 An administrative command economy simply does not operate like a market economy. A market economist cannot transfer indiscriminately his/her modes of thinking and

policy views and econometric models to the reform of a socialist economy – particularly the reliance on marginal analysis. For a short economic primer on the behavior of a prototypical CPE refer to Robert W. Campbell (1991). For a deeper understanding of the political economy of the communist system, see Janos Kornai (1992).

6 The macro-economic analysis of openness and growth in North Korea by Professor Jang C. Jin (2003) also points to the year 1974 as the beginning of the downturn of the North Korean economy.

7 To reflect overall social and economic change, demographers measure the *tempo* of urbanization as the annual rate of urban population growth *minus* the rate of rural population growth. The faster the rural population of a country declines, the higher the tempo of urbanization is.

8 In his recent "Costs of Utopia" (2001), Bertaud once again stresses that in the market city, urban planning only allocates precise functions to *public* spaces such as streets, avenues, parks and public buildings. Within that framework, the markets then decide who lives in what location and who opens a business where. The effects of *local* governance on land use regulations *and their interactions with markets* are critical to a sound city operation.

9 In socialist economies, housing statistics often use three measures of housing space: (1) *construction or total space* which includes all the area within the outside perimeter of the building, including common spaces like halls, stairways and public corridors; (2) *usable space* which is essentially the total inner area of the apartment; and, (3) *living space* which is the apartment less kitchen, bathroom and corridors. The net impact of using "living space" as the criterion for the allocation of units or registration on waiting list is to remove major quality dimensions from allocation decisions and to hide key housing differences across units. The housing services from 5 m^2 of living space with one's private kitchen are clearly not the same as 5 m^2 of living space and a communal kitchen. Yet this is what was happening in Leningrad where communal apartments were still common in 1990. For purely statistical purposes, 1 m^2 of living space can usually be converted to 1.45 m^2 of total space.

10 This section draws extensively on the analyses of Alain Bertaud in Bertaud and Renaud (1994).

11 Russian economists made highly suggestive analyses toward this ratio in 1990. In particular, given the broad range of pricing distortions in effect, it was estimated that the true resource cost of a new housing unit was actually six times the reported accounting cost of that unit used by construction *kombinats*.

12 See, for instance, Joseph E. Stiglitz, *Economics of the Public Sector* (1986: 375), or Arnold Harberger, "Taxation, Resources Allocation, Welfare," (1964).

13 In Moscow, 15.4 percent of the entire population was on the municipal and cooperative waiting lists in June 1990. The computerized management of this list was very complex. For its monitoring system, the Moscow government had identified fifty-six different categories of households and 120 different paths to achieve access in housing. The waiting period could extend up to ten years officially, but older applicants could be dropped from the list and registered again under a more recent date, (Renaud 1992).

References

Alexeev, Michael V. (1987) "The Effect of Housing Allocation on Social Inequality: A Soviet Perspective," *Journal of Comparative Economics*, vol. 12, 228–34.

Alexeev, Michael V. (1988) "Market vs. Rationing: The Case of Soviet Housing," *Review of Economics and Statistics*, 70(3), 414–20.

Bertaud, Alain (1988) *An Evaluation of Urban Planning in China*, unpublished mimeo, Washington DC: World Bank.

Bertaud, Alain (2001) "The Costs of Utopia", unpublished chapter in *Order Without Design.*

Bertaud, Alain and Renaud, Bertrand (1994) *Cities Without Land Markets: Lessons of the Failed Socialist Experiment*, Washington, DC: World Bank Discussion Paper 227.

Bertaud, Alain and Renaud, Bertrand (1997) "Socialist Cities Without Land Markets," *Journal of Urban Economics*, 41(1), January, 137–52.

Brumfield, William Craft and Ruble, Blair A. (1993) *Russian Housing in the Modern Age: Design and Social History*, Cambridge: Cambridge University Press.

Campbell, Robert W. (1991) *The Socialist Economies in Transition. A Primer on Semi-Reformed Systems*, Bloomington: Indiana University Press.

De Melo, Martha, Denizer, Cevdet, Gelb, Alan and Tenev, Stoyan (2001) "Circumstances and Choice: The Role of Initial Conditions and Policies in Transition Economies," *The World Bank Economic Review*, 15(1), 1–31.

Eberstadt, Nicholas and Bannister, Judith (1992) *The Population of North Korea*, Berkeley, CA: Center for Korean Studies.

Gros, Daniel and Suhrcke, Marc (2000) *Ten Years After: What is Special About Transition Economies?*, Munich: CESifo, WP 327, August.

Harberger, Arnold (1964) "Taxation, Resource Allocation and Welfare," in the *Role of Direct and Indirect Taxes in the Federal Revenue System*, ed. John Due, NJ: Princeton University Press.

Hughes, Gordon A. and Barry McCormick (1988) *Housing and Labor Market Performance.* Paper prepared for the IIESR Conference on Housing and the National Economy.

Hunter, Helen Louise (1999) *Kim Il-Song's North Korea,* Westport, CT: Praeger Publishers.

Jan C. Jin (2003) "Openness and Growth in North Korea: Evidence from Time Series Data," *Review of International Economics* (forthcoming).

Kornai, Janos (1992) *The Socialist System – The Political Economy of Communism,* Princeton, NJ: Princeton University Press.

Lee, Jeong-Sik, Jung, Hee-Nam and Cheong, Woo-Hyung (1997) *The Real Estate Reform Process in the Post-Communist Countries,* Seoul: Korea Research Institute for Human Settlements.

Lee, Jeong-Sik, Kim, Won-Bae and Jung, Hee-Nam (1996) *The Land Reform Process in the Post-Communist Countries,* Seoul: Korea Research Institute for Human Settlements.

Malpezzi, Stephen, Shilling, James D. and Wang, Yu-Yu (2000) *The Stock of Private Real Estate Capital in U.S. Metropolitan Areas*, Madison, WI: University of Wisconsin, School of Business, Working Paper, October.

Mayo, Stephen K. and James Stein (1995) "Housing and Labor Market Distortions in Poland: Linkages and Policy Implications," *Journal of Housing Economics*, vol. 4, 153–82.

Milanovic, Branko (1998) *Income, Inequality, and Poverty during the Transition from Planned to Market Economy*, Washington, DC: World Bank Regional and Sectoral Studies.

Noland, Marcus (2000) *Avoiding the Apocalypse: The Future of the Two Koreas*, Washington, DC: Institute of International Economics.

Noland, Marcus, Robinson, Sherman and Wang, Tao (2000) "Rigorous Speculation: The Collapse and Revival of the North Korean Economy," *World Development*, September.

Renaud, Bertrand and Barlow, Melinda (1989) "Housing Reform and Commercialization of Urban Housing in China," *Review of Urban and Regional Development Studies*, 1(1), 1–22.

Renaud, Bertrand (1991) *The Framework of Housing Reforms in Socialist Economies*, World Bank Discussion Paper 125, Washington, DC: the World Bank.

Renaud, Bertrand (1992) "The Housing System of the Former Soviet Union: Why Do the Soviets Need Housing Markets?," Washington, DC: Housing Policy Debate, 3(3), 877–99. Reprinted in Russian in a special issue of *Voprosy Economiki* (Economic Issues), Moscow, September 1993.

Renaud, Bertrand (1995) "The Real Estate Economy and the Design of Russian Housing Reforms," *Urban Studies*, 32(8), 1247–64 and 32(9), 1437–51.

Stiglitz, Joseph E. (1986) *Economics of the Public Sector*, New York: W.W. Norton & Co.

U.N. Population Division (1999) *World Urbanization Prospects 1999*, N.Y. New York.

World Bank (1995) *RUSSIA: Housing Reform and Privatization: Strategy and Transition Issues*, Report No. 11868–RU. vol. 1: Main Report and vol. 2: Annexes, Washington, DC: World Bank.

12 Inter-Korean cooperation in infrastructure development and territorial integration

Won Bae Kim

Introduction

The historic summit between the leaders of the two Koreas in June 2000 gave new hope for a gradual and peaceful integration of these two countries that have been separated for more than fifty years. If inter-Korean dialogue proceeds smoothly with the support of the major powers with interests in the Korean Peninsula, it will offer an opportunity to reintegrate the divided peninsula and reposition the area in the changing geopolitical landscape of contemporary North-East Asia.

However, many uncertainties still exist regarding the form and substance of inter-Korean economic cooperation. Questions also arise about the costs and benefits of economic cooperation for South Korea. The key issue is reciprocity: what can the South gain from the North as a result of such cooperation? More importantly, the South Korean public is not sure about the true intentions of Pyongyang – despite recent policy changes taken by the North with respect to relations with the South, the United States, and other Western countries. Skeptics in and outside South Korea interpret Pyongyang's recent external policy shifts as tactical moves rather than strategic changes. The past behavior of the North does not lend much credibility to the sustainability of its recent policy initiatives.

Despite the weight of those skeptical views, we cannot ignore the possibility of genuine policy shifts in the coming years. If Pyongyang continues its engagement with Seoul and is committed to normalizing its relations with Washington and Tokyo, it would be bound to make certain policy changes. A critical element in this policy shift is whether Pyongyang is willing to undertake major economic reforms needed to rebuild its economy. Although Pyongyang's new policies on security issues (such as the production and sale of nuclear devices and missiles) are important for the peaceful coexistence of the two Koreas and the North's relations with the United States and Japan, they are less threatening to the regime than economic reforms. Therefore, Pyongyang's commitment to economic and other systemic reforms will be the key indicator of the depth and sincerity of inter-Korean economic cooperation and integration in the coming years.

At this point no one can be certain about the future trajectory of inter-Korean dialogue, including the possibilities for economic cooperation. Assuming, however, that the momentum generated by recent events involving the Korean Peninsula continues without major setbacks, we can be reasonably certain that inter-Korean economic cooperation will expand and eventually lead to economic integration. With this prospect in mind, I would like to discuss the progress and key issues of inter-Korean economic cooperation including infrastructure development. Since any future inter-Korean economic cooperation and integration will inevitably touch upon territorial development, I will discuss immediate and long-term issues surrounding the territorial integration of the Korean Peninsula, with particular emphasis on balanced development. Using a German case as a reference point, I will consider a few strategic problems involved in inter-Korean economic cooperation and suggest ways to achieve balanced development.

Two Koreas in a snapshot

The economy

Although there is no reliable and undisputable statistical information about the economy of North Korea, we can safely say that North Korea has been in decline since the late 1980s. Moreover, North Korea experienced famine in the mid-1990s and food is still in short supply. Table 12.1 provides a few indicators by which we can compare the relative magnitude of differences in economic development between South and North Korea and between West and East Germany prior to unification.

Table 12.1 Comparison of South and North Korea with West and East Germany

Indicators		*Korea (1999)*		*Germany (1989)*	
		South	*North*	*West*	*East*
Population (1,000 persons)		46,858	22,082	62,063	16,614
Area (sq. km)		99,314	122,762	248,252	108,588
Labor force employed (1,000 persons)		19,837*	15,971*	27,742	8,886
Labor force distribution (%)	primary	13.6*	25.7*	3.9	10.8
	secondary	23.9*	48.0*	39.7	50.4
	tertiary	62.5*	26.3*	56.4	38.8
Gross National Income or Gross Domestic Product (billion US$)		402.1	15.8	1,196.8	97.0
Per capita GNI or GDP (US$)		8,581	714	19,283	5,840

Note: * figures are for 1994.

Sources: For Korea, all the figures are derived from the National Statistical Office of Korea (2001) and labor force figures are from Oh (1996: 143). For Germany, figures are from Bae (1994).

Based on these figures, we can readily see that the task facing the Korean Peninsula now is much more serious than the German situation in 1989. First, North Korea's population is almost half of South Korea's population, while the East German population was about one-quarter of the West German population. Although the Bank of Korea's estimate of North Korea's gross national income may contain a large margin of error, the size difference between South and North Korean economies is surely larger than that between West and East Germany before unification.[1] Therefore, the relative difference in per capita income between South and North Korea is much larger than that between West and East Germany. Reducing such a gap would be a formidable future task.

Compared to East Germany in 1989, North Korea has a higher proportion of its labor force in the agricultural sector and a smaller proportion of workers in the service sector. As happened in East Germany after unification, North Korea is likely to face a large shift of employment when it introduces a market economy and begins to engage in external trade (Maretzke and Strubelt 2000). Another important factor in North Korea is the large military force, estimated to be more than 1 million (Eberstadt 1997). When inter-Korean economic cooperation matures, there will likely be large-scale military reductions in both Koreas and the integration of this substantial group into the workforce will be a significant challenge.

The infrastructure

In addition to vast differences in the size of economy and employment composition, the two Koreas have sharply contrasting levels of infrastructure development, which has a direct bearing on the territorial integration of the two countries. On the whole, the North Korean infrastructure is underdeveloped and poorly maintained, indicating the need for a major restoration of infrastructure in order to revitalize the North Korean economy. The primary reason for North Korea's underdeveloped infrastructure lies in its overemphasis on heavy industries and relative neglect of infrastructure. Generally, the infrastructure has been regarded as a supplementary element of production rather than as an integral part of economic development. Investment in infrastructure has thus been kept to the minimum necessary to support production activities. As a consequence, North Korea faces infrastructure shortages as well as inefficient existing infrastructure due to poor maintenance.

As of 1999, North Korea had 5,214 km of railway, 23,500 km of road, 682 km of expressway, 7.4 million kilowatt electricity generating capacity, and 35 million tons of port handling capacity (see Table 12.2). Among these, electricity is known to be the most serious problem, with insufficient supplies hampering the normal operation of factories and railways. Total electricity generated in 1999 was only 18.6 billion kilowatt-hours, which was about one-thirteenth of that available in the South. Shortages in the country's coal supply are a direct cause of the low electricity generation. In addition, the deterioration of generating facilities and

Table 12.2 Comparison of infrastructure endowment between South and North Korea

Category		*Unit*	*South (A)*	*North (B)*	*Ratio (A/B)*
Road	Total length	km	87,500	23,500	3.7
	Road length/1,000 sq km of area	km/1000 km^2			
	Length of highway	km	1,996	682	2.9
	Percentage of pavement	%	77.8	8.1	9.4
Rail	Total length	km	6,683	5,214	1.3
	Rail length/1,000 sq km of area	km/1,000 km^2	66	42	1.6
	Total length of electrified rail	km	661.3	4,132.0	0.2
	Percentage of electrification	%	9.9	79.2	0.13
Port	Loading capacity	million tons	41,625	3,501	11.9
	Per capita loading capacity	tons	9.0	1.6	4.3
Electricity	Generation capacity	1,000kw	46,978	7,387	6.4
	Electricity generated	billion kwh	239.3	18.6	13.0
	Per capita electricity consumption	ton of oil equivalent	3.87	0.67	5.8
Telephone	Total number of lines	1,000 lines	14,570	820	17.8
	Lines per 1,000 persons	lines	33.68	3.57	9.4

Source: Statistical Office of Government of Korea, http://www.nso.go.kr

leakages in the transmission system are other reasons for electricity shortages (Cheong 1999).

The transport infrastructure also is underdeveloped and in poor condition. The total lengths of road and expressway in the North are about one-quarter and one-third of those in the South, respectively. Railways in the North are relatively well developed and are less deficient than other items. Two related problem areas in the North are neglected roadways and an undeveloped passenger transportation system. The demand for passenger transportation is suppressed by policies such as travel and migration control and assigning workers' residences within walking distance of workplaces. Instead, transport investment is concentrated on moving freight and North Korea's transportation system is centered upon railways. Road, air, and marine transportation play minor roles. For example, railways accounts for 86 percent and 60 percent of total freight and passenger transportation, respectively (Ahn 2000). This skewed modal distribution poses a major challenge in the future development of transport networks in the North.

Although the number of telephone lines does not represent the total picture of communication infrastructure, it offers a rough indication of the level of communication facilities. There are about five telephone lines per hundred persons in the North (as of 1998), which is about one-seventh of the total in the South. This is quite low even compared with eight lines per hundred persons in the Jilin Province of China, which is at a similar level of economic development as North Korea (Roh and Park 2000). In general, the present state of electricity, transportation, and communication facilities in the North is at the level of South Korea in the mid-1970s. Recognizing the importance of infrastructure in sustainable economic growth, South Korea has invested about US$50 billion, more than 2 percent of its gross national product (GNP) annually in the past three decades, on infrastructure (Oh 1998). These statistics suggest that infrastructure investment requirements for North Korea will amount to at least several billion dollars annually in the coming decades.

Progress in inter-Korean economic cooperation

There were few economic exchanges between South and North Korea till the late 1980s. The collapse of the Soviet Union and the break-up of the Eastern bloc in the late 1980s left the North with no choice but to engage in economic exchanges with the South. The Roh Tae Woo administration's northern policy in the late 1980s provided a channel for inter-Korean economic exchanges. In 1991, there was a breakthrough between the two Koreas. Both sides signed an agreement on reconciliation, non-aggression, and exchange and cooperation, although the terms of the agreement were not followed due to several unfavorable events including the death of Kim Il Song in 1994. Since then, however, inter-Korean economic exchanges have increased substantially. For example, the amount of inter-Korean trade in 1989 was US$19 million but it reached US$425 million in 2000 (Figure 12.1). Now, South Korea is second only to China among North Korea's trading partners.

Before 1999 inter-Korean economic exchanges were, however, heavily influenced by political and military factors. The exchanges followed a peculiar format of cooperation between the private sector of the South and the public sector of the North because Pyongyang refused to recognize Seoul as a legitimate political entity. Except for humanitarian aid by the South and the nuclear power plant project carried out by the Korean Peninsular Energy Development Organization headed by the United States,[2] economic transactions between South and North Korea were led mainly by South Korean business enterprises. The centerpiece was the Mt Kumgang tourism project, in which the South Korean industrial giant Hyundai took the lead in a major deal with the North.

Such strange arrangements also have incurred abnormally high transportation costs for South Korean enterprises. Without land connections since the Korean War, materials and goods have to be transported by sea, resulting in huge time and transport costs. These irregular aspects of inter-Korean economic exchanges have been changing since the summit in June 2000. After several

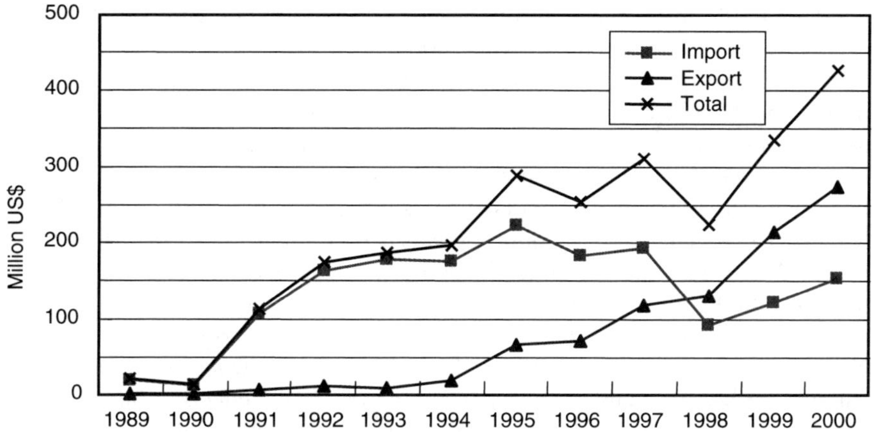

Figure 12.1 Inter-Korea trade, 1989–2000

Source: Ministry of Unification (2000)

ministerial and working group meetings in the latter half of 2000, Seoul and Pyongyang signed four treaties on economic cooperation. These treaties, establishing rules for taxation, investment guarantees, means of direct financial transactions, and settlement of trade disputes, created a legal framework that will enable South Korean enterprises to make investments in the North. As such, they elevated inter-Korean economic cooperation from an informal base to a more formal footing.

Another major change in 2000 was an agreement to link the disconnected rail and roadways passing through the demilitarized zone and to cooperate on flood prevention around the Imjin River that crosses the border. Rail and road connection projects were supposed to have been completed in the latter half of 2001. Even though South Korea completed the construction of the southern portion, North Korea did not fulfill its commitment. The future completion of these projects is not bright due to lack of Pyongyang's interest in these projects as well as its uncertain policy toward inter-Korean economic cooperation.[3] The North intends to open up the city of Gaesong (only 70 kilometers away from Seoul) as a site for South Korean tourists and to serve as an industrial park for South Korean enterprises (Hyundai is currently negotiating with the North on the details of the park). This means that the rail and road connections between Seoul and Gaesong will have significant economic effects on the North. Furthermore, as emphasized in President Kim's Berlin declaration in March 2000, the South is willing to help renovate the dilapidated infrastructure in the North.

The Pyongyang administration recognizes that infrastructure development, in particular energy and transportation, is vital for the rehabilitation of the ailing North Korean economy. It will not only create jobs but will also help modernize North Korea's dilapidated infrastructure such as power plants, railroads, roads, and ports. Rebuilding infrastructure will thus enable North Korea to re-engage in production activities and foreign trade. For these reasons, infrastructure development is one of the areas of economic cooperation on which both Koreas can easily reach an agreement (Kim 2000a).

Two critical questions regarding inter-Korean cooperation in infrastructure development involve, first, the extent and sequence of infrastructure building and, second, the means of financing. Skeptics point out that Seoul, given its limited financial capacity, cannot extend assistance beyond short-term, quick fixes such as the railway and road connections between the North and the South (Combs 1999). They also discount the effects of a major infrastructure build-up on the North Korean economy if it is not accompanied by economic reform (Noland 2000). As such, infrastructure development requires careful strategic planning since it is an integral part of inter-Korean economic cooperation. Moreover, the long-lasting and costly nature of infrastructure necessitates a careful cost-benefit analysis as well as an analysis of the effects of infrastructure development on regional development in the North and the territorial integration of the Korean Peninsula.

Issues of inter-Korean economic cooperation

The information on inter-Korean economic cooperation thus far highlights only the efforts on both sides that have been short-term and result-oriented rather than long-term and system-oriented. However, relying only on such a short-term, result-oriented approach will not be conducive to achieving the goal of balanced development between the South and the North called for in the 15 June 2000 agreement.

Understandably, Seoul's somewhat hasty attempt to engage with Pyongyang is derived from its belief that an engagement or "sunshine" policy is the only realistic option in inter-Korean relations. At that point, maintaining momentum by showing visible results to the North was more important than worrying about the long-term consequences of the actions taken. An assumption implicit in Seoul's approach is that changes will take place in the North's economic and military strategies. However, looking at Pyongyang's actions thus far, there is no conclusive evidence that major policy shifts will occur in the near future. Pyongyang is mainly interested in its survival as a regime and thus seems to be concentrating on extracting as much economic assistance as possible from the South. Pyongyang's strategy has been described as "muddling through" with *ad hoc* adjustments (Noland 1997). The leadership in Pyongyang is unwilling to take the risk of major reforms that could contribute to a collapse of the regime.

This attitude of Pyongyang is revealed clearly in its inter-Korean economic interactions. As seen in the case of the Mt Kumgang project, Pyongyang prefers package projects, whereby it can earn foreign exchange without making any significant investment or changes in its economic system. Pyongyang obviously wants to minimize any undesirable effects of economic cooperation with the South or foreign countries. This is apparent in its approach to opening up areas for foreign investment – first, setting up a special economic zone in an isolated area of Rajin-Sonbong and, second, opening up a remote and sparsely populated area of Mt Kumgang to South Korean tourists (see Figure 12.2). Even when a few South Korean joint ventures were allowed in the Nampo area (very close to Pyongyang), South Korean managers were not allowed to run them.

In a similar vein of what can be called economic self-interest, South Korean enterprises recognize that labor is the North's only comparative advantage and therefore contract processing has been and continues to be the dominant form of joint venture. Furthermore, given the poor infrastructure condition both institutional and physical in the North, southern enterprises prefer to invest in a few geographical pockets where labor is readily available and infrastructure is relatively well developed (e.g., Nampo, Pyongyang, Haejoo, and Wonsan are the preferred locations according to the Hyundai Research Institute 1999). Indeed, the merit of the Gaesong Industrial Park under negotiation comes from its geographical proximity to Seoul and availability of low-cost labor suitable for the labor-intensive industries to be relocated from the South. Combining these features with the likely pattern of infrastructure development in the North, we can anticipate with a reasonable degree of confidence the following outcomes:

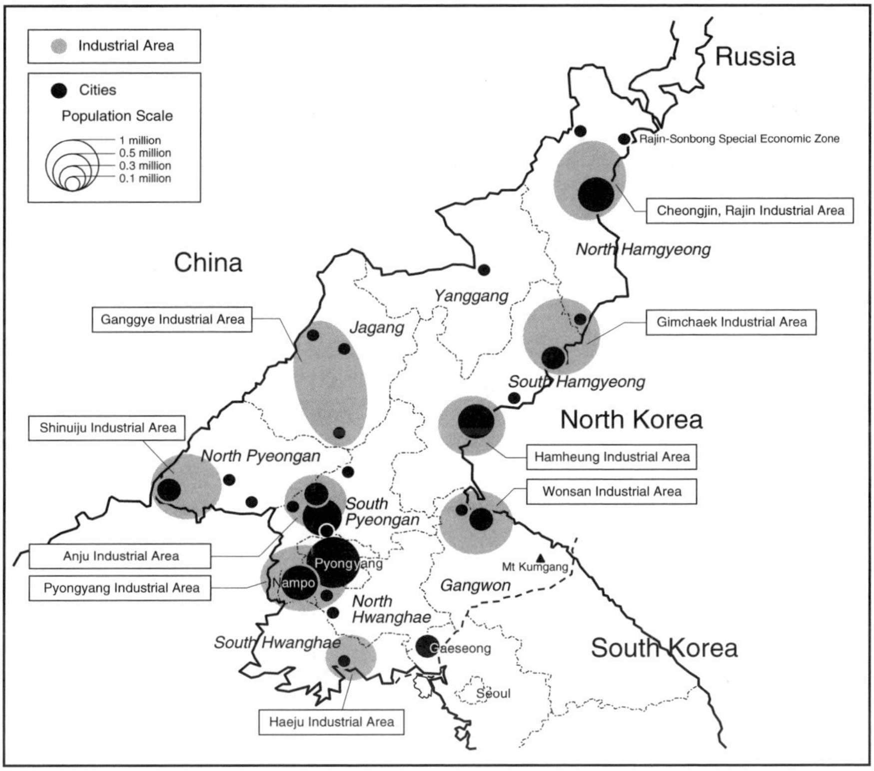

Figure 12.2 Major cities, provinces and industrial areas in North Korea

Note: Italics refer to administration.

1 South Korean investment will occur in processing and assembly industries as well as in tourism development, where North Korea can earn foreign exchange without making the significant political changes necessary for sustainable economic growth.
2 As a result, South Korean investment will concentrate in a few special economic zones in the North with relatively easy access to South Korea. South Korean government assistance in transport and other infrastructure also will concentrate on those special economic zones and transport links between them and Seoul.
3 Industrial conglomerates such as Hyundai will continue to be the major players in inter-Korean economic cooperation since they have the ability to mobilize financial resources.

The short-term, result-oriented approach has an advantage in terms of channeling South Korean investment into the North more efficiently and thus bringing quicker results. It also will be a likely pattern if left to market forces since it is generally palatable to the decision-makers involved. Figure 12.3 illustrates the geographical pattern that such a short-term, result oriented approach is likely to produce. However, the outcome produced by pursuing only short-run interests may have serious implications in terms of the balanced and resilient development of the two Koreas. Three issues are of particular importance: one regarding the industrial structure of the North; another with respect to the mode

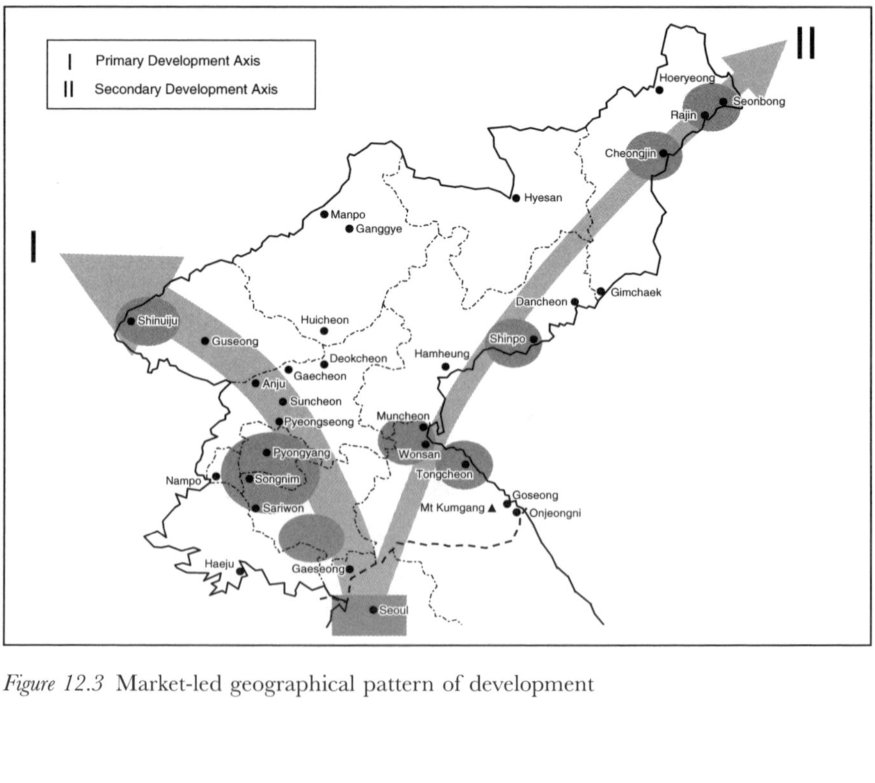

Figure 12.3 Market-led geographical pattern of development

of economic cooperation; and a third in terms of geographical patterns of development.

First is the question: what would be the long-term implications of the approach emphasizing the economic complementarity between the North and the South or, more specifically, the approach exploiting low-cost labor in the North? As suggested by private enterprises in the South, North Korea may become a low-cost production base for South Korean and foreign firms if the static comparative advantage of the North is emphasized (Korean Chamber of Commerce and Industry 2000). Two related concerns arise immediately. The first is whether North Korea can compete with China and other South-East Asian countries that have abundant low-wage labor. The second is the question of regional disparity between the North and the South. Would it be desirable for social integration in years ahead? Given the experience of Germany, where the west has spent an enormous sum of capital to raise the living standard of the east but regional disparity between the east and the west still persists, turning North Korea into a low-cost production base is not a desirable option.

Second, what would be the consequences of economic cooperation dominated by big industrial conglomerates or *chaebol* in the South? From the viewpoint of the current leadership in North Korea, using South Korean *chaebol* as a sort of cash cow is a preferred option. However, letting *chaebol* companies carry out the task of economic development in the North would involve both economic and political risks; economic risks in terms of reducing *chaebol* competitiveness internationally and political risks in the form of *quid pro quo* that the *chaebol* could be expected to establish (Noland 2000). Furthermore, the *chaebol* may not be as effective an agent as small and medium-sized enterprises in spreading market principles in North Korea.

Third, what would be the spatial consequences of investment concentrated in a few geographical pockets with easy access to South Korea? Investment concentration in a few areas seems inevitable in the initial stage of economic cooperation. However, if such short-run practices are allowed to continue, the endogenous growth potential of the North may be overlooked and as a consequence the self-sustaining growth potential of the North would be undermined. Furthermore, the concentration of investment in a few locations with favorable conditions will accentuate the development of the Seoul–Pyongyang corridor on the west coast of the Korean Peninsula. This will not only result in unbalanced development within the North but also in the Korean Peninsula as a whole.

Balanced development and long-term strategic considerations

In the short run, inter-Korean economic cooperation strategies will be limited in scope and contents. A result-oriented approach is very likely since both Koreas tend to focus on short-run benefits and costs. Economic cooperation, therefore, will take place in areas of mutual interest, for example, industrial parks and tourism projects that can quickly generate foreign exchange earnings for the

North. In other words, inter-Korean economic cooperation will begin in limited sectors of the economy and be geographically focused in a few pockets of the country.

When Pyongyang's commitment to economic reform becomes firmly manifest, successful inter-Korean economic cooperation will require a comprehensive strategy with a longer-term perspective. Investment priority should be placed on projects that will facilitate the endogenous growth potential of North Korea and promote the integration of two different systems. The need for a comprehensive strategy of inter-Korean economic cooperation stems from the longer-term objective of building diversified and balanced economies in the two Koreas. What does a diversified and balanced economy mean? First, it means an economy with a self-sustaining growth base. For example, making North Korea a low-cost production base for South Korean and other foreign firms would contribute little to building a self-sustaining economy. Second, it means the two economies should be complementary to each other. The same industrial structure of the South should not be reproduced in the North.

The complementarity, however, should not be interpreted here as simply accentuating the static comparative advantage of each side. For instance, defining low-wage, labor-intensive industries as the sectors of comparative advantage in the North and high-wage, technology-intensive industries as the sectors of comparative advantage in the South is missing the point. Disciplined labor and a relatively well-educated labor force are comparative advantages found in both northern and southern economies. Raising the level of knowledge and capital content in the industries in the North will not only complement the relatively knowledge-intensive industries in the South, but will also provide a basis for self-sustaining growth in the North. In short, building complementary economies means creating joint comparative advantages for both northern and southern economies.

Balanced development, which will be a critical element of economic cooperation in the long run, is not easy to define. The conventional definition is simply a quantitative equalization of living standards. Given the experience of Germany, we understand that equalization is neither possible nor desired in Korea. Despite a massive investment in the east amounting to US$540 billion over the past ten years, the east still lags behind the west. For example, per capita GDP in the east is about two-thirds of that in the west and the unemployment rate in the east is considerably higher (17.6 percent) than that of the west (7.9 percent) (Eltges and Maretzke 2000; *The Economist* 2000). Therefore, balanced development should be defined in qualitative terms, i.e., whether a region has a capacity for self-sustaining growth with its own distinctive characteristics. Balanced development does not mean an equalization of economic indicators across space. Nonetheless, the severe regional disparity between the South and the North would not be tolerable socially and politically after the two Korean economies are integrated. As a step toward lessening the severity of the disparity, an equal provision of basic social infrastructure should be considered a legitimate goal of balanced development.

Based on the preceding discussion, a comprehensive strategy for inter-Korean economic cooperation should acknowledge the following points:

1 Rehabilitation of regional economic bases to the extent justified economically and nurturing regional growth potential.
2 Promotion of new industries and joint ventures between local industries in the North and small and medium enterprises in the South.
3 Infrastructure development commensurate with industrial development and consistent with balanced regional development.
4 Reform and restructuring of the North Korean economy taking into consideration the issues of unemployment and migration consequences.

With respect to the first two points, a large proportion of the country's existing industries may have to be scrapped when North Korea eventually undertakes major economic reform (Kim 2000b). Selective retention of certain industries that have a strong local base and cluster should be considered based on their potential for self-sustaining regional economic growth.

In addition to utilizing low-wage labor for export-oriented industries, Pyongyang and Seoul together must consider the possibility of introducing and promoting new industries such as information technology and modern logistics in suitable locations within North Korea. Given the experiences of China, Germany, and the Eastern European economies, the growth of small and medium-sized enterprises is essential to maintain an employment base and to introduce market-type management (Naughton 1996; Strubelt 1997). Although the condition of local industries in the North is known to be poor, injecting capital and management know-how with the assistance of the South may partially salvage regional and local economic bases. Most of all, both sides need to determine how to harness the growth potential of North Korea and component regions within it.

Since infrastructure development is costly and has long-lasting impacts on the territory where it is built, infrastructure development strategy should be designed to maximize long-term economic and social benefits for the Korean Peninsula (Kim 2000a). But for the foreseeable future, the emphasis should be placed on raising the level of infrastructure in the North. Strategic planning is thus required to achieve short-term and long-term goals. In the short run, North-South transportation connections may be important to channel Southern investment into the North. These investment projects, however, should carefully consider the long-term effects on the territorial development in the North as well as on the whole Korean Peninsula, i.e., to avoid an excessive concentration in the Seoul–Pyongyang corridor.

Infrastructure investment strategies also require a staged approach. For example, a few essential energy, transport, and communication projects to make the North Korean economy begin to function should be given investment priority in the beginning. Major investment to expand Northern infrastructure should begin when inter-Korean economic cooperation occurs within a stable institutional environment accompanied by major economic reforms in the North. In the final stage, when the economic integration of the two economies takes place, major arterial transport network development including ports, airports, roads, and railways should begin. Improving the level of infrastructure in the North to reduce the gap between the North and the South will be the major task during the integration stage.

As the German experience suggests, unemployment and migration will be serious problems for North Korea after it undertakes reform measures (Maretzke and Strubelt 2000). Restructuring and reform will inevitably generate unemployment. Regions that specialize in heavy industries will suffer the most. High unemployment in a region will trigger outmigration. Without appropriate policy measures to counteract these tendencies, some areas will become problem regions. Judicious design of reform and restructuring policies may reduce the severity of these regional economic problems. Four policy areas are of particular importance: (1) agricultural reform; (2) policies regarding small and medium-sized enterprises; (3) restructuring of state-owned industries; and (4) reform of property ownership (Kim 2000b).

Even though agricultural reform would not have as great an impact in North Korea as it has in China, it could raise agricultural productivity. This would help relieve food shortages and provide surplus capital for the growth of new firms as it did in China. Another advantage would be that agricultural reform, by giving land and decision-making power back to farmers, could reduce the likelihood of migration from rural areas to urban areas in the medium term.

Local factories and private enterprises are reported to exist in North Korea (Chun 1998; Michell 1998). If Pyongyang adopts a dual pricing system and allows the purchase of inputs and raw materials from free markets, local factories would have much better prospects for survival and growth. Allowing service enterprises to grow in the Northern cities would provide a significant source of employment and thereby reduce the tendency for migration from one city to another by job seekers. Craft industries such as woodworking, plastic products, metal and motor repair, and catering trades such as food services, bakery, butchery, etc. would not only provide jobs for the unemployed but also environments for learning the market economy.

Many observers inside and outside Korea predict that most state-owned industries in the North will have to be scrapped if the North opens up to the outside world. Closing state-owned factories might be necessary but would cause massive unemployment since the North has a much higher proportion of state-owned factories than China did at the beginning of its reform. Restructuring rather than privatization might be more appropriate for the North. From the regional economy perspective, it would be necessary to retain some basic industrial activities, wherein Southern enterprises could render assistance for restructuring. In other words, severe local disruptions entailing high unemployment and heavy outmigration could be avoided by measures aimed at sustaining a regional economic base. A decision-making process should be developed regarding which industries and factories are to be saved for the recovery of the regional economy, including evaluating social costs and benefits.

Property reform may be the most important factor affecting migration propensity within the North and between the North and the South (McMillan 1996). Land and properties for farming and small-scale industrial and commercial activities should immediately be returned to or given to the existing tenants. Housing should be distributed to residents both in cities and in the countryside. This does not have to be an outright transfer of ownership. Granting use rights as China did would be sufficient for the short run. Distributing temporary ownership or usership to farmers, entrepreneurs, and residents would deter potential outmigration from the North to the South and migration between regions in the North.

Conclusions

No matter how the reunification of the two Koreas proceeds, either through the German style – the absorption of the North by the South – or through gradual and peaceful integration of the two, balanced development will be an issue of paramount importance. Massive transfer of capital – both public and private – from the South to the North is one way to move toward balanced development, as shown in the German case. However, the weak economic capacity of the South, which is much more limited than that of West Germany before the unification, is unlikely to allow South Korea to cover the financial costs and investments needed to reduce the yawning economic gap between the South and the North.

The situation obviously calls for a carefully planned strategy to address the current unbalanced level of development between South and North Korea. Since inter-Korean economic cooperation has just begun, policy-makers in the South and the North need to conduct both short-term and long-term strategic planning to address the various dimensions of inter-Korean economic cooperation.[4] A review of inter-Korean economic cooperation so far reveals that the sectors, places, and players involved in inter-Korean cooperation will be limited in the short run. These limitations, if not carefully considered from a long-term perspective, may produce adverse effects on the territorial integration of the two Koreas because the first step is likely to determine the steps which follow.

Perhaps Korea is fortunate in comparison with Germany because the two Koreas appear to have more time to prepare for economic integration and unification (assuming that the North will not collapse suddenly) and thereby to achieve balanced development.[5] Infrastructure development will serve as an important tool of policy leverage, whereby the public sector can steer private investment. Through frequent meetings, the two Koreas can pursue the optimum strategies of infrastructure development to help revive the North Korean economy and to enhance the competitiveness of the Korean Peninsula.

There will be another critical opportunity for planners and policy-makers to cooperate when the North decides to institute major reform and restructuring measures. Here again, both sides should carefully consider the territorial effects of various reform measures. Policy-makers need to consider several issues carefully, especially with respect to unemployment and migration. Besides the areas of industrial and infrastructure development, in which policy intervention may occur over a long period of time, reforms related to agriculture, enterprises, and property ownership will have one-time, perhaps decisive, effects on employment and migration. It is, therefore, worthwhile to spend as much time as needed to design policies to reduce the propensity for migration among North Korean residents and at the same time create job opportunities through direct investment from the South and abroad.

Aside from the regional dimensions of inter-Korean economic cooperation, Korean planners should pay attention to the environmental costs of physical development, ranging from factory construction to building arterial highways. Although not discussed in this chapter, environmental issues are important, as was seen in the case of Germany. Hasty decisions by the Pyongyang administration, which is desperate for foreign exchange, could potentially cause serious environmental damage.[6] It is also possible that the Seoul administration may overlook the environmental dimension of inter-Korean projects because of its preoccupation with the economic dimension. The seemingly bright yet challenging prospects for inter-Korean economic cooperation need to be carefully considered to ensure that the positive and negative effects including a variety of economic, social, and environmental effects can be optimized or mitigated to maximize the social benefits.

Notes

1 Noland (2000) raised doubts about the Bank of Korea's estimates of the gross national income of North Korea.
2 This organization was established in 1995 as part of the general framework agreed to by the United States and North Korea. South Korea, the United States and Japan are principal members of the organization.
3 Both rail and road connections go through the demilitarized zone and they are located near Seoul. Construction projects have been designed to restore the missing portions of rail (20 km) and road (19 km).
4 Both Koreas need to make institutional arrangements (including a peace treaty) to elevate inter-Korean cooperation to a firm legal footing.
5 Unification came suddenly to the German people. Political rationale was much more important than economic rationale in the process. In this regard, no one is sure when the reunification of the two Koreas will occur.
6 North Korea is reported to be renegotiating with Taiwan about the possible importation of nuclear waste from Taiwan into North Korea (*Chungang Daily*, 15 February 2000).

References

Ahn, Byung Min (2000) "Transport Infrastructure Development for Building an Integrated Economic Community," paper prepared for the Task Force on Building an Integrated Economic Community between the South and the North, Ministry of Construction and Transportation, Seoul (in Korean).

Bae, Jin Young (1994) "The Effects of Unification on Industrial Location and Structure in East and West Germany", Seoul: Korean Institute for International Economic Policy, (in Korean).

Cheong, Woojin (1999) "Inter-Korean Cooperation in Social Overhead Capital: Electricity and Energy," *Unification Economy,* October, 1–10 (in Korean).

Chun, Hong Tack (1998) "The Second Economy and Economic Reforms in North Korea", international conference on North Korea in Transition and Policy Choices: Domestic Structure and External Relations, 28–29 May, IFES/Graduate School of North Korean Studies, Kyungnam University, Seoul.

Combs, Gifford (1999) "The Role of International Finance in Korean Economic Reconstruction and Reunification," *National Bureau of Asian Research Analysis,* 10(5), pp. 1–15.

Eberstadt, Nicholas (1997) "Hastening Korean Reunification," *Foreign Affairs,* 76, 77–92.

The Economist (2000) "German Unification – Togetherness: A Balance Sheet," 30 October.

Eltges, M. and Maretzke, S. (2000) "Regionalpolitik in Deutschland: die Förderung der Ostdeutschen Regionen," unpublished paper, Bonn: BBR.

Hyundai Research Institute (1999) "Investment Environment by Region in North Korea", available (in Korean), http://www.hri.co.kr/nk (accessed 1 February 2002).

Kim, Won Bae (2000a) "Inter-Korean Cooperation in Infrastructure Development", paper presented at conference on New Challenges in Inter-Korean Economic Cooperation and Integration, 9–10 October, Stanford, CA.

Kim, Won Bae (2000b) "Transforming the North Korean Economy for Balanced Territorial Development," *Vantage Point,* 23(5): 38–49.

Korean Chamber of Commerce and Industry (2000) *Enterprise Survey on the Efficient Promotion of Inter-Korean Economic Cooperation,* Seoul: Korean Chamber of Commerce and Industry, (in Korean).

Maretzke, Steffen and Strubelt, Wendlin (2000) "Initial Situation in Germany in 1989 and the Experience of Regional Development in the Former GDR since 1990", paper presented at KRIHS-BBR joint workshop on the Experience of Regional Development in the Unified Germany and its Implications for Inter-Korean Integration, 18–19 October, Anyang, Geonggi.

McMillan, John (1996) "What Can North Korea Learn from China's Market Reforms?", paper presented at conference on the System Transformation of the Transitional Economies: Europe, Asia, and North Korea, Institute for Korean Unification Studies, Yonsei University, Seoul, 14 September.

Michell, Anthony (1998) "The Current North Korean Economy", in M. Noland (ed.), *Economic Integration of the Korean Peninsula,* Washington, DC: Institute for International Economics, Special Report 10, pp. 137–64.

Ministry of Unification, Government of Korea (2000), http://www.unikorea.go.kr.

National Statistical Office Korea (2001) "South and North Korean Society through Major Statistics", Seoul: National Statistical Office of Korea.

Naughton, Barry (1996) "Economic Reform in China: Macroeconomic and Overall Performance", paper presented at conference on the System Transformation of the Transitional Economies: Europe, Asia, and North Korea, Institute for Korean Unification Studies, Yonsei University, Seoul, 14 September.

Noland, Marcus (1997) "Why North Korea Will Muddle Through," *Foreign Affairs,* 76, 105–18.

Noland, Marcus (2000) *Avoiding the Apocalypse: The Future of the Two Koreas,* Washington, DC: Institute for International Economics.

Oh, Gil Nam (1996) "Labor Force Structure of North Korea", Seoul: Korea Labor Institute, (in Korean).

Oh, Jae-Hak (1998) "Strategies for Developing Transport Infrastructure in North Korea", paper presented at international conference on Developing Social Infrastructure in North Korea for Economic Cooperation between the South and the North, Seoul, 9–10 November.

Roh, Sung Jun and Park, Chong Bong (2000) "The Status of Information and Communication in North Korea and Policy Implications," Seoul: Atlas Research Group.

Strubelt, Wendlin (1997) "Die Sicherung der Arbeitsplöetze und Aktivierung der Stadtöekonomie in Ostdeutschland", paper presented at conference on Urban Policies after Unification. Korea Research Institute for Human Settlements, Anyang, Korea (in Korean translation) 6–8 November.

13 Economic transformation of North Korea

Lessons and "non-lessons" from Germany and Europe

Bernhard Seliger

Introduction

From the beginning of economic science, in Adam Smith's *Inquiry into the Nature and Causes of the Wealth of Nations* ([1776] 1952), economists have tried to learn by comparing economic systems. The transformation processes experienced in Central and Eastern Europe after 1989 and the East Asian financial crisis of 1997 heightened the interest in such comparative learning since both situations involved large-scale systemic change.[1] However, both events also were embarrassing for the economic profession because it was caught completely unaware by them.

Therefore, it seems to be necessary and legitimate to ask if an analysis of North Korea and its economic development process can benefit from the experiences of Central and Eastern Europe (CEE), and Eastern Germany, specifically. While the transformation process in Central and Eastern Europe provided economists with an invaluable amount of material for comparison and discussion of specific questions of economic transformation (such as privatization, monetary policy in transformation, or trade policy), the debate about the most advantageous strategy for economic transformation remained unresolved. After the supposed "Washington Consensus" was discredited as an easy universal blueprint for economic reform due to frequently disappointing attempts to implement it, competing explanations about the missing elements of transformation theory flourished.[2] Only recently, when stocktaking experiences began after ten years of transformation, some elements of a new view on economic transformation emerged.[3]

An application of European experiences to North Korea has to take into account the uncertainty surrounding the lessons from transformation. While a discussion of various options and alternatives of economic transformation is helpful, it cannot generate a uniform blueprint for economic reform. The interdependence of the economic and political transformation processes, or, as in the case of North Korea, the uncertainty about any political transformation process makes this kind of reform impossible.

A second necessary question asks how much North Korea's economy corresponds to the economic systems found in Central and Eastern Europe.

North Korea with its *juche* ideology is definitely a distinct breed of socialism.[4] But its distinctiveness is not so much a question of different quality of economic systems, but rather a question of degree, especially concerning autarky. Besides, North Korea shares many characteristics with other former socialist countries and notably strategic similarities with Eastern Germany.[5] Numerous articles have been written to compare the transformation experiences of Eastern Europe and especially Germany and North Korea, while developing diverse scenarios for change.[6] This article will not carry out this same exercise in scenario design again. Rather, it will try to identify those lessons in transformation theory which have not yet been learned and which also will present challenges to a possible transformation process in North Korea. To illustrate this different view on the North Korean transformation process, the lessons and "non-lessons" from more than ten years of economic transformation in Europe are compared and applied to North Korea.

Lessons and non-lessons from Europe and Germany

After ten years of economic transformation, important lessons about the success of transformation policies have been learned, yet governments still suffer from the "constitutional lack of knowledge". Hayek used this phrase to describe the difficulty that planning authorities and political decision-makers face when they attempt to centralize the information on millions of economic subjects, i.e. consumers and producers. Because of this difficulty any centrally planned economy is likely to be inferior to the spontaneous order of the marketplace where this information is incorporated in one single, highly informative figure, namely the price of goods (Hayek 1937, 1945).

For economies undergoing transformation, there also is a lack of knowledge about predicting and optimizing the implementation of a functioning market order. If one takes this lack of knowledge seriously (and the failure of early, neo-classical attempts to optimize the process of transformation urges us to do so), predictions can only be accurate qualitatively and limited to the "pattern prediction". Predictions cannot be stated accurately in concrete and quantitative terms of the transformation process.[7] The transformation process in particular may result in unintended consequences of "human action, but not of human design" (Hayek 1969).[8] With these warnings in mind, there are at least five lessons of economic transformation theory. However, there still remain unsatisfactory situations, where lessons have not yet been learned.

Lesson 1: Institutions matter

The failure to acknowledge the role of institutions in economic change was one of the great shortcomings of early transformation theory. This failure involved several misunderstandings. One of the important advisors in early transformation efforts in Poland and Russia, Jeffrey Sachs, estimated that it would take less than a year to introduce a new institutional framework, given the political will to do so (see Lipton and Sachs 1990: 108).

Policy-makers underestimated the time necessary for institution-building, especially to create the capacity to effectively support institutions. Institutions, even legal ones, were often extremely weak and weak institutions remain as one of the problems of transformation. Lack of knowledge about the application of laws and regulations continues to cause difficulty in transition economies.

The only country where an institutional "big bang" (i.e., an immediate and successful institutional transformation) did happen was the former German Democratic Republic. In East Germany, institutional change occurred mainly on two dates: the date of economic, monetary and social union in May 1990, and the date of political unification in October 1990. It also involved the transfer of sufficient personnel experienced in operating the new institutions. However, even in Germany there were numerous obstacles to establishing effectively functioning institutions. In that sense, the conclusion of Sinn and Sinn (1994: 141) that political transformation is almost child's play compared to economic transformation was wrong, even for Germany. It was even more inaccurate for other transition economies where institution-building took much more time.

Another misunderstanding concerns institutional variety. The Washington Consensus, which largely functioned as a blueprint for transformation in Central and Eastern Europe, originally contained no considerations relating to institutional change. Similar to neoclassical economic models of competitive markets, it assumed the existence of a functioning framework for the market economy rather than making it the central point of transformation theory. In reality, there emerged a multitude of institutional arrangements more or less able to cope with the challenges of the new market economy.[9] Finally, the problematic relationship between informal and formal institutions should not be ignored.[10] The long-lasting nature of informal institutions, such as the habits acquired in the period of socialist central planning, can inhibit the new, formal institutions and thus have unintended effects (see Mummert 1999).

Non-lesson 1: How to govern institutional change

While the institutional lessons learned are of great importance, we still know few things about how to govern institutional change, or how to install the "right" institutions in as little time as possible. As to the time aspect, those countries trying to achieve a "big bang" seem to have achieved better results on average (such as Estonia or Poland), but some, notably Russia, have performed poorly.[11] As for the "right" institutions, it is questionable whether any set of institutions can be said to be best suited for a particular country. Successful market economies are the outcome of an evolutionary process, where such institutions spontaneously developed. This seems to contradict the popular belief that politicians can achieve "economic miracles" by selecting the right institutions, as did Ludwig Erhard, the German economic minister, in West Germany in 1948. However, Erhard then merely freed an already existing economic system from strangling regulations.[12] This is different from a state's attempt to mimic the successful development of other states. Societies are complex phenomena which cannot deliberately be manipulated (see Hayek 1964).

For example, take private ownership as one of the cornerstones of the market economy. The lesson about the incentive function of private property has by now been well learned. But it still leaves two problems: the first is the time-consuming process of actually establishing private ownership in a transition economy. Even in East Germany, where the administration was heavily aided by Western civil servants, determining former owners of property or establishing new owners took several years and posed an important obstacle to new investment. Even more problems can be expected in North Korea, where most documents of former property ownership (on land) were destroyed in 1947 (see the discussion of Jung and Park 1998, especially pp. 196–201). Moreover, the need for a property ownership system to provide incentives for economic activity invariably will produce contradictions with other considerations, such as justice (for example, to former owners) or equity.

Lesson 2: Culture matters

Economic transformation does not take place in a cultural vacuum, but rather in a cultural environment, which influences formal and informal institutions, as well as the habits and behavior of people. I will not take up the "Confucian debate" once again even if it definitely is important for both Koreas' economic development.[13] But rather, I want to point out the more immediate interplay of an economic system and the developing economic culture. This has been a problem in Central and Eastern Europe and it will become a problem in North Korea.

While it is extremely difficult to define the exact nature of culture, the influence of culture on economic transition became an interesting research topic, when similar transition strategies resulted in vastly different outcomes.[14] The difference in growth rates and varying degrees of success in transition (as expressed by the "transformation index" of the European Bank for Reconstruction and Development) was explained by cultural differences between "Latin" countries in Central Europe and "Orthodox" countries in the Balkans and the former Soviet Union, except for the Baltic States with strikingly different results of transformation (see Panther 1997). This explanation focused on the long-term development of the civil society in Latin, i.e., Western and Central European countries, allowing the accumulation of trust as a precondition for anonymous exchange in the market (see Putnam 1993; Fukuyama 1996).[15]

Another view concentrates on the effects of central planning mechanisms and dysfunctional Fordism, manifested by the related phenomena of labor hoarding, bottle-necks in production, lack of material incentives and bureaucratic decision mechanisms, and on the economic ethics and behavior in post-socialist societies, and disregards the Western "homo oeconomicus" model with the socialist "homo sovieticus".[16]

The lack of entrepreneurship, responsibility, initiative, and will to govern one's own fate are attributed to the socialist, bureaucratic model of society (see Philipe

1995). Studies on the firms with foreign investments seem to confirm the existence of different perceptions and attitudes at the managerial level (see Vlachoutsicos 1999). The longer socialist rule influenced people's behavior, the more likely that problems will arise in the transformation process. Indeed, one of the differences between Russia and other transition economies is Russia's lack of entrepreneurship. This was expressed in a dearth of small and medium-sized enterprises, which in other countries such as Poland made a considerable contribution to growth and employment (Rautava 1999). But the states under socialist rule for only forty years also were deeply influenced by it. For example, after 1989 in East Germany, the perception of an industrious population living in the former industrial centers of Saxony and the general belief in hard-working Germans was in many cases contradicted by the reality of a population requiring "cradle-to-grave" protection. (For the attitudes in East and West Germany, see Roller 1992, and for a discussion, see Seliger 1999.)

This is an important lesson for North Korea. Koreans are generally proud to stress their 5000 years of common history and culture. But, despite this heritage, fifty years of Communist rule have imbued a different set of values and attitudes in people. Clearly, a different set of incentives also changes people's behavior. The striking growth of agriculture in China after 1978 and more recently under the Vietnamese *Doi Moi* policy show that a reversal of an apathetic attitude toward a more enterprising spirit also is possible.[17] But it should not be forgotten that both countries still have an important state-owned sector where change is incremental at best. When large-scale transformation begins and the state-owned and state-protected economy is dismantled, the problems will become more visible for those parts of the society unable to adjust to the market economy. This includes an age problem (in Eastern Germany people over fifty generally had extreme difficulty adjusting to new jobs), a skill and qualification gap and a motivation problem, which is especially difficult to address with transformation policy.

Non-lesson 2: How to mobilize the positive cultural features for change?

We know that the cultural setting for transition matters, but we do not know how the positive cultural features can be mobilized to promote a speedy transition, and ultimately, catching up with global progress. Perceptual differences in the market system and the role of the state are likely to be an important obstacle, especially for the acceptance of the market economy in North Korea, given the constant *juche* propaganda. Also, this may influence attitudes towards foreign capital, investment, and products and make it more difficult for them to contribute to North Korean economic transformation. However, the recent interest in foreign investment (since 1994, but especially in the last two years) will have an impact.

The Central and Eastern European lesson that attitudinal change takes time, perhaps at least one generation, is disappointing from the viewpoint of *transition policy*. However, policy-makers for North Korea can attempt to learn from the mistakes that Germany made during transition. An election pledge by the unification Chancellor Helmut Kohl to improve everyone's standard of living was supported by economists who were overly optimistic about the assets of the former German Democratic Republic (GDR) and the speed of mental transformation. Unfortunately, it ignored the inevitable hardships of structural change. There were two negative consequences (admittedly apparent with hindsight). First, it swelled the ranks of those who opposed the economic system of West Germany and at least partly desired a return to the elements of socialism ("Not everything was bad in socialism"). Second, it forced massive financial transfers to support real income in East Germany. This encouraged a subsidy-dependent mentality and posed obstacles to structural adjustment. At the same time it damaged business by fostering high government spending for consumptive purposes. The government subsidies were financed by debt and taxes and nurtured widespread expectations concerning the state's role in providing for the well-being of its citizens. This scenario tended to strengthen the survival of attitudes that hindered market economies.[18]

In its transition process, Korea cannot count on real or alleged cultural qualities of the North Koreans stemming from their long common cultural history. Instead, it has to cope with the different attitudes developed under central planning. Education might help to alleviate this problem, most probably for younger persons. And, the longer the duration of the pre-transition phase, the less urgent the problem is, a point we will return to later.

Lesson 3: Good governance matters

Another lesson from the Central and Eastern European transition experiences can be drawn, which is quite closely related to the first two and concerns the question of political and economic governance. Recently, the issue of good governance, i.e. a government guaranteeing the enforcement of institutions, acting impartially, with a low degree of corruption, following a policy sending clear signals to market participants (for example, by the enforcement of bankruptcy laws) has become the preoccupation of researchers and international agencies implementing and monitoring economic transformation processes.[19] All countries in transition have to cope with the problems of a large unofficial economy, discretionary application of laws, and the absence of effective enforcement mechanisms. Those countries experiencing an interdependent political and economic transformation process are especially prone to suffer from these problems. The Janus-headed role of the state – too weak to effectively enforce the law and too strong and interventionist to allow the unrestricted growth of business – also has been identified as a major problem (see Shleifer 1997; Herrmann-Pillath 1999). The capture of the state by special interest groups, for example via privatization, renders reform ineffective and results in continuing state intervention on behalf of specific firms (see Hellmann and Schankemann 2000).

Governance is not just the state's problem. An effective system of corporate governance also is important for successful transition. One lesson from transition experience is that privatization matters, but it is a necessary, rather than, a sufficient condition for successful corporate restructuring. The introduction of competition (by means of competition policy, dismantling of the *kombinat*-type conglomerates – a problem that also exists in North Korea – and allowing foreign competitors to challenge domestic monopolies) is of equal importance. The resulting industry structure is not separate from the path to privatization. For instance, a mass privatization strategy may not yield the same amounts of inflow of capital and know-how as another strategy aimed at selling assets to foreign investors.

In the Korean case (as in the German case), once it is possible, Southern companies are very likely to invest heavily in North Korea for obvious reasons. However, this also poses a problem. Most of the current investment by South Korean companies cannot be justified by economic rationality and in some cases, most notably for Hyundai Asan, clearly has a political motivation. While investment for "patriotic" reasons generally is not a problem (ultimately, the shareholders of company should be free to invest their money where they want), it becomes a problem if this investment is used as political leverage to gain favors from the South Korean government. In this respect, South Korean businesses should not be given any special consideration for investing in the North. Foreign capital interests should have first priority, thereby also challenging the oligopolistic market structure in the South.[20]

Non-lesson 3: How to achieve good governance

The problem of governance, of providing a fair, efficient, and transparent management of the public and the private sectors has haunted all transition economies. However, there are different degrees of difficulty, with some countries having fewer governance problems than others. These differences lead to another "non-lesson" from transformation: namely, if and how problems of governance can be solved, given the politico-economic reality of transition economies (such as the strong position of *nomenklatura* and bureaucracy). Even with a massive transfer of civil servants from the West, Germany was only able to partially avoid governance problems, including widespread difficulties with privatization (i.e., asset-stripping). The European Union and other international organizations tried to enhance the governance mechanisms in Central and Eastern Europe, by upgrading the education of civil servants. Ultimately, however, the reasons for "good" and "bad" governance are unclear. Cultural influences remain the most convincing available explanation (again the Latin/orthodox hypothesis), but offer no policy recommendations for future efforts.

Lesson 4: Capital matters

The capital stock in all of the socialist countries was degraded and worn-out, and there had been a lack of reinvestment to cover depreciation. While physical depreciation could not be denied under socialism, the ideas of obsolete economic assets and the "creative destruction" (Joseph A. Schumpeter) of investments that were still working physically did not exist. Additionally, with the introduction of the *T'ae-An* allocation system, investment had been concentrated in heavy industry, while the production of consumer goods and the service sector were neglected. [21] Thus, a transformation process has to change the industry structure, as well as modernize it.

Therefore, any catching-up process must take into account the massive need for building new capital stock. This concerns private investment as well as social overhead capital (SOC), mainly public investment in infrastructure.[22] An additional concern is that, in general, industrial capacity and the existing capital stock in Eastern European countries were greatly overestimated, even in the case of the former German Democratic Republic where after the rapprochement policy of the 1970s information was relatively abundant, compared to other Eastern European states, but especially compared to North Korea. Eastern European countries which lacked the possibility of a massive, state-led transfer of funds were more dependent on capital inflow through FDI. This is one of the reasons why some countries such as Hungary made FDI inflow a policy priority.

Non-lesson 4: How to manage the capital inflow efficiently

Here, the "non-lesson" is again best learned from Germany, where the capital inflow was highest. With an inflow of more than 1.5 trillion DM of public funding after 1990, Germany managed to raise the average net income of East German citizens far above the level of any other Central or Eastern European state to its current level of more than 80 percent of West German net income. Also, the country's capital stock was radically renewed. However, despite this inflow, the result was not a self-sustaining economic boom, but rather a short-lived bump, especially in the construction industry, followed by moderate or even low growth rates. After 1996 these rates were lower than in West Germany, so the catching up process during the first years after unification came to a halt. In 1999 GDP per capita still stood only at 56 percent of the West German level, while the net income per employee surpassed 85 percent in the same year.

A large part of the transfers was used to maintain the living standard of the East Germans rather than as investment, which is one of the reasons for the slow catching up. But what about the existing investment in the renewal of firms and in infrastructure, which is especially interesting from the viewpoint of transformation policy? While there were clearly some beneficial and urgent projects (e.g., re-linking East and West Germany by railway and road and upgrading the old or non-existing information and communication infrastructure), the term "infrastructure" is more ambiguous than usually assumed. Are large-scale environmental improvement projects (e.g., for water clearing) investments or consumption? From the point of view of accounting, they are public infrastructure investments. But they do not necessarily add to the productive capacity of the transformation country and could be seen equally as consumptive spending. In this sense, much of the infrastructure development has a dual character.

Again, the lack of knowledge on the part of the state decision-makers about the right amount and proper investment target for modernizing the economy becomes clear. Another earlier proper problem plagues the transition process, namely, the question of transfers of funds and investments, while still dealing with the old regime in North Korea. This is similar to the problem that West Germany faced in the 1970s. Will investment speed up the transition process, possibly by increasing personal exchange and opening up the minds of the North Korean authorities? Will it help modernize the debilitated industrial sector and thereby lower the eventual post-unification costs? Or, will it stabilize the existing system and then be used for non-productive purposes, like strengthening the military? Probably there are few alternatives to some form of engagement policy, but the questions raised are legitimate and still await an answer.

So, South Korea faces the two-fold problem of how to enhance economic modernization of the North. Before unification there is the problem of regime-stabilizing transfers of funds and technology. After unification there is the problem of organizing large-scale capital transfers to enhance self-sustaining growth. The East German experience shows that caution should be taken with the transfer of capital in the pre-unification phase and after unification the transfer of funds cannot substitute for painful economic change. This notion also is confirmed by the fact that many Central European states had higher growth rates than East Germany. However, these growth rates are linked to much lower real GDPs and lead to the disturbing conclusion that the state, i.e., the economically powerful South Korea, should rather not be too active in attempting to equalize real incomes in the North and South, since that would require a non-sustainable transfer of funds for consumptive purposes.[23] And, inevitably linked to this is the question of migration, which we will address in the last lesson and non-lesson of transformation.

Lesson 5: Wealth matters

This lesson is immediately derived from the German unification process and at first glance, it seems to be trivial. As soon as the borders were open, the difference in living standards between East and West rose to the top of the political agenda, superseding political topics (such as political freedom or unification) that once were more important. Given the promises of abundance under Marxist ideology and the system's clear failure to deliver abundance, the importance of the material side of unification is not surprising.[24] The transfer of wealth, which in East Germany led to living standards increasingly comparable with the West despite much lower productivity, was seen as instrumental in preventing mass migration from the East to the West. However, it also was used, for example by trade unions, to justify large wage increases unrelated to productivity increases, especially in the first post-unification years. A second factor preventing migration was the generous German welfare system, which compensates the unemployed with relatively high wage replacements through unemployment or social benefits.

However, migration itself is not necessarily a problem. Migration means a better allocation of production factors. It speeds up the process of human capital formation, for example, if East Germans learn and work in more productive West German firms. Migration also is vital for a self-sustaining transformation; it encourages people to compete in the labor market, and eventually enables them to create their own businesses. Indeed, the lack of mobility is seen as one of the problems in the highly rigid Western European (and especially, the German) labor markets. So, the lesson from the German unification process is that migration can be prevented by income subsidies and a generous welfare system, but doing so does not help the transformation process.

Non-lesson 5: How to overcome the freedom vs mass migration dilemma

As stated previously, migration helps to improve factor allocation in a market economy. But mass migration can become an intractable problem when it occurs without a functioning social system to govern the process. Then mass migration will upset the social structure in both regions. In the mass exodus region the least mobile will be left behind. In the inflow region social tensions and increased labor market competition will be created. In other words, where there are large differences in standards of living, a liberal border and migration policy may result in an unwanted shift of population towards the richer region. This is a particular problem for Germany and Korea, since both lacked cultural and language barriers to migration, but to some extent it also is a problem of Eastern European integration into the EU where migration is unfettered.[25]

What are the implications for North Korea? Should relatively free migration, one of the guiding principles of the market economy, be stifled to ensure long-term stable economic development? If political decision-makers had perfect foresight, as economic models often assume they do, they could determine the optimal rate of liberalizing border policy without creating mass migration, basically operating in harmony with the transitional productivity gains in North Korea. But, in reality this would deprive the North Koreans (at least for some time or to some extent) of their freedom of movement. Migration poses this dilemma: a German-style policy to curb migration leads to massive financial transfers without real economic growth and slows the adjustment process.[26] A conservative policy that restricts migration would be incompatible with true democratic unification. The consequence is that South Korean politicians are left hoping for an extended period of economic reform without political reform in North Korea. This transition strategy does not take into account the human costs of such a policy.

Conclusion

The lessons of economic transition and unification in Central and Eastern Europe and Germany remain ambiguous. On the one hand, transformation theorists now know all the ingredients that fuel successful market economies. On the other hand, there is little knowledge about a functioning "cooking recipe" to make these elements work together. When possible economic transition strategies for North Korea are discussed, the problem of a transfer of power often receives much attention, while the question of choosing the right transition strategy seems to be of minor importance. However, as this chapter shows, the conclusions from economic transformations of former centrally planned economies are far from obvious. Given the impact of selecting the "right" transition strategy on political and popular support, this issue should assume a more prominent place in unification discussions.

Acknowledgements

The author thanks the Asia Research Foundation for financial support for this research.

Notes

1 In this article, the notion of "transformation" is used deliberately. While the often-used term "transition" means the change from one well-defined state of nature to another equally well-defined one, the experience in Central and Eastern Europe shows that the process there was a transformation with an unknown and variable outcome.

2 The Washington Consensus emerged as a consensus among international economists working on successful economic transformation, first in Latin America and later in Central and Eastern Europe. It included the prescriptions of fiscal austerity, tax reform, liberalization of trade and finance, unified exchange rate regimes, attraction of foreign direct investment (FDI), privatization, and deregulation. For a discussion, see Williamson (1990, 1997) and more critically Kolodko (1999).

3 See Seliger (2002) for the theoretical aspects.

4 *Juche* (or *chuch'e*) is the specific application of Marxism-Leninism to North Korea, promulgated by Kim Il Sung and based on independence in politics, economics, national defense, and foreign policy. For the economy, it means the attempt to achieve autarky. It is opposed to "flunkeyism" (*sadaejuui*), the excessive dependence on foreign countries, which was seen in Chinese foreign relations before 1949. For a discussion, see Kim (1979) and Koo (1992).

5 For an overview of the North Korean economic system, see Hwang (1993) and Savada (1994). For the historical development of the North Korean economic system, see Kim (1997).

6 See, for example Lee (1993), Noland, *et al.* (1998), and Pollack and Lee (2000).

7 For the concept of pattern prediction, see Hayek (1952, 1964). Economists have found it highly tempting to predict exact outcomes based on detailed specifications of unknown facts. In the case of the North Korean economy, for example, Computable General Equilibrium (CGE) approaches exist for detailed calculations of migration streams. The failure of such calculations is not only due to the well-known difficulty of collecting reliable data about North Korea (for that problem, see Eberstadt 2000), but

moreover due to the general lack of knowledge of the data relevant to the actions of humans in the transformation process.

8 The study of consequences of unintended human action have often been neglected by economists postulating a clear relationship between ends and means in economic policy. However, for Hayek these unintended consequences are the focal point of social sciences; cf. Hayek (1979: 41). For a different methodological position, see Blaug (1992: 46–7).

9 For economic policy purposes, the focus on a specific and relatively small set of institutional key variables might seem advisable. However, recent research suggests that there is no "single institutional arrangement" guaranteeing efficiency, but rather a multitude of advantageous institutional arrangements. For an application to the labor market, see Freeman (2000).

10 Formal institutions are all institutional arrangements such as laws or regulations enforced by the coercive monopoly of the state. Informal institutions are enforced privately, e.g., customs, traditions, private negotiations on private court settlements, etc. Cf. North (1990).

11 See the discussions in Ellmann (1992), Murrell (1993), and Hall and Elliott (1999).

12 For the origins of the German social market economy, see Peacock and Willgerodt (1989).

13 See the overview of Köllner (1997).

14 In this sense, the cultural context of transformation was similar to the institutional development, a neglected dimension (see Raiser 1997). For a discussion of culture in the context of transition, see Boettke (1999), Herrmann-Pillath (2000) and Rosenbaum (1999).

15 It should be noted that this explanation to some degree contradicts Olson's theory of institutional sclerosis, since it postulates that long-term, stable societies with a dense network of interest groups are best able to adopt capitalism, while Olson points out the strangling effects of a dense network of interest groups on growth. Olson (1996) also applied his theory to the decline of socialism in Central and Eastern Europe.

16 The notion "*homo economicus*" is not without problems, since it sometimes refers to the mechanical, machine-like maximizing in neo-classical models. Here, it refers to a more complete and humane model of man, called REMM (resourceful, evaluating, maximizing man) by Karl Brunner (1987) and the even more complex model of "*homo agens*" by Ludwig von Mises (1959).

17 For the Chinese experience, see Shirk (1993), Schüller (1998) and Henning and Lu (2000). For Vietnamese *Doi Moi* policy, see Irvin (1995), Weeks (1998) and Boothroyd and Nam (2000).

18 It should be noted that this was not a problem of East Germany alone, but an all-German problem. It has led to a debate about the German "leisure park," with the shortest annual working time in the world, one of the most generous welfare systems and complementary decline in working ethics, and recently provoked a remark by the current chancellor about "lazy unemployed." The institutional problems (like the poverty trap of high marginal tax rates and rigid labor markets) have not yet been addressed in this debate.

19 See, for example, Camdessus (1997) for the role of the International Monetary Fund (IMF) in good governance. The OECD and the European Union founded the SIGMA (Support for Improvement in Governance and Management in Central and Eastern European Countries) initiative; see www.oecd.org/puma/sigmaweb.

20 In Germany, the level of foreign investment compared to Western German investment was low. The opportunity to establish more competitive economic structures, for example, in the all-German banking sector, was not acted upon.

21 See Lee (1993: 9). The neglect of light consumer industry and the "unproductive" service sector was a typical feature of all socialist countries. The year 1989 was designated by North Korea as the "year of light industry", but apparently with no success, because the

socialist trading system broke up soon after. However, light industry is one of those industries which due to low labour costs can and has already to some extent become a primary target for early foreign direct investment (FDI) in North Korea.

22 While infrastructure development is a "classical" task of the state or public authorities, experience from transformation countries shows that the need for capital can also lead to new models of public–private partnership in infrastructure investment, including private investment in roads, networks or bridges. For a discussion of the role of public and private sectors, see Stern and Stiglitz (1997).

23 For South Korea, this problem has an additional facet: South Korea is comparable to North Korea just as West Germany was to East Germany. However, South Korea itself has just undergone a massive financial and economic crisis requiring a not-yet-completed restructuring process, especially in the financial sector. This crisis also led to a massive debt build-up, which will be increased if more welfare state elements are introduced in South Korea. It poses an additional problem for possible unification strategies. South Korea urgently needs to reform its own fiscal system and maintain a sustainable fiscal policy. Japan with its debt problems provides a cautionary example.

24 North Korea's *juche* ideology, while it now stresses the importance of self-sacrifice for national independence, first operated under the premise of achieving material abundance through socialism and *juche*.

25 Currently, the EU nations most affected by migration after the accession of Central and Eastern European states have tried to implement a long transition period before freedom of migration is granted.

26 This policy allowed unrestricted migration, accompanied by massive income transfers, the creation of an identical social welfare system, and the introduction of the Deutschmark in Eastern Germany at an exchange rate that extensively revalued the savings of East Germans.

References

Blaug, M. (1992) *The Methodology of Economics, Or How Economists Explain*, 2nd edn, Cambridge: Cambridge University Press.

Boettke, P.J. (1999) *Why Culture Matters: Economics, Politics and the Imprint of History*, New York: New York University Working Paper.

Boothroyd, P. and Nam, P.X. (2000) *Socioeconomic Renovation in Vietnam: The Origin, Evolution, and Impact of Doi Moi*, Ottawa: International Development Research Centre.

Brunner, K. (1987) "The Perception of Man and the Conception of Society: Two Approaches to Understanding Society," *Economic Inquiry*, 25, 367–88.

Camdessus, M. (1997) *Good Governance: The IMF's Role*, Washington, DC: International Monetary Fund.

Chun, H.T. (1999) "The Second Economy in North Korea," *Seoul Journal of Economics*, 12(2), 173–194.

Eberstadt, N. (2000) "'Our Own Style of Statistics': Availability and Reliability of Official Quantitative Data for the Democratic People's Republic of Korea," *The Economics of Korean Reunification*, 5(1), 68–93.

Ellmann, M.J. (1992) "Shock Therapy in Russia: Failure or Partial Success?" in *Radio Free Europe/Radio Liberty research report*, 1(34), 48–61.

Freeman, R.B. (2000) "Single-peaked Versus Diversified Capitalism: The Relation Between Economic Institutions and Outcomes," National Bureau of Economic Research Working Paper 7556, Cambridge, MA: NBER.

Fukuyama, F. (1996) *Trust: The Social Virtues and the Creation of Prosperity*, New York: Simon and Schuster.

Hall, T.W. and Elliott, J.E. (1999) "Poland and Russia One Decade After Shock Therapy," *Journal of Economic Issues*, 33(2), 305–14.

Hayek, F.A. (1937) "Economics and Knowledge," *Economica*, 4, new series, 33–54.

Hayek, F.A. (1945) "The Use of Knowledge in Society," *American Economic Review*, 35(4), 519–30.

Hayek, F.A. (1952) *The Sensory Order*, London: Routledge.

Hayek, F.A. (1964) "The Theory of Complex Phenomena," in M. Bunge (ed.), *The Critical Approach to Science and Philosophy*, London: Collier Mcmillan, pp. 332–49.

Hayek, F.A. (1969) "Die Ergebnisse menschlichen Handelns, aber nicht menschlichen Entwurfs," in F.A. Hayek (ed.), *Freiburger Studien*, Tübingen: Mohr, pp. 97–107.

Hayek, F.A. (1979) *The Counter-Revolution of Science: Studies on the Abuse of Reason* (1952), 2nd edn, Indianapolis: Liberty Press.

Hellmann, J. and Schankemann, M. (2000) "Intervention, Corruption and Capture: The Nexus Between Enterprises and the State," *Economics of Transition*, 8(3), 545–76.

Henning, C. and Lu, X. (2000) "The Political Foundation of Chinese Style Gradualism: A Paradox of Too Strong Private Interest," *Journal of Institutional and Theoretical Economics*, 156(1), 35–59.

Herrmann-Pillath, C. (1999) "Staat und Transformation – Theoretische Reflektionen über einige offene Fragen der Forschung," in H.H. Höhmann (ed.), *Spontaner oder gestalteter Prozeß*, Baden-Baden: Nomos, pp. 371–90.

Herrmann-Pillath, C. (2000) "Was ist und wie betreibt man wirtschaftskulturelle Transformationsforschung?" in H.H. Höhmann, (ed.), *Eine unterschätzte Dimension? Zur Rolle wirtschaftskultureller Faktoren in der osteuropäischen Transformation*, Bremen: Edition Temmen.

Hwang, E.G. (1993) *The Korean Economies: A Comparison of North and South*, New York: Oxford University Press.

Irvin, G.W. (1995) "Vietnam: Assessing the Achievements of Doi Moi," *The Journal of Development Studies*, 31(5), 725–50.

Jung, H.N. and Park, H.J. (1998) "Reform Policy for Land and Property Ownership System," in Il Sakong and K.S. Kim (eds), *Policy Priorities for the Unified Korean Economy*, Seoul: Institute for Global Economics, pp. 193–222.

Kim, I.S. (1979) *On the Juche Idea: Excerpts*, Pyongyang: Foreign Languages Publishing House.

Kim, J. (1997) *Divided Korea: The Politics of Development 1945–1972*, revised edition, Seoul: Hollym.

Köllner, P. (1997) "Konfuzianismus und Wirtschaftsentwicklung in Korea: eine integrative Übersicht über die Literatur", in P. Köllner (ed.), *Korea 1997*, Hamburg: Institut für Asienkunde, pp. 215–48.

Kolodko, G.W. (1999) "Transition to a Market Economy and Sustainable Growth: Implications for the Post-Washington Consensus," *Communist and Post-Communist Studies*, 32, 233–61.

Koo, B.H. (1992) *Political Economy of Self-reliance: Juche and Economic Development in North Korea, 1961–1990*, Seoul: Research Center for Peace and Unification of Korea.

Lee, C.H. (1993) "Korean Unification: Issues in Transition and Economic Union," Kiel Working Papers no. 590, Kiel: Institute for World Economics.

Lipton, D. and Sachs, J. (1990) "Wirtschaftsreformen in Polen", *Europäische Rundschau*, 18(4), 97–113.

Mises, L. von (1959) *Human Action*, 6th edn, New Haven, CT: Yale University Press.

Mummert, U. (1999) "Informal Institutions and Institutional Policy: Shedding Light on the Myth of Institutional Conflict," discussion paper 02/99, Max-Planck-Institut zur Erforschung von Wirtschaftssystemen, Jena: MPI.

Murrell, P. (1993) "What is Shock Therapy? What Did it Do in Poland and Russia?," *Post-Soviet Affairs*, 9(2), 111–40.

Noland, M. (2001) "North Korea's external economic relations," in S.S. Kim and T.H. Lee (eds), *Northeast Asia: New Patterns of Conflict and Cooperation*, Lanham, MD: Rowman and Littlefield. Available on http://www.iie.com/PAPERS/noland0201-1.htm.

Noland, M., Robinson, S. and Liu, L.G. (1998) *The Costs and Benefits of Korean Unification*, Working Paper no. 98, Washington, DC: Institute for International Economics.

North, D.C. (1990) *Institutions, Institutional Change and Economic Performance*, Cambridge: Cambridge University Press.

Olson, Mancur (1996) *The Varieties of Eurosclerosis: The Rise and Decline of Nations since 1982*, Jean Monnet Chair paper no. 32, Florence: European University Institute.

Panther, S. (1997) "Cultural Factors in the Transition Process: Latin Center, Orthodox Periphery?," in J.G. Backhaus (ed.), *Issues in Transformation Theory*, Marburg: Metropolis, pp. 95–122.

Peacock, A. and Willgerodt, H. (eds) (1989) *Germany's Social Market Economy: Origins and Evolution*, London: Macmillan.

Philippe, M.P. (1995) "Le modèle de la société bureacratique, peut-il expliquer les difficultés de la transition?," *Journal des Economistes et des Etudes Humaines*, 6(2/3), 449–73.

Pollack, J.D. and Lee, C.M. (2000) "Preparing for Korean Unification: Scenarios and Implications," Rand Publication MR-1040-A, http://www.rand.org/publications/MR/MR1040/.

Putnam, R.D. (1993) *Making Democracy Work: Civic Traditions in Modern Italy*, Princeton, NJ: Princeton University Press.

Raiser, M. (1997) "Informal Institutions, Social Capital and Transition: Reflections on a Neglected Dimension," EBRD Working Papers no. 25, Available HTTP <http://www.ebrd.org/english/public/index.htm> (accessed 1 May 2002).

Rautava, J. (1999) "Small Enterprises: The Missing Engine of Growth in the Russian Economy," *The Month in Review*, January, p. 4.

Roller, E. (1992) *Ideological Basis of the Market Economy: Attitudes Toward Distribution Principles and the Role of Government in Western and Eastern Germany*, WZB discussion paper FS II 92–206, Berlin: Wissenschaftszentrum Berlin.

Rosenbaum, E.F. (1999) *Culture, Cognitive Models and the Performance of Institutions in Transformation Countries*, Frankfurt Institute for Transformation Studies Discussion Papers No. 1/99, Frankfurt/Oder: FIT.

Savada, A.M. (ed.) (1994) *North Korea: A Country Study*, Washington, DC: Federal Research Divison, Library of Congress.

Schüller, M. (1998) "Reform und Öffnung: Der chinesische Weg zur Marktwirtschaft," in C. Herrmann-Pillath *et al.* (eds), *Länderbericht China: Bundeszentrale für politische Bildung*, Schriftenreihe Bd. 351, Bonn: Bundeszentrale für politische Bildung , pp. 278–301.

Seliger, B. (1999) "Socio-cultural Change, Institutions and Transition Theory: Some Lessons from German Unification," *Zeitschrift der koreanisch-deutschen Gesellschaft für Sozialwissenschaften*, 9(2), 325–51.

Seliger, B. (2002) "Towards a More General Theory of Transformation?," *Eastern European Economics* 40(1), 36–62.

Shirk, S.L. (1993) *The Political Logic of Economic Reform in China*, Berkeley, CA: University of California Press.

Shleifer, A. (1997) "Government in Transition," *European Economic Review*, 41, 385–410.

Sinn, G. and Sinn, H.W. (1994) *Jumpstart: The Economic Unification of Germany*, Cambridge (Mass.): MIT Press.

Smith, A. (1952 [1776]) *An Inquiry into the Nature and Causes of the Wealth of Nations*, Chicago: Encyclopedia Britannica.

Stern, N. and Stiglitz, J. (1997) *A Framework for a Development Strategy in a Market Economy: Objectives, Scope, Institutions and Instruments*, EBRD Working Paper 20, London: EBRD.

Vlachoutsicos, C. (1999) *Internal Barriers in Transition of Enterprises from Central Plan to Market*, Davidson Institute Working Paper Series no. 277, Michigan: William Davidson Institute. Available HTTP <http://www.wdi.bus.umich.edu/> (accessed 1 May 2002).

Weeks, J. (1998) "Open Economy Adjustment and Transition in Vietnam," in P. Cook (ed.), *Privatization, Enterprise Development and Economic Reform: Experiences of Developing and Transitional Economies*, Cheltenham: Edward Elgar, pp. 100–7.

Williamson, J. (1990) "What Washington Means by Policy Reform," in J. Williamson (ed.), *Latin American Adjustment: How Much has Happened?*, Washington, DC: Institute for International Economics.

Williamson, J. (1997) "The Washington Consensus Revisited," in L. Emmerij (ed.), *Economic and Social Development in the XXIst Century*, Washington, DC: Inter-American Development Bank.

Part IV

Korean unification and economic integration

14 Beyond collapse

Continuity and change in North Korea

C. Kenneth Quinones

Introduction

North Korea's leadership faces a seemingly simple, but politically complex dilemma – pursue change or see their regime collapse. The smiling face of North Korea's deceased founding father, Kim Il Sung, beams from huge concrete billboards positioned at key intersections throughout the country. Each boldly proclaims, "Kim Il Sung is Forever With Us." The subliminal message is clear – Kim Jong Il's primary goal is regime survival. The younger Kim is determined to do whatever is necessary to perpetuate his father's legacy, even if this requires pursuing a carefully managed and quietly implemented program of change.

North Korea is changing. Kim Jong Il, in numerous essays since his father's death, has chastised "reformers" as traitors of socialism. He has condemned as "villains" the leaders of the former Soviet Union who advocated reform, and blamed such policies for the Communist bloc's demise. Yet at the same time, Kim has found in *juche,* his father's interpretation of Marxism and Leninism, ample rationale to distinguish between "reform" and "change." Some would label the distinction merely rhetorical. But if we delve into Kim Jong Il's mind through his writings, we can comprehend his distinction.

According to Kim Jong Il's essay "Socialism is Science," human beings, not Hegel's mechanical forces of dialectical materialism or Marx's economic determinism, drive history. Survival requires that the human species adjust to the constant changes of its natural and social environments. Humans analyze the change around them and respond with adaptations. For Kim Jong Il, like his father, the adaptations must reflect the specific aspects of conditions in Korea, not the universalistic formulations dictated by the ideologies and political philosophies of any superpower. To Kim, change is inescapable, and humans must adapt to it. So long as the changes or adaptations are formulated according to national conditions, rather than universal principles, change is acceptable. Kim rejects "reform" because it sacrifices nationalism for the sake of preserving Marxism or promoting capitalism. This also is to say that Kim is not striving to emulate any model, be it the so-called "Chinese model" or any other. The nationalistic Kim is seeking to synthesize various "changes" into a model he can proclaim to be his own.

North Korea appears destined to continue changing, but we should not anticipate change in some aspects of its politics and society. Authoritarianism has a long history in Korean society, dating from ancient Korea's adoption of Confucianism. Japanese colonialism early in the twentith century reinforced this authoritarian tradition in both halves of Korea. In the south, it has taken almost half a century of political turmoil to achieve democratization. Kim Jong Il is not about to relinquish political power during his lifetime. We can assume with considerable confidence that democratization is not on his agenda. Nor should we expect him to soon discard collectivism as the core of social and economic activity any time soon. Again, collectivism has deep roots in Korea's history. Confucianism emphasized selflessness for the sake of promoting the common good. Koreans' traditional reverence for their ancestors and kinship ties strengthens their preference for group rather than individual action. Kim Jong Il is certain to continue favoring socialism's collectivism over capitalism's individual gain.

Change is not, however, a one-way street. Those who observe North Korea in hopes of deciphering its conduct would also do well to recognize the need to change their perceptions of it and refine their methodology. Mentally, many Americans remain in a fortress constructed during the Cold War. Until we break out of that mindset, our perspective on North Korea will remain distorted. For example, most would agree that the Cold War ended a decade ago. Certainly the 1994 signing of the first diplomatic agreement between the United States and North Korea, the Agreed Framework, and the more recent visit of the US Secretary of State to Pyongyang have signaled the end of the Cold War between the two nations. Yet we persist in applying Cold War rhetoric to North Korea. Mention North Korea to Americans, especially some politicians and journalists, and they are prone to describe it as: "closed," "Stalinist," "aggressive," "authoritarian," and so forth. Negative images abound because of North Korea's past misdeeds. But most of these labels do not accurately describe the country today. Yes, it is an authoritarian regime, but it has not committed aggression against anyone for half a century and it is no longer closed to outsiders.

Rather than remaining focused on North Korea's past misdeeds, we would do well to assess what is compelling Pyongyang to change. Looking back, we can see that the changing international environment around the Korean Peninsula, specifically the collapse of the Communist bloc a decade ago, compelled Kim Il Sung to hasten the pace of North Korea's "opening" to the international community. Kim Jong Il has continued the process. Engagement of the international community perpetuates his father's legacy while furthering his foremost goal – regime survival.

At the same time, the younger Kim has far exceeded the level of change his father sanctioned. Much of this change is a reaction to the devastating floods of 1995. Nature did not initiate the decreases in food and industrial production, but it did quicken the pace of economic decline and necessitated relatively extensive adaptations. How we label this change and whether it is progress toward some imagined economic model is of minor importance. What is more important is that we recognize its occurrence, understand its causes and accurately assess its direction. Only then can we better influence the process of change in North Korea.

Students of North Korea in the United States would do well to shift their focus. For years they have debated whether North Korea was opening. All the while, the pace of its opening was quickening. Now the debate centers on the characteristics of the socio-economic model that North Korea is following or must follow. This discussion has outlived its usefulness. Possibly a more beneficial topic would be how to influence change in North Korea. In this regard, one thing is certain. We cannot influence that process unless we are actively engaged, diplomatically and commercially, with North Korea.

Kim Jong Il is mortal. The more openness and change he sanctions, the greater difficulty he will have to control and direct that change to serve his purposes. Ultimately, only two scenarios are inevitable; either the magnitude of change will overwhelm Kim's ability to control it, or he will die. Either way, North Korea will continue to change.

A matter of method

Any assessment of North Korea requires much more effort and caution than for other societies. It is a land of illusions where we must look beyond the obvious. The extreme secrecy there has severely obstructed the most earnest efforts to understand its inner dynamics. Since the Korean War, North Korea has sought to shield the reality of its weaknesses from the outside world while striving to project an image of strength, both military and economic. Driving this bizarre scheme are military need and a keen sense of insecurity on the one hand, and paradoxical feelings of shame and pride on the other. Secrecy shields weaknesses from both foes and subjects. It facilitates manipulation of perceptions with illusions of invincibility, prosperity, and ideological superiority. Beyond these illusions is the "real," unofficial North Korea today. Since 1995, North Korea's floods and droughts, food shortages, and crisis in public health have compelled it to reveal itself as never before to a virtual flood of foreigners. Today we know it as a land of bizarre contrasts: depressing poverty, pervasive food and medicine shortages, and crushing manual labor. Defending this grim reality is frightful military might in the form of ballistic missiles, hordes of armored vehicles, long-range artillery, and one million soldiers.

The potential pitfalls outlined above hint at the shortcomings of any comparative approach. A number of well-intended efforts in the late 1990s contrasted North Korea with small East European former communist states, and prematurely predicted its imminent collapse. Claims that Kim Jong Il is striving to emulate the "Chinese model" of change also have proven unfounded. The "model" approach compounds the analytical problems. The meaning of the "Chinese model" is usually assumed. Attempts to define it require compressing China's incredible diversity into a few brief paragraphs. On the other hand, some analysts are prone to assume the North Korean model can be quickly defined since it is a small, homogeneous society. Taken for granted is the accuracy of the limited information available about North Korea. But more problematic is the tendency of some assessments to include only evidence supportive of one's own foregone conclusion. This "inverted pyramid" approach consists of a broad generalization supported by a narrow base of evidence. Some analysts' reliance on this approach helps explain the increasing lack of relevance between debates whether North Korea will collapse, and whether it is adopting the "Chinese model."

Our approach will be less ambitious. To determine the degree, direction, and pace of change, we will focus on contrasting conditions in North Korea today with its recent past. Our analytical range will be narrow: its leadership's priorities, philosophy of change, and assessment of what has actually changed. This will not necessarily yield superior results. Our approach still shares many of the pitfalls of other comparative approaches. Nevertheless, we should benefit from the contrasting perspectives of past and present reality in North Korea.

Disciplined use of terminology will enhance clarity and analytical consistency. "Change" represents the process of human adaptation to circumstances altered by phenomena beyond the ability of a leader and his government to control. For example, the Soviet Union's demise was beyond Pyongyang's capacity to prevent. The new circumstances that phenomenon created compelled Pyongyang to "change" its international posture. "Reform" implies a rationally defined program of change intentionally formulated and implemented by a government. The process requires recognition that past human activities and policies produced undesirable consequences. To rectify the consequences, political leaders formulate and implement "reform." Maintaining this distinction between "change" and "reform" is essential to understanding why Kim Jong Il rejects "reform," while at the same time he seems willing to accommodate an impressive array of change.

Kim Jong Il on reform and change

Kim Jong Il rigidly distinguishes between "reform" and "change." His reasons are more than philosophical. Since 1990, the foremost challenge for him and his father has been perpetuation of their dynasty in the wake of the Communist bloc's demise. At a luncheon in New York City sponsored by the Asia Society in September 1992, someone asked then-North Korean Foreign Minister Kim Yong Nam how his homeland could expect to outlive the Soviet Union. Kim, a close confidant of then North Korean leader Kim Il Sung, paused momentarily. His nation would endure because of superior leadership and ideology, Kim Yong Nam answered confidently. Many of us at the time believed this was a hollow boast. Hindsight tells us his confidence in North Korea's will to survive was not misplaced. Whether its survival is a consequence of leadership and ideology remains, however, quite debatable.

North Korean leaders' preoccupation with survival is reflected in the Korean Workers Party (KWP) essays published since 1991 and credited to Kim Jong Il.

Key recurrent themes are *juche*'s infallibility, and condemnation of "reformers" and "reform" as having been responsible for the corruption and failure of socialism in Europe. The focus of this scorn is the Soviet Union's prime minister, Mikhail Gorbachev, and his reformers, as alluded to in the essay, "Socialism is Science." It is the first essay credited to Kim Jong Il after his father's death and appeared in the Party's foremost newspaper, *Nodong sinmun,* on 1 November 1994. The younger Kim opened by declaring that socialism, despite the claims of "imperialists and reactionaries," remains a science and has not failed. Conceding that socialism has crumbled in some countries, he counters that this is not a consequence of socialism's shortcomings, but of the "renegades of socialism," corruption and treason.

Kim Jong Il was more specific in his 25 December 1996 essay, "Respecting the Forerunners of the Revolution is a Noble Moral Obligation of Revolutionaries." He defended his Korean predecessors, "True revolutionaries who fight for the people and for the victory of socialism must not forget their revolutionary forefathers; instead, they must defend and develop their achievements" (ibid.: 8) The younger Kim placed his father above all others, "The communist morality of our people finds its highest expression in their unqualified respect for and absolute allegiance to the great leader Comrade Kim Il Sung" (ibid.: 9). Later Kim refers to "opportunists and socialist renegades," and accuses them of having "emasculated the revolutionary principles of Marxism-Leninism to please the imperialists." He calls them "traitors," and condemns them for having carried out "reform and restructuring for democracy and economic welfare" (ibid.: 15). Kim concludes that the "renegades" program, an oblique reference to Gorbachev, "was nothing but a reactionary theory for destroying socialism and reviving capitalism." Kim then links his rejection of reform to his premise that the Soviet Union's demise was a consequence of former Soviet leader Mikhail Gorbachev's reform program, *perestroika* (reconstruction or restructuring), and *glasnost* (openness). Gorbachev is condemned as a "traitor" to socialism and communism. To avoid falling into the same abyss, Kim and the KWP's ideologues have purged the word "reform" from their vocabulary. Instead, he repeatedly proclaims the infallibility of his father's *juche* thought.

But Kim Jong Il's rejection of reform extends beyond ideology. For him, reform poses substantial political problems. Gorbachev could justify the need for reform by criticizing his predecessors' work while proclaiming his intent to forge a better future for socialism. Doing so strengthened Gorbachev's legitimacy. The same can be said of Deng Hsiao Ping's call for reform to rectify Mao Tse Tung's excesses. Again, he could do so, after Mao's death, without adversely affecting his legitimacy. But for Kim Jong Il, his legitimacy is genetically bound to his father. Without his ancestry, he lacks legitimacy.

Kim Jong Il and his followers have declared his father's reign a "golden" age when Korean socialism achieved its greatest accomplishments under the "Great Leader." Kim Il Sung is more than the nation's father. He is credited with having surpassed the philosophical and scientific sophistication of Marxism-Leninism by formulating *juche.* The senior Kim is revered in North Korea for having driven the imperialists, Japanese and American, from the "fatherland." Under his leadership, according to the younger Kim, North Korea became a "workers paradise." Advocating reform would contest the perceived infallibility of Kim Il Sung's rule, and possibly tarnish the proclaimed brilliance of his accomplishments. The grand illusion of the Great Leader's superiority above all other communist leaders would be contradicted. Also, given North Korea's Confucian legacy, Kim Jong Il's filial piety would become suspect and his legitimacy gravely eroded.

Obviously, Kim Jong Il has little reason to pursue reform, yet ample evidence indicates he is comfortable with "change." To avoid any reference to "reform," North Korea's leaders and bureaucrats rely on an impressive array of synonyms to characterize their efforts to achieve change without reform. Thus Pyongyang makes frequent references to "modernization," "adaptation," "reinvigoration," "revitalization," "restoration," but not "reform."

Kim's formula for change

Juche is a paradox. In North Korea's highly centralized, authoritarian, and rigidly stratified political hierarchy, one would expect an ideology of similar features. After all, *juche's* antecedent, Marxism, imposes an inflexible logic on its followers. *Juche*, however, is amazingly pragmatic. Political reality nevertheless negates any possibility of any "gray" area in one's political loyalties and thought. An individual either submits totally to the perceived "collective" good and reveres the "great leader" and his thought as infallible, or is expelled from society. Yet *juche* permits loyal followers to explore, experiment, and even to alter and adapt foreign practices and materials to North Korea's internal conditions. *Juche* encourages change only so long as it conforms to the "Supreme Commander's" dictates.

Outsiders have long assumed North Korea's leaders were micro-managers. This illusion may be rooted in Kim Il Sung's practice of "on the spot guidance." During the Korean War and post-war reconstruction, he traveled frequently to the countryside and to factories to observe and comment on conditions. His visits were commemorated by a red plaque that noted in gold letters the date of his visit. His son has continued the practice. Since his father's death, the younger Kim has concentrated on the military, possibly to accent his concern for defense.

Kim Jong Il's performance and writings suggest he is more of a realist than a romantic, a person preoccupied with visionary planning rather than micro-managing implementation. Officials in Pyongyang talk with surprising candor about having considerable latitude to debate with one another how best to implement policy. As for the policy, they agree this is the exclusive preserve of "the highest level of their government," an allusion to Kim Jong Il and his small council of closest advisers. Party officials, bureaucrats, and military officers turn to the writings of the "Supreme Commander" for guidance on policy and the parameters for their debates about its implementation.

We should be cautious when drawing conclusions from Kim's public thoughts. They could have the dual intent of encouraging self-confidence in his followers while also inciting fear in his foreign audience. We can only guess at his real intentions. A reasonable possibility is that his public comments establish national priorities and set the parameters for discussion among the KWP rank and file about how best to achieve their leader's goals. Despite the inherent limitations, Kim's words remain our best avenue for peering into his thoughts.

In 1982, Kim Jong Il wrote in his landmark thesis, *On the Juche Idea*, "The Principles of Juche, independence, self-sufficiency and self-reliant defense are the guiding principles of realizing *Chajusong* (self-determination) in the spheres of ideology, politics, the economy and defense" (ibid.: 36). Since then, the only substantive alteration of these goals has been the elevation of defense to the top priority, possibly as a consequence of the Soviet Union's collapse and normalization of relations with South Korea. Similar themes are echoed in Kim's 19 June 1997 essay, "On Preserving the *Juche* Character and National Character of the Revolution and Construction."

Independence

In North Korea's political and ideological context, independence refers to the society's "inviolable" right to assert its sovereignty to protect itself from alleged imperialist exploitation and ideological subjugation. There is no room for individual independence or freedom. The individual is required to assimilate fully into society's collective whole and to submit to the common good. Ideological independence rejects Marxism's claim of infallible internationalism. Instead, it declares the superiority of Kim Il Sung's particularistic interpretation of it, i.e. *juche*. This declaration of independence from Marxism is the basis for the pragmatism of Kim Il Sung's thought. Unable to apply Marxism's urban industrial and capitalist-oriented criteria to Korea's essentially pre-capitalistic and agrarian society, Kim countered that he would guide Korea's struggle against imperialism according to conditions in his homeland. Those who criticized him were labeled "bigoted nationalists," "self-styled or bogus" Marxists, flunkeyists (those who allegedly revere foreign powers and their ideas more than those of their native land and people, specifically China) and "dogmatists" (theorists more faithful to Soviet Marxism than the teachings of the "Great Leader"). On the other hand, those who link their proposed solutions for North Korea's problems to the nation's indigenous conditions are lauded as heroes of the state.

Self-reliant defense

Kim declared in the same essay (ibid.: 50), "Self reliance in defense is a fundamental principle of an independent state." "Imperialism," of course, is his key villain. The best defense against "the imperialist war of aggression" is perpetual preparedness to counter its violence with violence. Supreme Commander Kim Jong Il makes frequent references to this in his contemporary calls for North Koreans to work harder so their nation can be a "strong and prosperous" nation. Kim emphasizes that a "self-reliant defense" requires mobilization of the entire population to support the nation's defense forces. He reveals his realistic side by sanctioning the need to "receive aid in national defense from fraternal countries and friends." Kim concludes that the potency of one's defense capability depends primarily on the domestic economy, but foreign assistance must be fostered simultaneously.

Self-sufficient economy

In 1982, Kim Jong Il could still speak confidently about a "self-sufficient economy." The nation's grain production was still yielding surpluses, exports of minerals were flowing steadily to the Communist bloc, and heavy industry was turning the North Korean army into a highly mechanized and mobile force. Kim proclaimed, "Building an independent national economy means building an economy free of dependence on others . . ." His "socialist independent economy" was to distinguish itself from capitalism by aiming "to meet the demands of the country and the people," not by generating personal profit. Heavy industry was to be the "pillar" of the economy. Light industry and agriculture were important, but less so probably because they did not contribute as directly to the production of arms and munitions.

Kim did not oppose learning and trading with the outside world. When he wrote his 1982 thesis (ibid.: 49), many outsiders still considered North Korea a closed and isolated society. It was closed, but mainly to the "Western" and non-socialist nations, but certainly not to the Communist and so-called "third world" or "emerging nations." Kim explained, "self-reliance does not mean building an economy in isolation." His "self-reliant" economy should, in his view, avoid foreign domination, but "this does not rule out international economic cooperation" (ibid.: 48). Here he was referring to retaining access to the technical and material wealth of the "socialist countries and newly emerging nations." Kim clearly did not foresee the collapse of the Communist bloc and China's gradual economic transition into a hybrid of socialism and capitalism.

Juche anti-Communism

Subsequent developments – the Communist bloc's collapse and North Korea's economic decline – required that Kim adjust some of his views. In his 1997 essay "On Preserving the *Juche* Character" he warns of a "sharp confrontation between socialism and imperialism." Kim's response to this new situation is an affirmation of his confidence in the validity of *juche*, "we must maintain the *Juche* character of the revolutionary struggle." He dismisses as a "shameless lie," "imperialists' allegations that socialism is inferior to capitalism." Again raising the banners of "self-sufficiency and self-reliant defense," he warns against tolerating "the capitalist 'Western' style in managing the state," a clear reference to decentralizing economic planning and replacing economic "collectivism" with "individual" incentives. North Koreans were still suffering from pervasive shortages of food and medicine when the essay appeared. Kim seems to make an oblique reference to his domain's woes, "The countries which are experiencing social problems, economic difficulties and disasters." For him, the way out of this harsh reality was to more resolutely muster one's indigenous efforts through political training. He rejected "so-called prescription that the imperialists are propagating." Given the broader context of his 1997 essay, he was probably referring to economic reforms.

Kim, apparently sensing growing ambivalence within his Korean Workers Party and bureaucracy toward imperialism, strikes out against it, "Aggression and plunder are the real nature of imperialism." The international community's food aid also seems to have had a positive impact on his subordinates. Apparently concerned, Kim strikes out against it as well, "Nothing is more foolish and dangerous than pinning hopes on imperialist 'aid'." He terms the aid "a noose of plunder and subjugation." He then dismisses South Korea's economic success as a consequence of its "flunkeyism," that is its perceived willingness to subordinate itself to the wishes of foreign powers in exchange for economic gain. He claims Seoul's "internationalization and globalization" are erasing its Korean qualities with a flood of American, Japanese, and West European preferences in politics, the economy, and culture.

Kim concludes that change is acceptable, but only so long as it opposes imperialism, preserves *juche* and the national character, and "strengthens international unity and cooperation among the progressive people of the world." This is an astonishing, almost unimaginable task for a tiny, lonely nation on the edge of economic collapse. But like his father, the Supreme Commander finds boundless pride and self-confidence in his sense of Korean nationalism. Having a million-man army certainly helps. Given Kim's demeaning attitude toward capitalism and blind faith in socialism, prospects would appear bleak that North Korea might adopt reforms aimed at a transition to capitalism, at least so long as Kim Jong Il rules.

Juche versus Marxism

Juche is a faint echo of Marxism. Kim Il Sung rejected Marx's internationalism and the universal and urban brotherhood of workers. He emphasized nationalism, and his assessments were rooted in local conditions. He rejected Engel's mechanical interpretation of history. Evolution toward communism was inevitable, Engel had claimed, because of the innate tensions of class struggle. Kim retained the concept of class struggle, but more in keeping with Mao Tse Tung's clash between peasants and landowners. Instead of Lenin's vanguard of the proletariat, Kim put soldiers and teachers in the forefront of his revolution. Man himself, rather than the inanimate and unthinking forces of history, Kim Il Sung argued, propels change within society and moves mankind toward a higher level of existence.

Juche verges on being the antithesis of Marxism. Kim Il Sung's thought is human-centered, nationalistic and rejects universal precepts. Solutions to problems are to be found in the analysis of indigenous circumstances and solutions are to be consistent with local conditions. Marx's theory minimized man's ability to determine his fate. Marx, like Kim, claimed universal validity and application for his views, but Kim rejected the idea that human activity must conform to a single ideology. According to Marx, urban workers were to unite behind the global outcry against capitalism's exploitation, and each state was to wither away as social classes dissolved.

But for Kim, the state is the encompassing and benevolent defender of nationalism and the national character. Society is rigidly stratified so the leadership can better manage class struggle, allocate obligations to the state, and determine awards and punishments. Kim shares Marx's appreciation for "collectivism," but in a very different way. Marx's collectivism was to provide materialistic equality and social egalitarianism. Kim sees collectivism as much more than the sharing of material goods. It means all individuals have a shared, collective obligation to serve the state and to act in unison with their peers. Kim's collectivism demands selflessness and self-denial. In his utopia, the individual ceases to exist as a separate entity and merges into the totality of the state and society. But in the view of Marx, the collective action of the multitude empowered workers to destroy their capitalist overlords and to seize political power.

Kim Il Sung retained the broad outlines of Lenin's view of imperialism. This fit comfortably with Kim Il Sung's hatred of Japanese colonialism of Korea from 1910 to 1945, and remained valid after Korea's division in 1945 and subsequent occupation by the armies of the United States and the Soviet Union. But Kim broadened Lenin's definition of imperialism to encompass ideological and cultural imperialism, tendencies Kim perceived in the ambitions of his two benefactors, the Soviet Union and China. To temper these impulses, Kim countered their interpretations of Marxism with his own, and sought to exploit their rivalry.

Juche's advantages

Juche concentrates all authority in the hands of the "Great Leader." Since man is perceived as the prime mover of reality, the younger Kim in his role as the "Supreme Commander" can sanction or commission adaptations in the name of compensating for changing circumstances. He does not have to conform to Marxism's supra-human historical forces. Nor has his father's philosophy taught him to believe that his subjects' conduct is a consequence of economic determinism and materialism, another Marxist precept that limits a leader's authority. *Juche* empowers its foremost advocate to mold human activity through his example, instructions, and political education. *Juche* also teaches Kim's followers to suppress their individual impulses, to merge their being with the collective whole of society, and to conform to his dictates. Hence Kim Jong Il can proclaim himself the *de facto* Supreme Commander in his society.

For the younger Kim, linking his personal preference to his father's precedent is politically the safest way to propose "change," or to select one "adaptation" over another. For example, many foreign observers have misinterpreted the appearance in the mid-1990s of "farmers' markets," sometimes also referred to as "black markets," as evidence that a second, "underground capitalistic" economy was emerging in North Korea. Actually, Kim Il Sung condoned such "peasant" markets whenever domestic conditions required. (See Kim Il Sung's 1 March 1969 essay, "The Questions of the Peasant Market in a Socialist Society and of the Way to Abolish It." As we will see later, Kim Jong Il has relied extensively on his father's precedent in the areas of foreign and unification policy.

Juche's pragmatism enables Kim Jong Il to experiment with an impressive range of new, even alien methods. It allows him to draw on any ideological and cultural tradition to address the underlying causes for problems at home, so long as the method is first tested and adapted to conditions within North Korea. Any one of these might be taken from a "capitalistic" society and contain traits of "capitalism." For *juche,* the "capitalistic" characteristics are less a concern than the capacity to adapt to indigenous conditions without adversely affecting the "national character." Such reasoning enables Kim to consider diverse adaptations, even from "imperialists" in West Europe, North America and Japan.

Juche alone, however, cannot explain Kim Jong Il's ability to adapt his father's political and economic system to changing circumstances. Kim also has demonstrated impressive political acumen by focusing the blame for North Korea's woes on "the schemes of the imperialists nations to strangle socialism" and natural phenomena. North Korea's economic decline is not a consequence of shortcomings in its ideology and failings of its leadership, Kim Jong Il claims. Rather, it is a consequence of US economic sanctions and the "betrayal of socialism" by Moscow's leadership. Flood and famine are not a consequence of incorrect past policies, such as the excessive use of chemical fertilizers to boost grain production and deforestation to allow for the planting of more corn on hillsides. Instead, Pyongyang blames nature for its food shortages.

Doing so has enabled Kim to avoid personalizing his rationale for change. Because of the hereditary basis of his power, he cannot contend that his father had misinterpreted *juche.* By not having blamed his "elders" for his regime's problems, Kim has avoided one of the major pitfalls of the Soviet Union's reform program. The Soviet effort to assess blame splintered the Soviet Communist Party and the bureaucracy into warring factions. Kim's approach has preserved the cohesiveness of his primary bases of support, the Korean People's Army and the Korean Workers Party, his emphasis on blaming natural phenomena and "imperialist schemes" motivates his elite followers to accept his changes with minimal resistance.

Continuity

Kim Jong Il has made impressive progress in perpetuating his father's legacy. Some minor adjustments have been made, such as Kim's formal title and institutional rearrangement within the bureaucracy. Otherwise, the essential structure of North Korea's self-proclaimed "*Juche* system" is being preserved much as it has existed for nearly half a century.

The political system

The political system continues today much as it did under Kim Il Sung. Kim Jong Il monopolizes political authority, regardless of the titles he confers on himself. Deferring to his father, the younger Kim has left the title "Great Leader" for his father and instead prefers to be called the Supreme Commander. Whether he is called president or secretary or whatever, he and his followers know he shares power with no one. In the eyes of the society's most powerful groups – Korean People's Army, the Workers Party, the bureaucracy – Kim Jong Il stands alone at the pinnacle of power. He monopolizes their energies and determines their fate, and that of the entire population. Despite rumors that circulated in the years immediately after Kim Il Sung's death, we are unaware of any concerted challenge or opposition to Kim Jong Il's authority. He had consolidated his rule by the fall of 1998, and all indications point to his having the full support of the most powerful group in the society, the Korean People's Army (KPA). The same can be said for the even larger Workers' Party (KWP). As discussed earlier, *juche* remains the state's uncontested and unaltered ideology.

Key political practices continue largely unaltered. Some laws have been revised, but they remain essentially assertions of state power. There is no evidence of greater respect for human rights. Some of the content of the mass media has changed since 1994, but still the government dominates the mass media and uses it to educate the people for its own purposes. Some of the harsher labels assigned to the United States, Japan and South Korea have been moderated, but the duration of these changes has been brief and a reading of the back pages of the nation's leading newspaper, *Nodong sinmun,* reveals persistent references to "American imperialists," etc. Museums, places devoted to educating the young and old alike about the regime's glorious accomplishments and the evil deeds of its foes, remain just as they were ten years ago. Images of Americans and Japanese remain disturbingly negative. Nor has the similarly charged content of school textbooks been changed.

Defense

North Korea's defense posture remains much as it was at the time of Kim Il Sung's death, except for its nuclear-related programs. Defense continues to be the top priority. Kim Jong Il maintains a formidable conventional military force, much of it forward deployed just north of the demilitarized zone (DMZ). Backed by an awesome concentration of long-range artillery, this force could lung toward Seoul on a moment's notice. Dozens of short- to middle-range ballistic missiles could wreak instantaneous havoc on South Korea. The Korean People's Army's (KPA) combat capability and sustainability, however, have suffered in recent years. The nation's economic decline, total dependence on imported oil, inability to upgrade some military technology, and persistent food shortages have taken their toll. Nevertheless, the KPA retains a fearsome ability to inflict terrible suffering on South Korea. North Korea also remains a potent threat to peace in the Middle East because of its ballistic missile exports and potential to develop nuclear weapons. Also unchanged are Pyongyang's foremost enemies: the United States, Japan, and South Korea. One significant change since Kim Il Sung's death has been discontinuation of North Korea's nuclear weapons program, a change Kim Il Sung sanctioned on the eve of his death. The US–DPRK Agreed Framework talks resumed with his approval, and he had even outlined the terms of the agreement several months earlier. Kim Jong Il nevertheless deserves credit for remaining faithful to his father's wishes in this regard.

Reunification

The June 2000 North–South Korean summit in Pyongyang suggests there has been some significant movement toward reconciliation. Yet, in spite of appearances, Kim Jong Il has retained the essence of his father's reunification policy. Nothing accomplished at or since the Pyongyang summit was unprecedented, except the meeting between the two men. All the accords leading to and after the summit continued a process that commenced in 1972, and that reiterate previous agreements. The summit's 15 June 2000 accord, Article I, reiterates the 4 July 1972 accord; articles 2, 3, and 4 refer to items in the December 1991 Basic Agreement on Reconciliation, Peace, Social Exchange and Economic Cooperation. The June 2000 accord pledges Kim Jong will visit Seoul, a promise originally agreed to in principle in June 1994 by Kim Il Sung and his South Korean counterpart.

Continuation of Kim Il Sung's unification policies is evident in his son's writings. Of particular interest are his 4 August 1997b essay, "Let Us Carry out the Great Leader Comrade Kim Il Sung's Instructions for National Reunification," and a 1998 essay, "Let Us Reunify the Country Independently and Peacefully Through the Great Unity of the Entire Nation." Kim Jong Il's deeds support these goals. In these essays, he begins by carefully linking his views to those of his father, "The Juche-oriented idea of great national unity elucidated by the respected Comrade Kim Il Sung . . .". The younger Kim proclaims that his father formulated the "original idea" on this topic. He asserts that, "It is inconceivable to talk about national unity apart from the principle of national independence." Kim Jong Il urges that, "All the Koreans in the north, south and abroad must unite closely under the banner of patriotism." He claims, "successive south Korean authorities [i.e., previous presidential administrations in Seoul] have obstructed harmony between the north and the south with their anti-North confrontation policy." Kim Jong Il, like Kim Dae Jung, advocates coexistence of each side's "different ideologies and systems."

To confirm faithfulness to the "Great Leader," Kim Jong Il ties his views to his father's essay, *The Ten Point Programme of the Great Unity of the Whole Nation for the Reunification of the Country*. This Kim Il Sung essay appeared in 1993 at the beginning of former South Korean President Kim Yong Sam's administration. At an October 1993 meeting with US Congressman Ackerman, then the chairman of the US Congress' House Foreign Affairs Committee Sub-committee on East Asian and Pacific Affairs, Kim Il Sung autographed a copy of the essay on reunification. He asked the Congressman to deliver it to South Korean President Kim Yong Sam with the message that a North–South summit was in order. Unfortunately, Kim Yong Sam chose to ignore the invitation. Not until the two Koreas were on the verge of war did Kim Yong Sam finally accept Kim Il Sung's offer. Former US President Jimmy Carter conveyed the invitation to Kim Yong Sam as part of a deal to resolve the nuclear crisis, but Kim Il Sung died before the meeting could take place. When Kim Yong Sam publicly labeled the deceased Kim Il Sung a "war criminal," Kim Jong Il refused to meet the South Korean leader. Six years later, Kim Jong Il's summit with Kim Dae Jung fulfilled his father's wishes.

Change

North Korea has not stagnated since Kim Il Sung's death. Changing circumstances around the Korean Peninsula and within North Korea's borders have compelled numerous adjustments. North Korea's external relations have undergone the most obvious and extensive alteration. There also have been some changes in the economy's agrarian sector, and it appears Kim Jong Il is assessing ways to better link the North's internal economy to the international market.

External relations

External forces began altering North Korea's foreign relations prior to Kim Jong Il's succession. His policy of opening North Korea and engaging its enemies continues his predecessor's work, yet he deserves credit for continuing the process. The pace has been uneven, and North Korea remains uneasy with the growing number of foreigners within its borders. Also, Pyongyang's foreign posture has vacillated between respect for international norms of diplomacy and commerce, and its more conventional reliance on coercive rhetoric and saber-rattling displays of military power to intimidate its antagonists.

Some milestones in North Korea's changing external relations have been:

- The 1990 resumption of North–South political dialogue and beginning of Japan–DPRK normalization talks.
- 1991 admission of both Koreas into the United Nations, North–South Declaration on the De-nuclearization of the Korean Peninsula, and accords on reconciliation, non-aggression and social and economic cooperation.
- January 1992 US–DPRK high level dialogue in New York and North Korea's subsequent safeguards agreement with the International Atomic Energy Agency.
- 21 October 1994 US–DPRK Agreed Framework.

- March 1995 establishment of the Korean Peninsula Energy Development Organization (KEDO) to implement the Agreed Framework, and related protocols, and September 1995 start of the international humanitarian effort to prevent famine in North Korea, and admittance of private, non-governmental organizations.
- May 1996 agreement between the United States and North Korean armies to jointly recover the remains of US servicemen who died in the Korean War, and Pyongyang's December expression of regret to Seoul for the intrusion of North Korean commandos and submarine.
- June 1998 visit by South Korean Hyundai Corporation founder Chong Ju-yong to North Korea with gifts of cows and trucks, and the autumn start of South Korean tourist visits to North Korea's Diamond Mountain area.
- September 1999 US–DPRK agreement on ballistic missile test moratorium.
- June 2000 South–North Korea summit, September visit by North Korea's Defense Minister to South Korea, October 2000 visit by KPA General Cho Myong Nok to Washington, DC, and November 2000 visit by US Secretary of State Madeline Albright to North Korea.
- 2001 normalization of relations between North Korea and Australia, Canada, and most members of the European Union.

Each spurt of diplomatic progress has succumbed to a period of severe tension. The nuclear crisis of 1992–94 followed the North–South basic agreements of 1991–92. The US–DPRK Agreed Framework of October 1994 prevented nuclear proliferation and reduced the risk of war. Yet a series of armed clashes commenced shortly after the Agreed Framework took effect and continued until the summer of 1999.

The Russian and Chinese normalization of relations with Seoul severely undercut Pyongyang's confidence in its traditional supporters. North Korea attempted to compensate by intensifying efforts to engage its primary foes, Japan and the United States. The results have been mixed. At the same time, Russia's economic crisis halted its once considerable economic and military aid to North Korea. Russia has diluted its military commitment to Pyongyang's defense by requiring cash payment for all arms purchases and by revising its defense treaty. No longer is Russia committed unconditionally to North Korea's defense. It has limited that commitment to assisting only in the event of aggression against North Korea.

Relations with China also have undergone significant change. Gone are the days when Pyongyang could maximize gains from its two socialist partners by playing one off against the other. China's economic engagement of Seoul and preoccupation with its own economic development severely strained Beijing's relations with Pyongyang during the mid-1990s. Beijing–Pyongyang relations have warmed considerably since 1998, but still North Korea can no longer take Beijing for granted. China now expects its small dependency to provide something in return for food aid and economic assistance in the form of technology transfer and investment.

Engagement

Never before has North Korea been so accessible to foreigners from "capitalist" nations. Until 1995, visits were carefully managed political events, crafted to accent North Korea's positive aspects and to veil its shortcomings. Now a growing number of foreigners visit and reside in North Korea. They include businessmen, engineers, technicians, and even diplomats from most of the European nations, South and South-East Asia, Australia, and North and South America. Resident representatives of UN humanitarian agencies represent: the United Nations Development Program (UNDP), the Food and Agriculture Organization (FAO), the World Food Program (WFP), UNICEF, and the International Atomic Energy Agency (IAEA). Other residents are foreigners affiliated with KEDO, a small number of German, Swiss, Swedish, Italian, and Japanese business representatives, plus the US Army Joint Recovery Team. WFP monitors are assigned to all of North Korea's provinces. Temporary foreign visitors have been able to visit all the provinces. Even the US Army is permitted access to the nation's Northern provinces to seek out and recover the remains of hundreds of American soldiers who died there during the Korean War. Some areas of the nation remain closed, primarily because of military related concerns, but never before have so many foreigners been allowed such extensive access inside this once closed society.

Old habits die slowly, especially in North Korea, and ample restrictions remain on travel inside and outside Pyongyang for both foreigners and natives. Visiting Pyongyang is not a simple matter. Non-residents of Pyongyang still must obtain a travel permit to visit their capital. Foreigners must have a sponsor, and must fulfill other sometimes rather arbitrary requirements before they can receive a visa. Once in Pyongyang, so-called "guides," usually young men eager to prove their loyalty to the Korean Workers Party and who speak any one of several foreign languages, still accompany most foreign visitors everywhere in Pyongyang and beyond. Going anywhere, even shopping in a department store, still requires an advance request.

In stark contrast to these old practices are some surprising new ones. More and more North Koreans are willing to acknowledge foreigners in public. Occasionally there are exchanges of smiles and hand waves, pleasantries and social chitchat, even on the street. Taken singly, these small changes of personal conduct hint at a gradually changing view of the outside world. Relative to 1994, they are significant steps for North Koreans who were raised to despise foreigners, especially Americans. Twice in 2000, when landing at Pyongyang International Airport aboard an American Boeing 747 cargo plane, which proudly displayed an American flag over its forward door, sentries jumped to attention and saluted. Children bowed and adults waved enthusiastically as humanitarian relief workers rumbled through the countryside in imported vehicles. In Pyongyang, children in the street boldly walked up to me, bowed and asked if I were an American. In hotels and stores, the staff were friendly and helpful. The welcome on farms has been equally hospitable. All of this is a far cry from just five years ago when no one wanted to be seen talking to a foreigner.

Likewise, North Korean officials from increasingly diverse quarters of the bureaucracy are venturing abroad in growing numbers. Until 1998, most delegations to foreign lands were dispatched to engage in diplomatic representation and negotiations, or to advocate North Korea's ideology and policy point of view. These remain the reasons for most official foreign travel, but a growing number of experts are going abroad to learn. Particular areas of interest are agriculture, business, and international trade. A few young North Koreans are even allowed to enroll in year-long academic programs abroad. China still attracts the largest number of students, but small groups are currently enrolled in universities in Australia, Germany, Sweden, the Netherlands, and Italy. Short-term study programs in various areas of agriculture, law, and international business have been conducted in the United States. In 2000, there were at least four agricultural study tours to the United States. Despite the still small numbers, each returning group has a substantial impact on its peers and family members because of the ripple effect of their stories, the gifts they distribute and the photographs they share.

The economy

Kim Jong Il's confidence in *juche* rules out his conversion to capitalism, at least in the foreseeable future. Since his father's death, particularly 1995–97, Kim has appeared aloof while his subjects suffered chronic shortages of food and medicine. His utterances about the economy denied any sense of urgency despite the incredible suffering around him. But looking back, we can now appreciate the profoundness of the steps he took in the winter of 1995–96. He did what his father had never done – sought aid from the international community. The torrential rains of August 1995 wreaked havoc on the country's agriculture. Rice paddies were flooded, preventing pollination. The corn turned as hard as stone. Vegetables rotted in the ground. Landslides covered houses and fields with dirt and stone. Roads and bridges were washed away. Most coal mines were flooded. North Korea was on the verge of famine. Kim dispatched a North Korean Air Force helicopter with the resident UNDP Representative Faruq Akizad aboard to witness and record the scope. Concerns of secrecy were forgotten, and a videotape was made of the destruction. UN relief aid soon followed. South Korea and Japan quickly sent grain. The United States government reacted hesitantly. Some believed the damage had been grossly exaggerated. US food aid was not sent until the spring of 1996.

Despite North Korea's claims of "self-reliance," acceptance of foreign aid does not contradict Kim Il Sung's teachings. He commented in his 1992 essay, "On Further Developing the Taean Work System," that, "Self-reliance does not mean refusing to use machinery made by others. Nor does it mean opposition to learning from others, nor total rejection of foreign aid. The point is that self-reliance should be the basic principle guiding our activities." Significantly, this passage is highlighted in "Second Thematic Roundtable on Agricultural Recovery and Environmental Projection in the DPR Korea," jointly authored by representatives of the North Korean government and the UNDP in June 2000. Kim's son and heir used the disaster to open his country as never before, not just to foreign visitors, but also to a range of information and concepts previously unknown in North Korea's history. As with North–South dialogue, the process of opening remains slow with uneven progress, but it is continuing.

Changes in North Korea's economic posture have not impressed most economists. No fundamental reforms have been initiated. Despite its highly dysfunctional condition, the economy remains under centralized management. Private property and the rewarding of individual enterprise remain unknown. But rather than focus on what we believe Kim Jong Il needs to do, we will assess what he has done.

Agriculture

Changes in the economy are not readily apparent to outside observers, but the economy's focus is shifting. North Korea's economic planners have moved away from the Soviet example. The debris of this failed system still clutters North Korea's economy, but finally it is being cleared. Simultaneously, as mentioned above, a variety of specialists are traveling the world to assess alternative economic practices. Agricultural revitalization and light industrial production have taken the lead over heavy industry. The agricultural system is in transition. Unorthodox farming methods have been introduced. Foreign advice and technical assistance are eagerly sought from UN agencies and non-governmental organizations from around the world.

The essence of collectivism has been retained in the form of state ownership of all land and group efforts, but with an element of individual incentive. Centralized supervision of all farming activity, however, has been loosened. Local and middle-level managers, those who supervise the nation's 3,000 collective farms, are shouldering more responsibility to determine the kind and distribution of crops in accordance with their assessment of local conditions and needs. No longer does Pyongyang's bureaucracy dictate these decisions. The same is true for the increasing diversification of livestock. Rabbit and poultry farming techniques have been introduced from Italy, aquaculture from Thailand and Malaysia, and geese and duck raising from China. Collective farms are able to retain any produce in excess of quotas established by Pyongyang. When available, work teams allocate any surplus to members according to the amount of time they invested in cultivating crops.

The entire process, however, disrupts farming. The collective farm managers no longer can rely on the Ministry of Agriculture for agricultural inputs – fertilizer, pesticides, seeds, and fuel. They must use surplus farm production to purchase or barter trade for these essentials. Individual farms must find their own means to transport surplus food to urban and foreign markets, particularly the so-called farmers markets in major urban areas and in North-East China.

Nevertheless, farm productivity has been increasing gradually. Adoption of double cropping, efforts to replenish the soil's nutrients naturally through crop selection and rotation, increasing access to fertilizers, particularly from South Korea, and reduction of land erosion have helped.

An ambitious program is underway to improve the agricultural infrastructure. Reconfiguration of all rice paddy land began in 1999 and will continue at the pace of one province per year until completed across the nation. This requires taking large tracts of land out of production so the paddies can be graded into regularly shaped rectangles using heavy machinery. Roads, electricity and communication lines, and irrigation ditches also must be realigned. The work has been completed in Kangwon and North Pyongan Provinces, and is showing multiple benefits. Productivity will rise while reliance on electricity will decline. The larger paddies will more readily accommodate modern tractors, planters and harvesting equipment. More efficient use of farm labor will increase the capacity to double crop more land. Double cropping is now limited by the fact that most farming is done by hand. The reconfigured irrigation system will rely on gravity to channel water into fields instead of relying on the electricity-dependent pumping system built under Soviet tutelage in the 1960s. Additionally, a new system of gravity-fed irrigation ditches is under construction in South Pyongan Province. The project, now in its second year, relies on gravity instead of electric pumps to distribute water to rice paddies north and west of Pyongyang. The International Fund for Agricultural Development (IFAD) is providing the funding.

None of these changes will make North Korea self-sufficient in food production any time soon. Actually, such a goal is unrealistic given conditions on the Korean Peninsula and the size of the population that inhabits North Korea. Adverse weather conditions, plus chronic shortages of fuel, machines, and agricultural inputs such as fertilizers and pesticides, will perpetuate the nation's dependence on external supplies of grain. Since 1992, North Korea has imported at least 20 to 25 percent of its food grain needs either as commercial purchases or, since 1995, as food aid. Like South Korea, it will have to purchase increasing amounts of food from the international market as its population grows. The only way to pay for these food imports is for North Korea to become a producer and exporter of internationally competitive light industrial goods just as South Korea did in the 1970s and 1980s.

Commerce and industry

Kim Jong Il has recognized the need to link his domestic economy to the international market place. This process has been underway since the early 1980s. Progress has been sporadic, but the pace appears to have quickened since 1998. Here too Kim seems to have a plan in mind – induce Koreans outside his domain to invest in North Korea's light industry. Initially, North Korea hoped Koreans resident in Japan would turn the northeast port area of Najin-Sonbong into an enclave of capitalism. Japanese currency would be converted into factories to produce and export textiles and house wares to Japan and China. The effort faltered and has yet to match expectations. Since 1997, Kim Jong Il has shifted the focus to attracting investment from Koreans living in North-East China and South Koreans. Some Korean Chinese have invested in small-scale textile and food processing joint ventures. But North Korea can hardly compete with the booming economic conditions that have prevailed in North-East China for the past five years.

South Korean interest has waxed and waned since 1990, but President Kim Dae Jung's June 2000 summit with Kim Jong Il has energized prospects for the future. Since the summer of 1998, South Korean investment in North Korea has boomed. Hyundai multinational corporation founder Chung Ju Hyong led the way with 1,000 cattle and 500 trucks in June 1998. He followed with a massive investment in developing tourism for South Koreans in the Kumgang or Diamond Mountains, a spectacularly rugged mountain area at the eastern end of the demilitarized zone (DMZ). In addition to an upfront cash payment of US$972,000,000, North Korea earns US$300.00 for each tourist who visits the area from South Korea.

So-called "enclave capitalism" also is occurring in at least two other areas of North Korea. Again, Hyundai is preparing to develop a major industrial park at Kaesong, a provincial city in North Korea located about thirty miles due north of South Korea's capital. South Korea's other major multinational, the electronics giant Samsung, is investing in computer and color television production facilities west of Pyongyang. With the South Korean government's strong encouragement, several South Korean small and medium industries are planning to set up shop in Kangso, an industrial town southwest of Pyongyang.

None of these ventures will convert North Korea into a capitalist economy, but in combination they will significantly enhance North Korea's capacity to earn hard currency from tourism and the production and export of light industrial goods. As a consequence, North Korea's government will have to sanction increasing interdependence with the outside world in all areas of endeavor. Change will continue, even if there is no formal program of economic reform.

Conclusion

Looking back, we can see the outline of an apparent program of change designed first to stabilize and then to recharge North Korea's flagging energy. The priorities appear to be: secure the nation's defense, complete the succession from father to son, and revive the economy, beginning with agriculture. All of this can be accommodated within *juche,* without resorting to reform, because of its innate pragmatism. The torrential rains and floods of August 1995 severely disrupted this program and the timetable for implementation. By September 1998, however, the program appeared to have gotten back on track. Kim Jong Il celebrated the consolidation of his succession with the launching of a three-stage ballistic missile, the Taepodong. The launch jarred the world because it came at a time when many nations believed Kim's regime was on the verge of collapse.

Though the launching fell short of its avowed goal, it achieved its psychological objective of putting the world on notice that Kim was prepared to perpetuate and defend his regime. His summit with Kim Dae-jung, the January 2001 visit to Shanghai, and the July trip to Moscow indicate in a highly visible way that Kim Jong Il is willing to do what ever is necessary to save his father's legacy.

Kim's "managed change" may stagnate, or even reverse itself temporarily, but if his regime is to survive, North Korea must continue to embrace change, and intimately engage the outside world. We only fool ourselves if we believe that he would go so far as to abandon authoritarianism and collectivism. At the same time, however, we would do well to recognize that *juche* is not a barrier to change. On the contrary, it is his rationale for change. So long as he remains steadfastly loyal to his father's legacy of *juche* and nationalism, a concerted challenge to his legitimacy is not likely.

At best, we should hope to see him lead his country into the society of nations and away from reliance on war and coercive diplomacy as means to promote his nation's interests. Whether he will fulfill North Korea's commitments under the US–DPRK Agreed Framework remains to be seen. Likewise, getting Kim to forego other weapons of mass destruction, such as ballistic missiles and chemical/biological weapons, remains an uncertain endeavor. Prospects that he would do so might be improved significantly if his regime's survival depends more on its growing interdependence with the international community, and less on maintaining the military capability to either deter or to counter a perceived armed threat.

Kim Jong Il resists foreign pressure because of his faith in *juche*. Succumbing to outside pressures would discredit him. Yet for half a century, Washington has relied on sanctions, diplomatic and economic, to force North Korea's leaders to submit to its aims. South Korea and the European Union now recognize the futility of this effort. Since 1990, the trend internationally and for North Korea has been toward engagement, economic and diplomatic. Washington, nevertheless, persists with sanctions. Doing so enables Kim Jong Il to exploit US policy by deflecting blame for his nation's economic woes away from himself and his father, and onto the United States.

The present Bush Administration would do well to emulate its previous policies, particularly those of the former Bush Administration, which initiated engagement with North Korea. As a first step, all economic sanctions should end. This would enhance the ability of American private enterprise to influence directly the future of economic change in North Korea.

References

Kim Il Sung (1992) "The Question of the Peasant Market in a Socialist Society and the Way to Abolish It," *On the Management of the Socialist Economy*, pp. 290–294, Pyongyang: Foreign Languages Publishing House.

Kim Il Sung (1993) *The Ten Point Programme of the Great Unity of the Whole Nation for the Reunification of the Country*, Pyongyang: Foreign Languages Publishing House.

Kim Il Sung (1992) "On Further Developing the Taean Work System," *On the Management of the Socialist Economy*, pp. 160–176, Pyongyang: Foreign Languages Publishing House.
Kim Jong Il (1982) *On the Juche Idea*, Pyongyang: Foreign Languages Publishing House.
Kim Jong Il (1994) "Socialism is Science," Pyongyang: Foreign Languages Publishing House.
Kim Jong Il (1996) "Respecting the Forerunners of the Revolution is a Noble Moral Obligation of Revolutionaries," 25 December. Unpublished essay.
Kim Jong Il (1997a) "On Preserving the *Juche* Character and National Character of the Revolution and Construction," 19 June. Unpublished essay.
Kim Jong Il (1997b) "Let Us Carry out the Great Leader Comrade Kim Il Sung's Instructions for National Reunification," 4 August. Unpublished essay.
Kim Jong Il (1998) "Let us Reunify the Country Independently and Peacefully through the Great Unity of the Entire Nation," Pyongyang: Foreign Languages Publishing House.

15 The foreign policy framework of Korean unification

Felix Philipp Lutz

Introduction

In the immediate future an implosion or collapse of North Korea is fairly unlikely so long as the Communist regime continues to retain total control over all aspects of public life and especially since the vague policy of cooperation is likely to continue. Nor is South Korea working towards a scenario which is tantamount to such a collapse; the associated threats and difficulties in the military, economic, and social areas are simply too great (Hong 1999: 8).

The rapprochement between the two Koreas in 2000 was both a pleasant surprise and a puzzling new development for most of the countries and parties involved in Korean affairs and the situation on the peninsula. However, the political impetus of the summit did not last very long. North Korean reluctance to support the agreements and intentions of the summit finally caused another stalemate on the Korean Peninsula.

In addition, the terrorist attacks in New York City and Washington, DC, in September 2001 resulted in the designation of an 'axis of evil' in a speech by US President George Bush in February 2002. Here North Korea is linked with Iran and Iraq. Though the Bush administration does not plan military action against the Democratic People's Republic of Korea (DPRK), the speech stirred some unrest and concerns in South Korea.

The DPRK is obviously more stable and politically flexible than anybody imagined. Furthermore, neither the economic crisis, which has now persisted for many years, nor the ongoing catastrophic famine (Natsios 2001) has been able to destabilize the Communist dictatorship.

North Korea finds itself in desperate straits. But the somewhat macabre demonstration of poverty and destitution serves a political end, namely to obtain financial and humanitarian help, especially basic foodstuffs. The past policy of continually provoking its neighbors also seemed to have the same goal, namely, to secure concessions, compromises, and aid. North Korea's seeming unpredictability has been deliberate (Snyder, 1999). It helped to make North Korea a serious negotiating partner, and at the same time secured a kind of attention that transcends the regional significance of the Korean Peninsula. Yet, we should not immediately deduce from this that there is now a fundamental willingness on the part of Pyongyang to cooperate to any extent with foreign or western powers or with South Korea, for that could threaten the existence of the regime. However, there are indications that the North Korean regime is prepared to undertake certain steps in order to overcome its economic difficulties.

A sudden collapse or a progressive disintegration similar to that in the former East Germany will not favor a predictable unification process. The actual course of German unification cannot serve as a model for a similar series of events in Korea. Too many parameters relating to the historical development of the two countries over the past fifty years are fundamentally different, as are the basic economic, social, and demographic frameworks.

Furthermore, neither South Korea nor North Korea is ready for unification. The ongoing financial and economic crises in Asia and South Korea probably make it impossible to embark on anything now and for the foreseeable future that is even remotely as expensive as the reunification process in Germany.

Against this background, this chapter makes a plea for a long-term foreign policy strategy designed to sustain the gradual involvement of North Korea in a large number of agreements and various kinds of cooperative endeavors. These would go hand in hand with the establishment of communications structures. Together their goal would be to work toward the time when it will be possible to speak in realistic terms about embarking on a reunification process in an atmosphere of security and trust.

The constellation of foreign policy interests pertaining to the Korean Peninsula

The history of relations between the two Korean states was determined by the nature of the Cold War. Under the cover of the East–West conflict, North Korea was able to use its rhetorical (and to some extent terrorist) militancy, its diplomatic and contractual unreliability, and its policy of switching between its protectors, China and Russia, to shut itself off from the outside world. Regional factors, the East–West conflict, and the policy of switching allegiances together conspired to encourage North Korea to develop its own nuclear program (whereas Seoul was forced to give up its plans in this regard), and facilitated the survival of the North Korean regime after the collapse of most other Communist countries. The anachronistic situation on the Korean Peninsula is partly due to the absence of any institutions or peacekeeping forces. The main actors have not yet declared or defined their own specific role in the Korean Peninsula.

North Korea is aware of the fact that "to reform is to die." The present structure clearly cannot survive. Pyongyang will not be able to prevent a slow and gradual reform process and the evolution of an increasingly open society. Since the end of the Cold War, it also has become apparent that comprehensive aid to North Korea from Peking for ideological reasons is no longer a given. For a long time North Korea deliberately played on the fears of its neighbors and the international community about its unpredictable behavior. However, in the very near future some of these political options will no longer be available. "Pyongyang's foreign policy alternatives are limited in the security environment of the mid-1990s" (Kihl 1997: 61) and thereafter. The relationship between North Korea and China certainly became more difficult when Peking established diplomatic ties with Seoul. A considerable part of North Korea's foreign policy clout and room for maneuvering has disappeared on account of the weakened links to its two former protectors and allies, Russia and China. Though this might change again in the light of the planned US National Missile Defense (NMD)-program, which is indirectly leveraging support for North Korea from Russia and China.

In the following outline, the constellation of foreign policy interests of the major actors relating to the Korean Peninsula and Korean reunification will be described. This leads to suggestions for the future setting and environment of a unified Korea and ways and means to reach that goal.

Japan, a difficult partner

For Japan, the Korean Peninsula is of special importance within the Asian region. On account of its geographically strategic location, Korea is "the dagger aimed at the heart of Japan." Japan has a decided interest in ensuring Korean stability and security. Furthermore, a divided Korea performs valuable functions for Japan. As a result of the American presence in South Korea it forms a buffer between Japan and its regional rival, China. On the other hand, since the demise of the Soviet Union as a potential opponent, it has helped to ensure a continued US interest in the stability of the Asian region (Olsen 1994: 199). However, relations between Japan and the Korean Peninsula are often rather strained. The problems facing the two countries are

- The burden of the past, and Japan's role as a particularly brutal colonial power which tried to "de-Koreanize" Korea, exploited its natural resources, used it as a market for its own products, and did whatever it could to destroy Korean culture.
- Japan's brutality during the Second World War has not been forgotten. Nearly 1.5 million Koreans were taken to Japan, where they were forced to work in mines, in the armaments industry, and on large building projects. In addition, 365,000 Koreans were forced to serve in the Japanese army. Korean women who were abused by Japanese soldiers during the Second World War are still waiting for compensation.

However, there also are a number of more recent problems:

- The territorial disputes between South Korea and Japan concerning a number of small islands and the associated maritime and fishing rights (Green 1998: 206).
- South Korea has blamed Japan for devaluing the yen during the Asian crisis, which led to the collapse of its own currency, the won (Feldstein 1997; Lincoln 1997).

- South Korea also has complained that during the crisis Japan did little to promote renewed confidence in the South Korean economy.[1]
- Furthermore, differing assessments of the regional security situation make it difficult for the two countries to reach agreement. Japan views the rise of China with suspicion, whereas this is less important for South Korea.
- Resurgent nationalism in both Japan and South Korea has led to growing mutual mistrust (Green 1998: 205). Also Japan's difficulty in coming to terms with its own past is a constant source of political trouble, offending both China and the Republic of Korea (ROK).[2]
- Currently, relations between Japan and North Korea cannot be described as particularly good. Apart from the question of the whereabouts of Japanese women who had married North Koreans, which remained unresolved until 1997 (Ahn 1993: 264), relations are strained primarily on account of North Korea's missile tests and Pyongyang's dubious nuclear strategy (Green 1998: 212).

However, in the recent past there also have been attempts to normalize relations between North Korea and Japan. For example, North Korea permitted Japanese women who had married North Koreans to leave the country. Nevertheless, this failed to fundamentally improve relations between the two states. In 1998, Japan reacted to North Korea's nuclear provocations by canceling badly needed supplies of food. At an international level, Japan opposed the Democratic People's Republic of Korea's envisioned membership with the Asian Development Bank, the International Monetary Fund (IMF), the World Bank, and other international financial institutions.

Relations between South Korea and Japan have improved in recent years under Kim Dae Jung. As late as 1997 Japan assumed that South Korean troops would immediately open fire on the Japanese self-defense force if it were to attempt to resist a North Korean attack.[3] The Asian economic crisis may bring about fundamental improvement in the relations between Japan and South Korea. As a result of the open markets which the IMF has imposed on South Korea, and to which Japan, albeit with some hesitation, also has subscribed, there is a chance for greater economic interaction between the two countries (Green 1998: 213).

Japan's interest in a united Korea may be summarized as follows:

1. Japan prefers a unification scenario which is not preceded by violence, for example, "ignited" by a disintegrating and leaderless North Korea.
2. A united Korea could become a significant economic player and possibly even a military power. In order to keep a united Korea from threatening its interests, Japan will support the adoption of the present alliance between South Korea and the United States by a united Korea.
3. However, on account of its specific geo-strategic location, Japan will always press for a nuclear-free Korea.

4 Japan, no doubt for economic reasons, but also because of existing but unpaid reparations claimed by North Korea, will play a key financial role in the construction of an improved infrastructure in northern Korea.

Japan will likely maintain its alliance with the United States and manage its regional foreign and security policy within the current framework provided and supported by joint US–Japan security arrangements (Gong 2000). "However, the details of maintaining the joint US–Japan security arrangement and the continued presence of US military forces in Japan are expected to emerge as hot topics of debate."[4] Therefore, it will be crucial at the outset to integrate Japan into a regional regime or framework of arms control, security and trust.

The USA: ally and hegemon

For almost half a century the United States has played a dominant role on the Korean Peninsula as an ally of South Korea. After the Korean War, US policy on the Korean Peninsula was determined by bi-polarity and China's changing role in the region. Containment was the dominant goal and the basis of US and allied policy. All other goals were subordinate to this. Against this background the United States' primary objectives were to ensure stability on the Korean Peninsula and avoid an armed conflict with North Korea and/or China.

Since the end of US–Soviet conflicts, the problem areas have shifted, and with them the goals of American foreign policy in the region. An important goal is to prevent the proliferation of weapons of mass destruction (WMD) and the corresponding delivery systems or missiles. For years, the United States, working with Japan and China, has attempted to negotiate corresponding agreements with North Korea (and China), partly to prevent cooperation between the DPRK and states such as Pakistan and Iran in the field of missile systems.[5] Other US goals are the retention of the troops stationed as a forward base on the Korean Peninsula, and the containment of China, Russia and Japan (though in a different sense with regard to Japan). At the same time, the United States acts as protector of both South Korea and Japan.

The United States will attempt to remain the dominant power on the Korean Peninsula (Chung 1998: 224). The primary US goals are closely connected with the basic tenets of American foreign policy. These include the liberalization of regional markets and support for a prosperous economy in South Korea. The establishment of a liberal world economic order has been an important goal of American foreign policy since the beginning of the twentieth century (Lutz 1999: 644). Moreover, the United States wishes to retain unimpeded access to the regional maritime routes, and to keep open all channels of communication. Short-term US goals on the Korean Peninsula include greater political coordination with Japan and South Korea[6], deepening US–Chinese consultations concerning North Korea. At the top of the agenda are contacts with North Korea at a higher administrative level, and a comprehensive package with the DPRK with respect to regional and bilateral problems.

The Perry Report and the Berlin Agreement were two major steps by the Clinton administration toward normalizing relations with the DPRK (Moon and Kim 2000). However, in the past few years, there has been no bipartisan consensus with regard to US foreign policy on North Korea. In order to minimize the effect of US domestic politics on the diplomatic and political process on the Korean Peninsula, Seoul should make it clear to Washington that it lays claim to a leadership role regarding Korean unity. This does not mean that South Korea should call into question the US military and strategic role in the Far East. However, in the future, the decisive steps toward a long-term policy of rapprochement, which could lead to unification, must come from Seoul. Recurrent anti-US sentiments in South Korea could be reduced if the United States were to step back and permit its allies, the South Koreans, to play a leading role in diplomatic and military matters on the Korean Peninsula. This also would finally end persistent South Korean fears that the United States might negotiate its own agreement with the DPRK. American efforts at stabilizing North Korea and, conversely, Pyongyang's attempts to negotiate with the United States on its own would damage the partnership between Seoul and Washington only if Washington failed to keep South Korea informed or if it were to pursue a fundamentally different policy on the Korean Peninsula.

However, South Korea can use the persisting differences in interests and priorities between Seoul and Washington to take the lead on the Korean Peninsula with regard to security and diplomatic matters. For this, South Korea needs a clear-cut American commitment toward its security, and the option of a unification policy on the Korean Peninsula. The content of this commitment in diplomatic and political terms must be just as clear-cut as it was in the case of German unification. It should involve the following elements:

- Permanent and automatic consultation of South Korea in all matters related to foreign policy and unification, ideally through a high-level task force/ standing committee both in the foreign ministries and also at the presidential level in both countries.
- US support will be given to South Korean concepts and policies which, inasmuch as they do not endanger peace and stability in the region, and are aimed at rapprochement and unification of the two Korean states. The Perry Report and/or following US strategies and policies will support South Korean efforts aimed at a peaceful process of change. With such a visible commitment, South Korea will no longer be in a position where neither North Korea nor Japan considers it to be a fully-fledged and functioning actor. Such a commitment certainly fits with the formulation of future US foreign policy in the light of change in the region. The Far East will play a large role in international politics, and above all in the future global economy. Even if one assumes only modest growth rates, the Far East states, and China in particular, especially since it has joined the World Trade Organization (WTO), will cause a shift in relative importance of the various parts of the global economy. The US policy towards Asia must acknowledge

> these developments. It is in America's interest to remain as a central power in the Far East region. At the same time, it must retain its military presence and ability to project its power, and, if possible, to avoid extraneous influence. However, prior to Korean unification it is unavoidable that, in the course of multilateral negotiations and the necessary balance of the respective security needs, US forces also will be included in the agreements. The United States itself can steer this process most effectively by participating in the establishment and implementation of consultation or similar organizational forms at an early stage.

In the future, the strategic US advantages over China in terms of military power and capability will be limited. China will eventually become a very strong regional power trying to project its influence far beyond the current sphere, if only on account of its sheer size (Swaine and Tellis 2000). Although China currently does not have the real military capability to invade Taiwan, in the long term China's growing military might will have to be taken seriously (Tow 1997). Up to now, China has restricted itself to expanding and maintaining its economic capacities and resources. However, this could change in the course of the build-up of even a modest US NMD (Roberts *et al.* 2000: 57).

For decades North Korea has attempted to sidestep South Korea and negotiate directly with the United States on foreign policy and security aspects of the Korean Peninsula. South Korea's mistrust, which is being and has been fueled in this way, has not exactly improved relations between the United States and the ROK. But even if North Korea were to succeed in improving and strenghtening its direct relations with the United States and Japan, this does not constitute a danger or a disadvantage for South Korea. If the United States were to favor an explicit commitment with regard to a South Korean leadership role, then closer US–North Korean contacts would even be advantageous for stability on the Korean Peninsula. The United States should be prepared for a scenario in which Japan and China might use either the negotiations for a multilateral security system or the sudden collapse of North Korea to increase their influence and leverage to harm US interests on the Korean Peninsula.

The United States is the only one of the involved powers for whom the unification of Korea has no objective or subjective disadvantages. Even in the unlikely event of withdrawal of American troops from Korea, US military influence in the region would remain for a long time. The technological and logistical superiority of the United States together with (South) Korea and Japan would in the long term be able to stabilize the balance of power in the Far East. The United States would derive numerous benefits from Korean unification or even from a unification process, which could be linked with an agreement or even cooperation with China. Therefore the envisaged NMD program of the United States must be considered as a potential threat to any regional arms control effort in the near future. Such a move could motivate China to make strategic adjustments in doctrine and at the same time compensate by building larger forces and developing counter-measures (Roberts *et al.* 2000: 57).

It will be difficult for the United States to fulfill or reject China's demands with regard to Taiwan if Beijing makes concessions to support Korean unification. Thus, the US alliance and Far East policy will be subjected to severe strains and pressures. However, there is a distinct possibility of support from Washington for a leading role for South Korea. Parallel to Seoul's leading role, the United States, as the "benevolent hegemonic power," could continue to perform an important function in the trilateral Japan–US–South Korea relationship. Although the South Koreans may view an overly close US–Japan partnership with suspicion, this alliance also helps to strengthen any security policy and military efforts. Furthermore, the United States should ensure that Japan will play a positive and supportive role in the process of Korean unification.

China, the future superpower

Analysts' and security experts' descriptions of how to deal with China, the largest and strongest power in the East Asian region, still tend to be characterized by Cold War concepts such as engagement and containment. In reality, outmoded approaches no longer represent opposing concepts. Indeed, they can be regarded as long-term complementary strategies for the cooperative integration of China as part of a predictable East Asian development process.

For historical reasons, China's chief interest and foreign policy goal is national security, in political, military, and economic terms (Hinton 1994). The need for sovereign dignity also should be seen against the background of the Western and Japanese colonial policies. This explains some of Beijing's especial sensitivity with regard to Taiwan.

North Korea has been and still is a permanent threat to the stability of all power relationships and balances in the East Asian region. Though China currently seems to prefer a divided Korean Peninsula with North Korea as a buffer between South Korea and US troops, this is not necessarily a long-term policy. Actions by unpredictable North Korea could still trigger a regional arms race, with South Korea developing medium-range missile capabilities and Japan building up a TMD (Theater Missile Defense) system. Neither development suits China. However, the division of Korea also is obviously of strategic advantage to China. As long as the division persists, and North Korea is dependent on Chinese support, South Korea will not pursue or support anti-Chinese policies, either of its own accord, or together with Japan and the United States. Nor is it in Seoul's best interest if Japan or the United States have a bad relationship with Beijing. From a Chinese point of view, the three states are allies, and thus form a united political front. South Korea's "northern policy" has been a success in that both Russia and China have embarked on a new-style relationship with South Korea. At the same time they have changed their focus from a one-sided, ideology-based show of support for North Korea, and have moved toward more extensive diplomatic and economic relations with South Korea (Kotch 1997).

Yet China has a special role to play in Korean unification. For some time China has maintained full diplomatic ties with both South and North Korea. But it also is linked to North Korea by the 1961 alliance treaty which, in case of a conflict, obliges China to give military support to the North. To date, China has not exerted any pressure on Pyongyang, although the relationship with North Korea is no longer as close as it used to be.

Chinese–North Korean relations show signs of the change in Chinese foreign policy since the 1990s. The gap between the allies increases on a daily basis as China introduces economic liberalization and reforms, while North Korea clings to its old, semi-Stalinist economic and industrial habits. Furthermore, China seems to be growing tired of having to exert pressure on the unpredictable North Korean regime at the behest of the international community when the latter has once again threatened or carried out one of its missile launches.

There are earlier examples of Beijing withdrawing support from a partner state. In the middle of the 1970s, China quickly parted company from its long-standing satellites, Albania and Vietnam. The reasons for the split were China's changed foreign policy, and its interest in improving relations with the United States (Harding 1997: 391). Thus, the possibility exists that depending on the scenario, China might be prepared to give up its erstwhile closest ally Pyongyang. Currently, China's primary interests are expanding its trade relations, and earning hard currency needed for the modernization of its economy. An economically bankrupt and politically unpredictable North Korea could be a severe detriment to those plans.

Nevertheless, one should not overlook the fact that North Korea serves a strategic function for China; it forms a buffer between China and the US troops stationed in South Korea. It is safe to assume that China, in the event of Korean unification, will link its assent to the withdrawal of US troops.

It is likely that in the long term China would prefer a reunited and predictable Korea under American and Chinese "supervision" to the present uncontrollable situation. In addition, China derives advantages from its economic cooperation with South Korea. China's growth will continue to depend to a large extent on export markets, technological imports, and capital inflows. From the Chinese point of view, a reunited Korea with conventional armed forces cannot pose a (strategic) threat, as long as the (remaining) American troops on the Korean Peninsula do not constitute more than a subjective potential danger. With the weapons systems at its disposal, the United States can project military power over long distances and at short notice. Because of this, American and Korean troop levels should not pose an insurmountable problem for either side in the context of a peace treaty. Furthermore, through negotiations on a peace treaty or upon the reunification of Korea, China will gain an instrument by which it can influence the nature and the number of American troops in Korea and in the East Asian region as a whole. Currently, Peking is wholly unable to influence either the number or the composition of US troops in South Korea. By becoming involved in intra-Korean negotiations, China would be able to make an active contribution to the long-term structure of a regional agreement on security policy, and to receive additional controls via instruments such as confidence-building measures (CBMs).

The overall situation could, however, also suffer a severe setback from current US calls for the build-up of a National Missile Defense (NMD) which would be aimed at rogue states such as North Korea and Iraq. Unless US missile defenses, US–Russian nuclear diplomacy, and Chinese nuclear modernization are given careful consideration, decisions by the Bush administration could lead China to initiate a major build-up of its nuclear forces, increase Sino-Russian strategic cooperation, and jeopardize both the efforts at arms reduction and the effectiveness of any American missile defenses that are eventually deployed (Roberts, *et al.* 2000: 53).

One could almost say that the United States and China need each other in order to attain their respective goals in the East Asian region since they share a series of economic, political, and security interests. Thus, it benefits China if it turns the United States into a strategic partner (and vice versa!) rather than proceeding against or without the Americans. China needs an environment which supports its social and economic development, both domestically and regionally (Gill 1999: 67).

In August 1996, China's balance of trade surplus with the United States exceeded that of Japan for the first time. China's annual exports to the United States are about to reach US$ 50 billion. And in future, China is hoping to import more new technology and attract even more capital. China and the United States will become important partners in different areas of cooperation. Security questions, problems associated with the proliferation of nuclear weapons and nuclear technology, and a range of other regional and international issues will make such cooperation necessary and beneficial for both sides. China's relations with the United States are characterized by pragmatism and a clear desire to cooperate where possible, demonstrated by the reaction of the Chinese government after the September 11 attacks in the United States. However, Peking considers Washington's attitude towards Taiwan and Chinese unity to be a problem. This could play a very significant role in negotiations leading to Korean reunification, and should thus be accorded the importance it deserves.

In conclusion, it appears that China is adopting a wait-and-see approach toward unification and related matters. The region's security situation will not be altered by Korean unification unless it is subject to overall negotiations and changes in the attitudes of the nations participating in such an agreement. China will have a number of options for influencing regional military structure, troop deployments, and economic benefits. The price tag for Chinese involvement includes economic cooperation with neighboring states both as export markets and for the import of technology and capital, the involvement and containment of Japan, and a predictable and non-nuclear Korea and US presence with fewer troops and bases in the region.

Russia

Since the end of the Cold War, Russian influence in the Far East has declined. The international accord between the superpower United States and the former superpower Russia has ended the ideological and military rifts of the twentieth century. Russia currently is not in a position to play a decisive role on the Korean Peninsula, despite the 2001 efforts of Russian President Putin to exploit reservations about the American missile defense program in South Korea. Russia could regain its status only if it were to provide massive support for Pyongyang, become the mentor of the North Korean regime, and help to stabilize the country in financial and economic terms. The political and economic benefits of such a policy would be rather dubious. Moreover, it is doubtful whether North Korea would depart from its unpredictable patterns of behavior and submit to Russian hegemony.

However, Russia could clearly benefit from a multilateral approach to a security policy solution in East Asia while making only a relatively small contribution of its own. For this reason, Russia, of all the countries potentially affected, has in the past pressed most strongly for the establishment of such a dialogue (Kang 2000). Russia would favor a neutral unified Korea in a nuclear weapons-free region, e.g., Japan and Korea. Given the persistent economic problems and difficulties with nationalist tendencies and independence movements in its own back yard, Moscow would welcome Chinese involvement in a multilateral arms control structure. But the recent rapprochement between Moscow and Beijing has done little to clear up the fundamental suspicions and mistrust on both sides. The US–Chinese interest in East Asia has replaced the former Soviet Union–US conflict (Ross 1999) and eases Moscow's burdens in a variety of ways. Thus, although Russia will not play a role, it will attempt to promote its interests amid the shifting political alliances in East Asia. Russia is currently working to strengthen its strategic role in East Asia. President Putin's visit to North Korea was not only meant to support Pyongyang and help revive the former ally, but also had an explicit strategic component. Moscow might in the long run, try to work towards a 2+4 formula concerning negotiations on Korean unification as it did in the mid-1990s (McDougall 1997:167). Russia will not stand aside while the Koreas, Japan, China, and the United States negotiate a new peace and security arrangement in the region. Like China, Russia is deeply worried about the American plan to build a National Missile Defense system. This could cause the two great East Asian powers to line up against the United States and thereby endanger the process of future rapprochement between the two Koreas.

A comprehensive approach towards unification

The long-term planning of political projects such as the reunification of a country (in this case Korea) is not a utopian vision or something that should be consigned to the realm of science fiction. While he was in office, Konrad Adenauer planned and pursued a long-term policy which comprised internal, foreign, and economic policy segments, and which above all *also* aimed to reunite Germany eventually. Of course, integration into the West, the Cold War, and other developments seemed to lead in a direction which was the exact opposite of what was likely to bring about a reunion between the two German states. However, in retrospect, it was the basic tenets of Adenauer's foreign policy, coupled with the *Ostpolitik* of the Sozialdemokratische Partei Deutschlands (SPD)–Freie Demokratische Partei (FDP) coalition in the 1970s and the dissolution of the Soviet bloc, which made the reunification of the two German states possible. Thus, as we have seen, it is certainly not absurd to suggest pursuing a strategic plan that will lead to the reunification of the two Korean states within the framework of a long-term policy. The result – a united Korea – will depend very much on what the individual steps in the plan look like. It also will depend on which of the steps, institutionalized and formalized arrangements, political mechanisms, and various kinds of international integration, can in fact be designed and subsequently implemented. A policy of Korean unification might be based on the following modified formula: keep the Chinese out, the Japanese down (in military terms), and the Americans in. This will guarantee security and the possibility of steady economic development within a friendly network of economic, political, and cultural regional structures. Against the background of the foreign policy situation and current political and economic developments, a comprehensive foreign policy approach that has as its goal a long-term cooperative and integrative process seems the most promising. The following foreign and security policy goals constitute the framework within which a process of this kind could be tackled:

- reconciliation and stabilization of North Korea;
- fostering economic growth in both Koreas;
- establishment of political leadership (leadership by competence) of South Korea.

Reconciliation and stabilization of North Korea

In the current phase, cocooning signifies the development of a set of small steps whose aim would be to gradually integrate North Korea in various different segments, and at the same time enable it to achieve economic stability (Jee 1994). Such a policy is justified not only on account of its obvious practicality which will make it easier to attain the goal (and cause less frustration), but also because of the financial and economic difficulties which still beset South Korea. Unless the country is given more time, it will not be able to make available even a fraction of the resources needed for renunification. South Korea is in a much less favorable situation than West Germany was during the breakdown of the German Democratic Republic (GDR). Therefore, Seoul and the South Korean people need time to prepare economically for the gigantic burden of rapprochement, economic/political federation or even unification of the two Koreas.

The erratic and unreliable nature of North Korean diplomacy and its militant rhetoric of the past must be overcome through a process of cooperative communication. To this end, readiness to cooperate and reliability can be tested within the framework of a number of agreements; initially these could be "sideshows", i.e., less important or even unimportant areas. North Korea could be integrated into a network of treaties and cooperative agreements step by step with increasing degrees of complexity and economic, diplomatic, and foreign and security policy significance. Within the current process of rapprochement, hopefully only temporarily interrupted, the construction of a highway and a railway line, family reunions, meetings between North and South in the ASEAN Regional Forum (ARF), and other contacts will all work toward greater understanding between the two Koreas. An important side-effect is that more contact between North Koreans, foreigners, and South Koreans will help to reduce suspicion and mutual distrust, an element that should not be underestimated in the relations between North and South Korea. South Koreans must bear in mind that stabilizing North Korea does not mean maintaining the dictatorship or the poor quality of life in North Korea. It is just a means to encourage engagement on all levels and thereby induce change.

Fostering economic growth in both Koreas

The most important element within any larger Korean unification effort is the strength and stability of the South Korean economy and this is among the major Southern concerns about the financial and economic burdens to be placed on South Korean people (Kim, 2000)[7] by a hasty unification process, for example, caused by an unexpected collapse of the North. Though South Koreans long for national unity, they are realistic enough not to overestimate the capacity and financial resources of the South Korean economic system at present. Recent surveys in South Korea show more critical and fewer positive opinions concerning a unification process. Younger people in particular show less enthusiasm about sacrificing for national unification.[8] This is due to a generational change with fewer people having experienced common ties with people in the North and also due to fears about the future standard of living. According to German surveys at the time of unification, the situation there was similar to that of South Korea now, with younger people showing less enthusiasm for unification. Nevertheless, unification and support for unification itself were never seriously questioned in Germany.

A booming economy can leverage domestic and international support for the cause of unification. Therefore, a far-sighted economic policy is extremely important for any strategic approach to unification. Including measures to make the ROK's economy more competitive globally will attract foreign investment and thereby also strengthen the cause of unification. A prudent approach toward unification also could include efforts and strategies to leverage economic as well as financial support. A specific political commitment by the European Union (EU) to assist the unification process on the Korean Peninsula would be helpful. Here, Germany could speak in favor of such a process within the EU due to its historical experience as a divided country experiencing hardships similar to the two Koreas. An initial sign of the EU's involvement in and support for a process of rapprochement and reconciliation on the Korean Peninsula was demonstrated by the declaration for peace in Seoul at the Asia-Europe Meeting (ASEM) in

South Korea in October 2000. Though for the time being this is nothing more than a declaration, it could well develop into some kind of political, economic, or financial support in the future.

Establish political leadership in the East Asian region

While progressing economically and technically and continuing the sunshine policy toward the North, South Korea seems likely to emerge as a leading East Asian nation. For many historical and political reasons, neither Japan nor China can assume such a role which also serves as a mediator between Asia and the West (the United States and the European Union). South Korea (and a united Korea) are not hindered by a history of nationalism, aggression, or colonialism and therefore could emerge as a natural leader in such a multi-purpose role. However, such a role is greatly dependent on the long-term economic performance and the extent of economic and financial reforms carried out in South Korea. A strong and prosperous South Korea will be much more readily accepted as a leading nation.

An international framework for unification

Currently, peace and security on the Korean Peninsula are guaranteed through bilateral arrangements and alliances within a process of "multipolarization" of East Asian power relations (Lee and Hong 1997: 188). Unification, however, will require new structures due to Chinese participation and interests as well as Japan's expanding role in the region. To balance these two actors, a multilateral mechanism needs to be established which can integrate both while at the same time safeguarding Korea's interests and position. Whatever solution is implemented through negotiations by the relevant powers, it cannot replace bilateral relations and especially not the US–ROK alliance which will be the nucleus of any solution to the current situation. The actual number of US forces stationed in Korea after unification will not be as important[9] as the commitment of the United States to act as a reliable ally of South Korea (and also a united Korea) as a friendly hegemon, and as a competitor, not an adversary of China, in the region. Thus, the United States has to play different roles (which it already does anyway): alliance partner for Korea and for Japan; mediator between nationalist tendencies and historical reservations; friendly, benevolent hegemon to support Korea on the Korean Peninsula; guarantor of open skies, sea lanes, and communications; and at the same time, strategic partner of a rising China.

The fundamental aim

The fundamental aim of any policy toward the North should be to establish a stable and unified Korea. In this context, order does not signify the division and allocation of power. It refers to the establishment of structures and the implementation of rules. Furthermore, the fundamental aim of establishing a new order pertains both to the current situation and to a future united Korea. It can be seen in the institutionalization of contacts and talks between the North and the South, the implementation and enlargement of existing agreements and forms of cooperation, and the networking of existing negotiations and initiatives. Vital interests of a unified Korea will be to maintain territorial integrity, sovereignty, and independence. According to already formulated goals, a unified Korea's status in the global economic system also should be secured and improved. Most important will be the establishment of a security environment which will reduce the threat posed by weapons of mass destruction in the region and on the Korean Peninsula, including a viable arms control regime governing nuclear weapons and delivery systems (Finnegan 1999). Viewed in the long term, the agreements and forms and structures of communication that have materialized should culminate in a new order which will link regional and multilateral structures on the Korean Peninsula.

The basis would have to be an East Asian mechanism which could safeguard the transitional process during unification, oversee the dismantling of North Korean forces (eventually also a larger number of South Korean forces), monitor any regional arms reductions, and also function as an overall forum for bilateral and multilateral communication. Taking into account the history of regional power politics, alliances, conflicts, and interests, a modified approach similar to the current US–ROK alliance would probably prove to be the most promising model for the security and foreign policy structure of unified Korea.

Structures and processes would include the following:

- A clearly non-confrontational (from a Chinese point of view) alliance with the United States (with an option of including Japan in some way).[10] A nuclear weapon-free, united Korea, which at the same time would be strong enough in military terms to inflict incalculable/or very high cost-harm to any aggressor, could become the champion for a nuclear-free East Asian region.
- A regional security structure, including at least the major powers (China, the United States, Japan, Russia) and a unified Korea serving as a forum of communication, negotiation and mediation. Such a conference/regime or even organization would in addition work out confidence building measures (CBMs), set up a regional non-proliferation regime for any kind of weapons of mass destruction (WMDs), cooperate with other relevant organizations (United Nations, ARF), settle territorial disputes, and be the relevant institution in any security matters. The full array of CBMs would have to be applied to allow East Asian nations to focus on their economic development.
- A diverse set of economic structures designed to foster economic growth in a unified Korea, generate financial aid, and attract direct long-term foreign investment (Asia-Pacific Economic cooperation (APEC), Association of South East Asian Nations (ASEAN), WTO, new regional free trade zone) to subsidize the long period of recovery and development needed in the northern part of a then-unified Korea.

- Complete international integration in all relevant existing bodies and organizations concerning security, economics, finance, trade, and research.

The most important initial function of a multilateral structure or mechanism would be to build up confidence between the two competing powers, China and the United States, in order to avoid another arms race in the face of the US NMD and envisaged theater missile defense (TMD) programs with Japan and Taiwan. ASEAN is not suited to serve as a forum for security issues in the emerging Korean unification process (Choi 1996). Suggesting a multilateral mechanism for security and consultation in the East Asian region is not meant to copy the Commission on Security and Cooperation in Europe (CSCE) structure or organization. The history and current situation on the Korean Peninsula are quite different from that in Europe during the Cold War where the bipolar conflict between the North Atlantic Treaty Organization (NATO) allies and the Soviet Union focused on Germany. A conference on security and cooperation, which would include ASEAN, the important regional powers, and the United States and Russia, could create the framework for solving numerous conflicts. Above all, it would involve North Korea in a process which could reduce tension on the Korean Peninsula and make it possible for both countries to shift from military confrontation to fruitful cooperation.

The UN also could make an important contribution by providing a public forum for any policy of unification. Since 1947, the UN has played a limited, though at times significant, role in the relations between the two Korean states.

It will be critical for South Korea to construct mutually beneficial scenarios with each of the powers involved in reunification. South Korea's diplomatic task will be to integrate these scenarios and political realities into a homogeneous foreign and unification policy. Since it will prove impossible to take into account all Chinese and US interests, a list of priorities should be drawn up. This list will reflect the interests of all those involved and suggest solutions. The various approaches can be seen as part of a larger strategy which, through a deliberate policy of rapprochement, paves the way for further constructive negotiations between the two Korean states.

Chinese involvement is necessary in order to prepare it for a cooperative role, and to prevent it from assuming an unduly important role, which could even extend to intervention or some kind of military aid for North Korea. Seoul should start talking to China about unification long before it occurs. Since China is both the immediate geographical neighbor and also the most important actor with an interest in the Korean Peninsula, it is absolutely essential that it should be on good terms with both Korean states, and later with a reunited Korea. The most important goal in negotiations on unification, arms control or disarmament will be to integrate China as a guarantor (and no more) in the context of a CBM (confidence-building measures) structure. Furthermore, China's long-term role also will have to be redefined. Provision must be made for a possible collapse of North Korea, and also for a civil war scenario in the North. South Korea should retain the initiative at all times, and, on account of the close involvement of the

United States, should always be seen to "dominate" any type of negotiations or respective scenario (2+2, 2+4, etc.). In addition to the obvious purpose of defending Korea, the presence of US troops also should be seen as a positive influence on China. A sizable American presence will not pose a serious threat to China in conventional terms or in the size of its ground forces, but it can prevent Japan from ever feeling threatened by China or by a reunited Korea.

Furthermore, China has a special interest in the problems of divided countries, for it also defines itself as a divided country. The reincorporation of Taiwan is an important foreign and domestic policy goal of Chinese politicians. Two conclusions are of importance for any South Korean policy of reunification: First, by playing a positive role in a Korean unification process, China could demonstrate its cooperative and peaceful intentions towards Taiwan and therefore reduce tensions within its own sphere of influence. In foreign policy terms, it would enable China to demonstrate that it is prepared to assume a constructive role which corresponds to its geographical situation, size, and importance in the region.

Second, China's relations with the United States could well be enhanced by a (successful) process of this kind. This, in turn, would lead to the establishment of mutual trust, and, in the long term, could lead to greater stability in the Pacific Rim region. Clearly, there is a realistic future scenario in which China plays a cooperative role in the unification of the two Koreas, especially since China now and for the foreseeable future enjoys its most comfortable position in terms of national security since the Second World War. China's role on the Korean Peninsula, however, depends heavily on its bilateral security relations with and expectations of the United States. Therefore, it is even more important for Seoul to assume the leading role in unification security and diplomacy in East Asian affairs.

Outlook

High expectations in South Korea and elsewhere in the aftermath of the presidential summit of the two Koreas in 2000 were dampened by the complete retreat of the DPRK, leading to the current stalemate in bilateral relations between North and South. The events of September 11, further strained relations between the United States and the DPRK. The Bush administration gradually increased diplomatic pressure on North Korea in spring of 2002. First, President Bush included North Korea in his famous "axis of evil" speech on terrorism. Then, a published nuclear policy review listed six countries, including North Korea, as possible American nuclear targets. Only a few days later, Washington decided not to certify North Korea as compliant with the 1994 accord that was to allow North Korea two proliferation-proof reactors in return for international inspections.

Soon after the Bush speech the North reacted, trying to revitalize relations with Russia, and agreeing to take up negotiations with the South again. Also in March 2002, after US pressure escalated, North Korea for the first time provided details about Japanese citizens believed missing in North Korea.

Despite the progress achieved by South Korea and the United States with North Korea in the 1990s, and also in the light of the unfulfilled hopes of the presidential summit of 2000, it remains obvious that the DPRK views any kind of regular communication, contacts, or other means of dealing with others as a fundamental threat to its existence. Under these circumstances, it looks as if any attempt to enmesh the North in a web of cooperative instruments is set to fail. However, at the same time, as long as North Korea is economically desperate, Seoul can count on the eventual return of the North to the negotiating table.

The "sunshine policy", together with the fostering of economic growth and technological advancement, and the effort to make South Korea a leading nation in the region offer great potential for stability, détente, and a new role for Korea in East Asia. This threefold approach can serve as a reliable basis for North Korea and South Korea's allies to calculate Seoul's intentions. Any government in power after the 2002 presidential elections will continue to deal or negotiate systematically with the North. Both South and North Korea currently seek to maintain the status quo (Choi 2001). But even to achieve that low-level goal, they need to communicate and negotiate with each other on a continuing basis. "Memories of a famine's horror are long and undying" (Natsios 2001). Any government involved in the seemingly endless diplomatic process of negotiating with the North Korean regime will have to deal with the historical consciousness and the memories of the North Korean people after unification. Most of the North Koreans will not remember happy times in a unified country, but rather who helped them during times of starvation and suffering and who did not. Therefore, any policies of disengagement or confrontation will not be rewarded in the long run.

It should not be forgotten that North Korea is still a dictatorship oppressing its people and threatening South Korea and other states with immense military power. Therefore, the most important thing is still the need for the North Korean regime to fundamentally change its political system, its ideology, and the treatment of its own people. The South Korean people will not negotiate about their freedom and their political and social achievements while entering into a new and dynamic process with the North Korean regime. A realistic view on new developments will predominate over the strong emotional desire for national reunification. Therefore it is necessary to safeguard any process of détente and rapprochement. This requires ongoing and intensified diplomatic efforts and long-term strategies directed towards all the regional actors. North Korea has become a member of the ASEAN Regional Forum and is thus incorporated into a framework dialogue which will serve Seoul's interests by further opening up North Korea and safeguarding the ongoing process of change.

Notes

1 See Hangyerae Sinmoon, Editorial, 10 January 1998; Moonhwa Ilbo, Editorial, 29 February 1998, after Green, (1998: 213).

2 The dispute about Japanese history textbooks has troubled Sino-Japanese and Korean-Japanese relations.

3 "Chinese Views on the Guidelines," 1997 Defense Research Committee Report, Tokyo, 7 November 1997, p. 9.
4 Ibid.
5 As of spring 2002, however, no substantial agreement has been reached between the United States and North Korea during the last round of negotiations on the North Korean missile program.
6 Already initiated with the TCOG (Trilateral Coordination and Oversight Group) between the three countries.
7 Cost estimations for the current process leading to unification range from US$1 trillion to raise the standard of living in the North up to a level of 1:3 for the next ten years and US$50 billion for the next five years, see *Wirtschaftswoche*, 48, 9 November 2000.
8 Ibid.
9 Quality and composition of troops will be decisive and also part of any arms control or security regime.
10 See Finnegan's (1999) discussion of a broad variety of options and scenarios for a unified Korea.

References

Ahn, Byung-Joon (1993) "Japanese Policy toward Korea," in Gerald Curtis (ed.), *Japan's Foreign Policy after the Cold War: Coping with Change*, New York: M.E. Sharpe, pp. 263–73.

Blackwill, Robert D. and Dibb, Paul (eds) (2000) *America's Asian Alliances*, Cambridge MA: MIT Press.

Choi, Kang (1996) "Unified Korea's Security Policy: Balancer of Multilateral Security Cooperation," in Tae Hwan Ok and Gerrit W. Gong (eds), *Change and Challenge on the Korean Peninsula: Past, Present and Future,* Seoul: The Research Institute for National Unification, pp. 71–86.

Choi, Sukyong (2001) "Divided States: Reunifying without Conquest," in I.William Zartman (ed.), *Preventive Negotiation: Avoiding Conflict Escalation*, Lanham, MD: Rowman and Littlefield, pp. 91–112.

Chung, Oknim (1998) "Regional Perspectives and Roles on the Korean Peninsula," *Korea and World Affairs*, 22, 222–41.

Curtis, Gerald L. (ed.) (1993) *Japan's Foreign Policy after the Cold War: Coping with Change*, New York: M.E. Sharpe.

Defense Research Committee (1997) "Chinese Views on the Guidelines", Tokyo: Defense Research Committee, 7 November, p. 9.

Drennan, William M. (1998) "The US Role in Korean Reunification," *Korea and World Affairs* 22: 159–76.

Dujarric, Robert (2000) *Korean Unification and After: The Challenge for US Strategy*, Indianapolis: Hudson Institute.

Ellings, Richard J. and Simon, W. Sheldon (eds) (1996a) *Southeast Asian Security in the New Millennium*, New York: M.E. Sharpe.

Ellings, Richard J. and Simon, W. Sheldon (eds) (1996b) "A Postscript on US Policy," in Richard J. Ellings and W. Simon Sheldon (eds), *Southeast Asian Security in the New Millennium*, New York. M.E. Sharpe, pp. 221–6.

Feldstein, Martin (1997) "Japan's Folly Drags Asia Down," *The Wall Street Journal*, 25 November.

Finnegan, Michael J. (1999) "The Security Strategy of Unified Korea and the Security Relations of North-East Asia," *The Korean Journal of Defense Analysis*, 9, 121–48.

French, Howard W. "North and South Korea to Resume Dialogue," http://www.nytimes.com (accessed 25 March 2002).

Gill, Bates (1999) "Limited Engagement," *Foreign Affairs* 78, 65–76.

Gong, Ro-myung (2000) "Japan's Northeast Asia Policy in the 21st Century," *Korea Focus Online*, 9 February.

Green, Michael J. (1998) "Japan and the Future of the Korean Peninsula," *Korea and World Affairs*, 22, 199–221.

Harding, Harry (1997) "China's Cooperative Behaviour," in Thomas W. Robinson and David Shambaugh (eds), *Chinese Foreign Policy: Theory and Practice*, Oxford: Clarendon Press, 375–400.

Henriksen, Thomas H. and Lho, Kyongsoo (eds) (1994) *One Korea? Challenges and Prospects for Reunification*, Stanford, CA: Hoover Institution Press.

Hinton, Harold C. (1994) "China as an Asian Power," in Thomas W. Robinson and David Shambaugh, (eds), *Chinese Foreign Policy: Theory and Practice*, Oxford: Clarendon Press: pp. 348–74.

Hong, Soon-young (1999) "Thawing Korea's Cold War: The Path to Peace on the Korean Peninsula," *Foreign Affairs* 78: 8–12.

Jee, Man Won (1994) "Forging a Common Security View: Prospects for Arms Control in Korea," in Thomas H. Henriksen and Kyongsoo Lho (eds), *One Korea? Challenges and Prospects for Reunification*, Stanford, CA: Hoover Institution Press, pp. 81–97.

Kang, Bong Koo (2000) "South Korea–Russia Relations and Presidential Summitry," *Korea Focus Online*, 10 February.

Kihl, Young Whan (1997) "Why the Cold War Persists in Korea: Inter-Korean and Foreign Relations," in David R. McCann (ed.) *Korea Briefing: Toward Reunification*, New York: M.E. Sharpe, pp. 49–69.

Kim, Yung-Bong (2000) "Conditions for Unification in the 21st Century," *Korea focus*.

Kotch, John Barry (1997) "Korea's Security Dilemmas and the Diplomacy of an Emerging World Power," *Korea and World Affairs*, 21, 628–52.

Lee, Young-Sun and Hong, Yong-Pyo (1997) *Unified Korea and New Strategies for National Survival*, in Kim Dalchoong, Moon, Chung-in (eds) History, Cognition, and Peace in East Asia, Yonsei University Press, Seoul, pp. 177–99.

Lincoln, Edward (1997) "Maybe It's the Teacher's Fault," *U.S. News & World Report*, 15 December.

Lutz, Felix Philipp (1999) "Europa und Amerika," in Werner Weidenfeld (ed.), *Europa-Handbuch*, Bundeszentrale für politische Bildung: Bonn, pp. 633–52.

McDougall, Derek (1997) *The International Politics of the New Asia Pacific*, Boulder, CO: Lynne Reiner Publishers.

Moon, Chung-in and Kim, Juchan (2000) "The Perry Report and the Future of the Comprehensive Approach: A South Korean Perspective," in Chung-in Moon, Masao Okonogi and Mitchell B. Reiss (eds), *The Perry Report, the Missile Quagmire, and the North Question*, Seoul: Yonsei University Press, pp. 115–27.

Moon, Chung-in, Okonogi, Masao and Reiss, Mitchell B. (eds) (2000) *The Perry Report, the Missile Quagmire, and the North Question: The Quest of New Alternatives*, Seoul: Yonsei University Press.

Natsios, Andrew S. (2001) *The Great North Korean Famine: Famine, Politics, and Foreign Policy*, Washington, DC: United States Institute of Peace Press.

Olsen, Edward A. (1994) "Korea's Reunification: Implications for the US-ROK Alliance," in Thomas H. Henriksen and Kyongsoo Lho (eds), *One Korea? Challenges and Prospects for Reunification*, Stanford, CA: Hoover Institution Press Publication.

Roberts, Brad, Manning, Robert A. and Monteperto, Ronald N. (2000) "China: The Forgotten Nuclear Power," *Foreign Affairs*, 79, 53–63.

Robinson, Thomas W. and Shambaugh, David (eds) (1994) *Chinese Foreign Policy: Theory and Practice*, Oxford: Clarendon Press.

Ross, Robert S., *The Geography of the peace, East Asia in the Twenty First Century.* International Security, vol. 23, no. 4 (Spring 1999), pp. 81–118.

Snyder, Scott (1999) *Negotiating on the Edge: North Korean Negotiating Behaviour*, Washington, DC: United States Institute of Peace.

Swaine, Michael D. and Tellis, Ashley J. (2000) *Interpreting China's Grand Strategy*, Santa Monica: RAND, Project Air Force.

Tow, William (1997) "China and the International Strategic System," in Thomas Robinson and David Shambaugh (eds), *Chinese Foreign Policy: Theory and Practice*, Oxford: Clarendon Press, pp. 115–57.

Zartman, I. William (ed) (2001) *Preventive Negotiation: Avoiding Conflict Escalation*, Lanham, MD: Rowman and Littlefield.

16 Openness and growth in North Korea

Evidence from time series data

Jang C. Jin[1]

Introduction

Until recently, the beneficial effects of increasing openness for the North Korean economy were believed to be ambiguous, with a strong assumption that free trade would be more harmful if the economy were more open to the world. In particular, greater openness and globalization of the economy were seen as a threat to the solidarity of the Communist Party that could weaken the political leadership in North Korea. Since the early 1990s, North Korea has attempted to implement a policy of limited openness to trade in designated geographic areas. However, it has not been very successful in attracting foreign capital due to inadequate infrastructure in these areas, as well as the accumulation of a huge, non-payable foreign debt. More recently, however, the economy seems to be showing signs of growth, and, at the same time, international trade tends to rise (see Figure 16.1). Are these trends linked, and, if so, what is the nature of the link? Does the co-movement of the two series reflect the new growth theories in which an economy's openness stimulates economic growth through its impact on technological improvement?[2] Despite the major implications of such a linkage and the challenge of new trade policy for North Korea, very few rigorous studies have been done.

The aim of this chapter is to examine empirically the sources of growth for the post-war North Korean economy. A fairly pragmatic approach is taken for this study. Rather than developing an explicit theoretical model, implications that emanate from a number of alternative models are considered in the empirical analysis. The short-run dynamic relationship between openness and growth is examined using the concept of Granger causality that investigates whether changes in one variable precede changes in another. Tests of Granger causality are purely statistical methods that allow data themselves to speak whether the data are consistent with what the theory implies. Should Granger causality run from openness to gross national product (GNP), it would imply that trade liberalization is a desirable policy instrument for economic growth. But if no causal orderings were found between the two variables, the sources of growth must be something other than openness; in this case, the sources would be domestic. Thus, the extent to which increasing openness precedes economic growth in North Korea is an empirical question.[3]

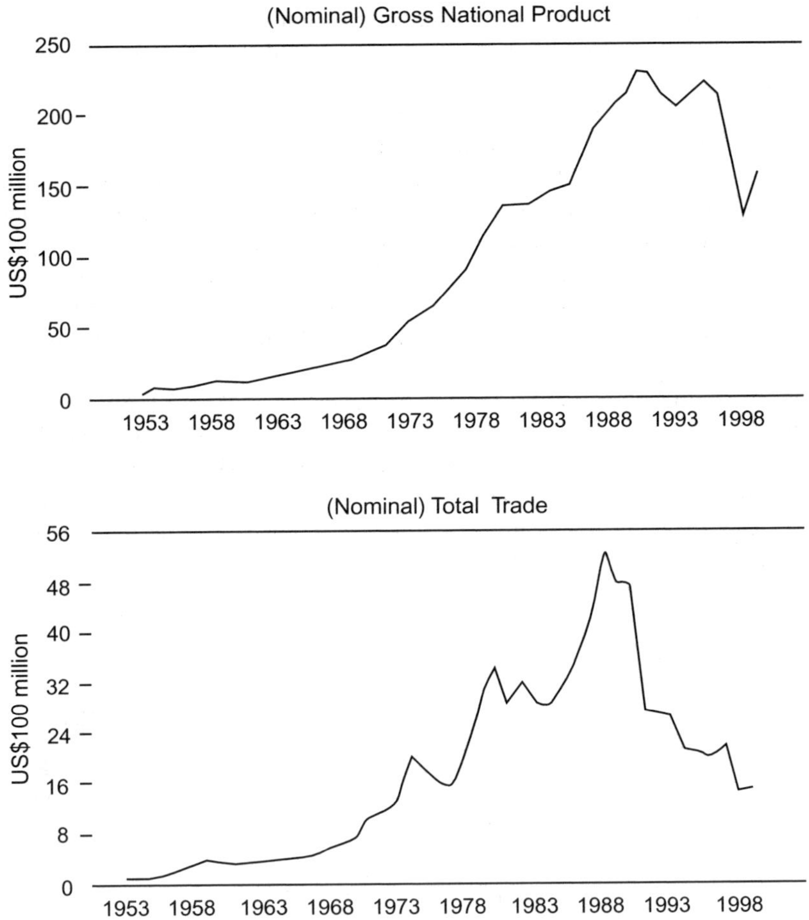

Figure 16.1 Nominal GNP and total trade in North Korea, 1953–98

The chapter is divided into five sections. The second section describes the data series. The third section discusses the empirical results of Granger tests, and the next section examines the robustness of the results using alternative methods. Conclusions follow.

Data

Annual North Korean data for the period 1953–99 are used for the analysis. The data begin in 1953, the year following the end of the Korean War and the time from which the series are available. All data except the GNP series are obtained from South Korea's National Statistical Office (2000). The GNP in North Korea was originally estimated in South Korea's Ministry of Unification. But for the years after 1990, the Bank of Korea (the central bank in South Korea) has estimated the GNP series that is consistent with the ministry's series. The combined series of nominal GNP figures estimated by the central bank and the ministry are now generally acknowledged to be the best measures currently available.

However, real GNP is difficult to measure, since historical price indices are not available for North Korea. It is well known that commodity prices in North Korea are controlled by the government and once set by the government, these prices seldom change for several years. On the other hand, informal market prices are determined by supply and demand in farmers markets, which will reflect the price movements in North Korea better than the government-controlled prices. It would be desirable to combine these two series and construct a weighted price index for North Korea, but information on the prices is not available to the public.

As an alternative, we construct two different series of real GNP: one is real GNP deflated by the world consumer price index (CPI), and the other is deflated by the CPI in China (Figures 16.2 and 16.3). Using the price level in China would be a more conservative option since the degree of government control over prices was similar in these two countries. However, recent economic development in China has been quite different from that of North Korea. Therefore, we use the

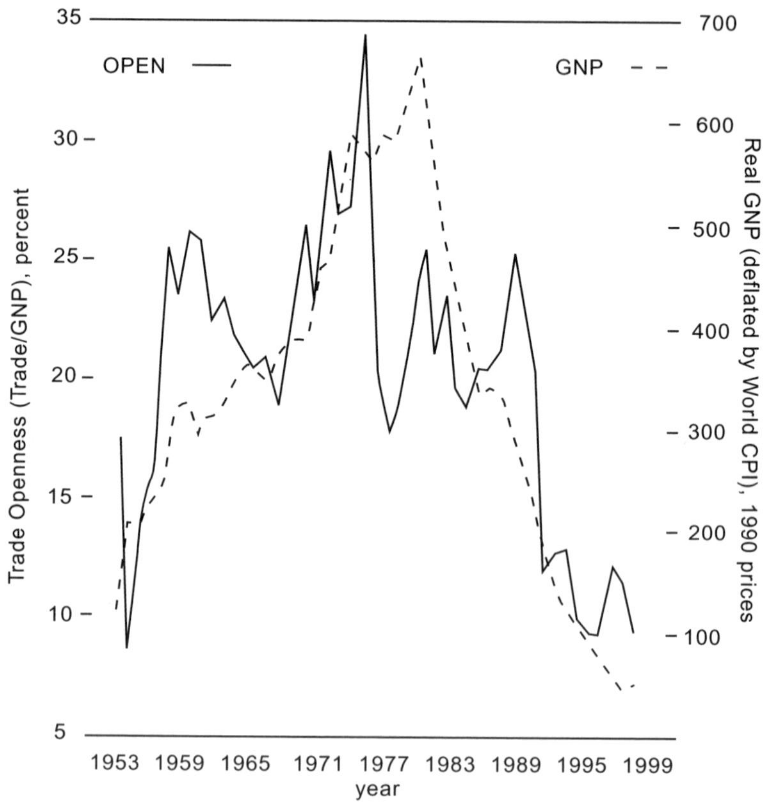

Figure 16.2 Trade openness and real GNP deflated by the world CPI, 1953–99

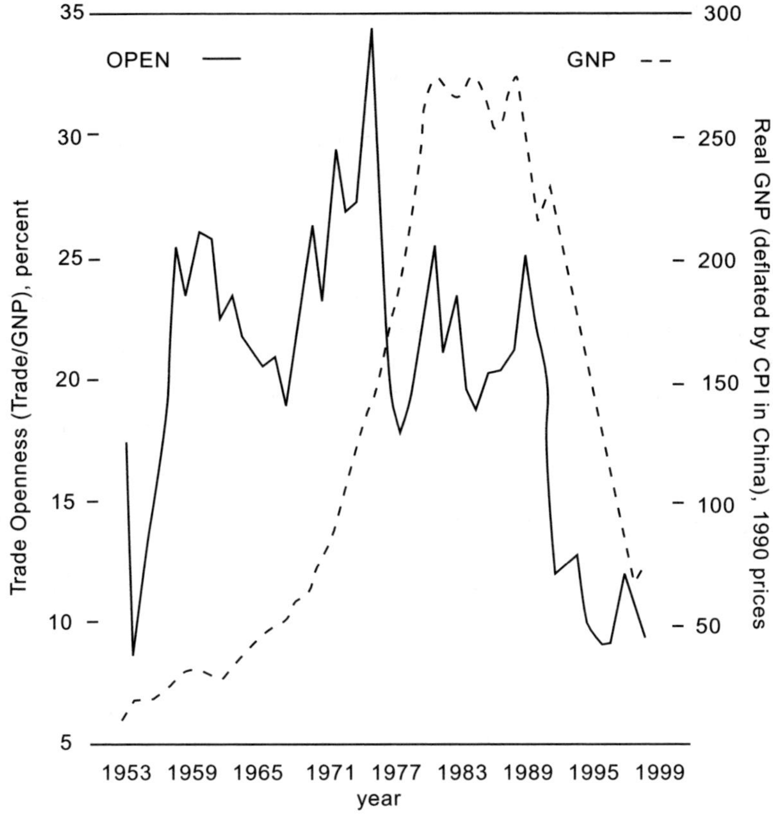

Figure 16.3 Trade openness and real GNP deflated by the CPI in China, 1953–99

world CPI, which changes more slowly than the CPI in China, for the following two reasons. One is that North Korea is a highly regulated economy; in most cases, the government controls prices, and thus inflation rates are presumed to be moderate. The second reason is based on a desire to minimize any problems with the use of high inflation rates like other Asian Countries. The data for the world CPI are obtained from *International Financial Statistics* (International Monetary Fund), and the data for China's CPI are taken from *China Statistical Yearbook* (National Bureau of Statistics, People's Republic of China).

The imports/GNP ratio is used as a proxy for openness of an economy (e.g., Romer 1993). Since even protected economies like Japan and South Korea have expanded exports to other countries, the export share is removed from total trade. The import share in GNP then reveals import penetration that represents the degree of a country's openness: a more open economy has fewer restrictions in world trade, and thus higher import shares in GNP. An alternative measure of openness – the average share of trade (imports plus exports) in GNP – will also be discussed.

Prior to specification and estimation of the model, augmented Dickey-Fuller tests were employed to check for first-order unit roots. These tests suggested that the first differences of the logarithm of GNP and the differences of OPEN should be used in specifying and estimating the model. Based upon the arguments of Engle and Granger (1987), cointegration tests were also performed for the two variables that required differencing to achieve stationarity. Since no evidence of cointegration was found, the model was estimated with differences of OPEN and log differences of GNP, and error correction terms were not included.

Basic results

Although increasing openness has long been believed to be independent of economic growth in North Korea as well as harmful to political solidarity, trade openness has a tendency to move toward a fraction of real GNP. Figures 16.2 and 16.3 show that the North Korean economy grew rapidly in the 1960s and 1970s accompanied by a noticeable growth in international trade. Economic development during this period is in striking contrast to the 1980s and 1990s, during which both trade and real GNP fell steadily. More recently, however, trade openness began to rise, followed by a symptom of economic growth in 1999. Rather than constructing a structural relationship of the variables, a reduced-form approach is employed to investigate the short-run causal orderings between openness and growth.

Granger (1969) defines the causal orderings such that X Granger-causes Y if the current value of Y can be predicted more accurately, in the sense of mean square error, with the use of past values of both X and Y rather than past values of Y only. Based upon the definition of Granger causality, a simple bivariate autoregressive (AR) model is specified as:

$$GNP_t = a + \sum_{i=1}^{p} \alpha_i GNP_{t-i} + \sum_{j=1}^{q} \beta_j OPEN_{t-j} + \mu_t, \tag{16.1}$$

$$OPEN_t = b + \sum_{i=1}^{r} \gamma_i OPEN_{t-i} + \sum_{j=1}^{s} \delta_j GNP_{t-j} + \nu_t, \tag{16.2}$$

where GNP is the real gross national product, and OPEN is the imports/GNP ratio which is used as a proxy for trade openness; μ_t and v_t are serially uncorrelated white-noise residuals; and p, q, r, and s are lag lengths for each variable in each equation.

Using the same lag length for the variables in each equation, the model is estimated by least squares. To help infer the causal orderings, the Granger test employs F-statistics within a framework of restricted and unrestricted models. For the Granger causal links from openness to growth, past values of openness are used as a zero restriction, and vice versa. F statistics are computed as:

$$F = \frac{(RSS_r - RSS_u)df_u}{RSS_u(df_r - df_u)}, \tag{16.3}$$

where RSS_r and RSS_u are the residual sums of squares in restricted and unrestricted models, respectively; and df_r and df_u are, respectively, the degrees of freedom in restricted and unrestricted models.

Table 16.1 shows the results of the Granger causality test for three cases. First, nominal GNP is used as an income variable. The growth rate of GNP causes (in the Granger sense) the changes in openness if one to three years are used for the lag lengths. When the lag lengths are extended to four to six years, relatively smaller test statistics are observed and they are all statistically insignificant at the conventional significance levels. A similar pattern of causal inference is found when real GNP deflated by the CPI in China is used. However, the Granger causal link from GNP to openness is in general invariant across lag lengths when real GNP is deflated by the world CPI.

Table 16.2 further reports the results of the Granger test that uses the ratio of trade to GNP as an alternative measure of openness (Harrison 1996, among others). The results are even stronger than in our earlier findings. The zero restriction in the OPEN equation is statistically significant at the 5 percent level, and the results are robust across lag lengths. This suggests that domestic growth in North Korea Granger-causes trade openness of the economy, but the reverse causation is not found.[4]

Table 16.1 Basic results, 1953–99

Income lag (year) *Variables*		*F statistic*		*Causal inferences*
		GNP Eq (16.1)	*OPEN Eq (16.2)*	
Nominal GNP	1	1.42 (0.24)	5.49 (0.02)	OPEN $\Leftarrow$ GNP
	2	0.55 (0.58)	2.39 (0.10)	OPEN $\leftarrow$ GNP
	3	0.53 (0.66)	2.97 (0.04)	OPEN $\Leftarrow$ GNP
	4	1.09 (0.37)	1.83 (0.14)	OPEN ... GNP
	5	0.57 (0.72)	1.11 (0.37)	OPEN ... GNP
	6	0.67 (0.67)	1.05 (0.42)	OPEN ... GNP
Real GNP (deflated by China CPI)	1	2.29 (0.13)	5.13 (0.02)	OPEN $\Leftarrow$ GNP
	2	0.56 (0.57)	2.20 (0.12)	OPEN ... GNP
	3	0.46 (0.70)	2.22 (0.10)	OPEN $\leftarrow$ GNP
	4	0.98 (0.43)	1.19 (0.33)	OPEN ... GNP
	5	0.61 (0.68)	0.71 (0.61)	OPEN ... GNP
	6	0.41 (0.86)	0.43 (0.84)	OPEN ... GNP
Real GNP (deflated by World CPI)	1	2.40 (0.12)	9.28 (0.01)	OPEN $\Leftarrow$ GNP
	2	0.47 (0.62)	4.48 (0.01)	OPEN $\Leftarrow$ GNP
	3	0.39 (0.75)	3.96 (0.01)	OPEN $\Leftarrow$ GNP
	4	1.34 (0.27)	3.09 (0.02)	OPEN $\Leftarrow$ GNP
	5	0.74 (0.59)	2.22 (0.07)	OPEN $\leftarrow$ GNP
	6	0.61 (0.71)	2.12 (0.08)	OPEN $\leftarrow$ GNP

Note: The F-statistics are computed with restricted and unrestricted models. Numbers in parentheses represent p-values. The imports/GNP ratio is used as an openness measure.

Table 16.2 Alternative measure of openness: trade/GNP, 1953–99

Lag (year)	*F statistic*		*Causal inferences*
	GNP Eq (16.1)	*OPEN Eq (16.2)*	
1	3.44 (0.07)	10.54 (0.01)	OPEN ⇐ GNP
2	0.76 (0.47)	4.54 (0.01)	OPEN ⇐ GNP
3	0.42 (0.73)	3.46 (0.02)	OPEN ⇐ GNP
4	1.12 (0.36)	3.38 (0.02)	OPEN ⇐ GNP
5	0.61 (0.68)	2.98 (0.02)	OPEN ⇐ GNP
6	0.46 (0.82)	2.92 (0.02)	OPEN ⇐ GNP

Note: The F-statistics are computed with restricted and unrestricted models. Numbers in parentheses represent p-values. The trade/GNP ratio is used as an openness measure. Real GNP is deflated by the world CPI (1990 = 100).

Further investigation

Two sub-samples

To check on the robustness of the results, the sample is split into two sub-periods based upon the degree of openness of the North Korean economy. Figure 16.2 shows that the economy grows rapidly in the 1960s and 1970s, and at the same time the degree of openness tends to rise until 1974. After that, the degree of openness declines, and output also falls. Table 16.3 shows results for the two sub-samples. In the open-economy sub-sample (1953–74), increasing openness to trade leads (again, in the Granger sense) to the growth rate of GNP in most cases. The feedback effect from output growth to openness is also found for the open-economy sub-sample. On the other hand, no causal orderings are observed for the closed-economy sub-sample (1975–99).

The feedback effect in the open-economy sub-sample (1953–74) is consistent with the general belief that increased openness to trade will stimulate economic growth, perhaps due to an increase in the effective size of the market facing producers. Enhanced economic growth then provides access to international markets and promotes international competitiveness in tradable goods, and

Table 16.3 Two sub-periods, 1953–74 and 1975–99

Lag (year)	*1953–74*		*1975–99*	
	GNP Eq (16.1)	*OPEN Eq (16.2)*	*GNP Eq (16.1)*	*OPEN Eq (16.2)*
1	2.66 (0.12)	3.73 (0.07)	0.32 (0.57)	1.62 (0.21)
2	3.09 (0.07)	3.93 (0.04)	0.06 (0.93)	1.13 (0.34)
3	6.26 (0.01)	3.71 (0.04)	0.20 (0.89)	2.36 (0.11)
4	4.65 (0.03)	2.20 (0.15)	0.70 (0.60)	1.64 (0.22)

Note: The F-statistics are computed with restricted and unrestricted models. Numbers in parentheses represent p-values. The imports/GNP ratio is used as an openness measure. Real GNP is based on 1990 prices, deflated by the world CPI.

hence exports rise. Therefore, the findings of the feedback relationship between openness and growth lend support to the policy implication that openness and growth were reinforcing each other in the process of economic development in North Korea during the post-war reconstruction period.

Multivariate Granger causality

The bivariate AR models provide evidence that the feedback relationship between OPEN and GNP is fairly robust across lag lengths for the open-economy sub-period (1953–74), but the causal orderings do not appear in the post-1974 sub-sample. For this reason, we further investigate the interrelationship between imports and exports, and the imports of goods and services in North Korea may not be directly related to export expansion. If this is the case, the domestic economy will not be stimulated.[5]

Following Sims (1980), a small macro-model is employed. A vector autoregressive process of order p, VAR(p), for a system of k variables can be written as:

$$X_t = A + B(L)X_t + u_t, \tag{16.4}$$

where X_t is a $k \times 1$ vector of system variables, A is a $k \times 1$ vector of constants, B(L) is $k \times k$ matrix of polynomials in the lag operator L, and u_t is a $k \times 1$ vector of serially uncorrelated white noise residuals. The standard Sims VAR is an unrestricted reduced-form approach, and hence no restrictions are imposed on the coefficient matrices to be null.[6]

A three-variable VAR model includes imports, exports, and GNP. All variables are in real values, deflated by the world CPI (1990 = 100). Real imports are included in the model to examine its effect on real exports which in turn may affect real GNP. This also allows us to investigate a direct impact on real GNP. Since there is little consensus on what the appropriate structural model is and how the model variables interact, the standard unconstrained VAR is employed. Specifically, all model variables are treated as jointly determined, and no *a priori* assumptions are made about the exogeneity of any of the variables in the model.

The VAR order is set to three years to reduce serial correlation of the residuals. The marginal significance levels of the Ljung-Box Q statistics range between 0.27 and 0.98. Using other lag lengths merely reduces the significance levels of the Q statistics.[7]

Table 16.4 provides F-statistics to infer direct Granger causality from one variable to another, using the estimates of equations from the VAR model.[8] The results indicate that the predictive role of changes in imports appears to be insignificant for export growth, and the effect of exports on GNP is also insignificant. While the growth of GNP Granger-causes changes in both imports and exports, the reverse causal orderings are not found to be significant. Neither direct nor indirect causal orderings from imports to GNP are observed for the entire sample period. However, for the open-economy sub-sample (1953–74), strong causal relations are observed between exports and imports, whereas the relations appear insignificant for the years

Table 16.4 Multivariate Granger causality

Dependent variable	*Causal variables*			*Q-statistics (p-values)*						
	1953–99				*1953–74*			*1975–99*		
	Imp	*Exp*	*GNP*		*Imp*	*Exp*	*GNP*	*Imp*	*Exp*	*GNP*
Imp	0.27 (0.84)	0.10 (0.95)	4.15 (0.01)	21.07 (0.27)	0.15 (0.70)	4.75 (0.04)	18.62 (0.01)	1.07 (0.31)	0.76 (0.39)	2.18 (0.15)
Exp	0.37 (0.76)	1.73 (0.17)	5.84 (0.01)	12.18 (0.83)	3.81 (0.06)	0.75 (0.39)	3.81 (0.06)	0.78 (0.38)	1.87 (0.18)	5.34 (0.03)
GNP	0.32 (0.80)	1.03 (0.39)	0.86 (0.46)	7.50 (0.98)	2.32 (0.14)	2.83 (0.11)	0.04 (0.82)	0.01 (0.99)	0.20 (0.65)	1.87 (0.18)

Note: The F-statistics are computed with restricted and unrestricted models. Numbers in parentheses represent p-values. All variables are in real terms, deflated by the world CPI (1990 = 100). The lag length is determined at three years.

after 1974. This suggests that the imports of goods and services in North Korea are not related directly to the production of goods and services for export expansion, but are used for other purposes, perhaps, for example, militarization that is independent of economic growth.

Conclusion

The results of Granger causality tests generally support the causal implications of the openness–growth relationship in the case of the North Korean economy. The possibility that the ultimate source of declining real GNP since 1974 is a decrease in trade liberalization of the North Korean economy cannot be rejected. The results are more convincing when the sample is split into two sub-periods (pre-1974 and post-1974). In particular, a strong feedback relationship between openness and growth has been found for the open-economy sub-sample in North Korea, but the effect appears to be insignificant for more recent decades. One plausible explanation for this finding would be that increased imports were not related directly to export growth in recent years. Further investigation of these links is possible if more reliable price indices can be constructed for North Korea.

Notes

1 This is a reprint of my article (2003) in *Review of International Economics* (forthcoming).

2 The theoretical foundations of the new growth theories are discussed in Romer (1986) and Lucas (1988), and the theoretical ambiguity of this view is found in Grossman and Helpman (1991), Rivera-Batiz and Romer (1991), Stokey (1991), Young (1991), and Levine and Renelt (1992). Theoretical disagreement on the role of openness is matched by mixed empirical evidence. Surveys of the empirical evidence are found in Frankel and Romer (1999) and O'Rourke (2000).

3 Granger's definition of causality does not refer to causality, as it is usually understood. Some critics suggest using 'precedence' rather than 'Granger causality' (see Basmann 1988, among others). In practice, however, we would like to know whether a time series X precedes a time series Y, or Y precedes X. This is the purpose of Granger causality. Thus, the test for Granger causality can be used for policy evaluation, but its interpretation should be exercised with care (see Granger 1988).

4 For the robustness of the results, some proxies for financial market openness such as foreign direct investment, interest rate differentials, and foreign holdings of government debt can be used, but no series of this type is available.

5 In contrast, South Korea has increased the imports of raw materials as well as intermediate inputs to boost exports and hence output.

6 The drawback of the VAR, of course, is that it is difficult to distinguish sharply among different structural models, since the VAR technique is a reduced-form approach. Cooley and LeRoy (1985) and Leamer (1985) have pointed out the limitations of the VAR approach.

7 No attempt has been made to select optimal lags for the VAR model, since the degree-of-freedom problem will be especially serious.

8 Since most hypotheses in a VAR are cross-equation in nature, variance decompositions (VDCs) and impulse response functions (IRFs) are commonly used in the literature. Rather than computing the VDCs and IRFs, direct Granger causality between two variables of interest is the focus in this paper (see, e.g., Marin 1992).

References

Basmann, R.L. (1988) "Causality Tests and Observational Equivalent Representations of Econometric Models," *Journal of Econometrics,* 39, 60–104.

Cooley, T.F. and LeRoy, S.F. (1985) "Atheoretical Macroeconomics: A Critique," *Journal of Monetary Economics,* 16, 283–308.

Engle, R.F. and Granger, C.W.J. (1987) "Cointegration and Error Correction: Representation, Estimation, and Testing," *Econometrica,* 55, 251–76.

Frankel J.A. and Romer, D. (1999) "Does Trade Cause Growth?", *American Economic Review,* 89, 379–99.

Granger, C.W.J. (1969) "Investigating Causal Relations by Econometric Models and Cross-spectral Methods," *Econometrica,* 37, 424–38.

Granger, C.W.J. (1988) "Some Recent Developments in a Concept of Causality," *Journal of Econometrics,* 39, 199–211.

Grossman, G.M. and Helpman, E. (1991) *Innovation and Growth in the Global Economy,* Cambridge, MA: MIT Press.

Harrison, A. (1996) "Openness and Growth: A Time-series, Cross-country Analysis for Developing Countries," *Journal of Development Economics,* 48, 419–47.

International Monetary Fund (various years) *International Financial Statistics,* Washington, DC: International Monetary Fund.

Leamer, E.E. (1985) "Vector Autoregressions for Causal Inference?", *Carnegie-Rochester Conference Series on Public Policy,* 22, 255–303.

Levine, R. and Renelt, D. (1992) "A Sensitivity Analysis of Cross-Country Growth Regressions," *American Economic Review,* 82, 942–63.

Lucas, R.E. (1988) "On the Mechanics of Economic Development," *Journal of Monetary Economics,* 22(1), 3–42.

Marin, D. (1992) "Is the Export-led Growth Hypothesis Valid for Industrialized Countries?", *Review of Economics and Statistics,* 74, 678–88.

National Bureau of Statistics (various years) *China Statistical Yearbook,* Beijing: National Bureau of Statistics, People's Republic of China.

O'Rourke, K.H. (2000) "Tariffs and Growth in the Late 19th Century," *Economic Journal,* 110, 456–83.

Rivera-Batiz, L.A. and Romer, P.M. (1991) "Economic Integration and Endogenous Growth," *Quarterly Journal of Economics,* 106, 531–55.

Romer, D. (1993) "Openness and Inflation: Theory and Evidence," *Quarterly Journal of Economics,* 108, 869–903.

Romer, P.M. (1986) "Increasing Returns and Long Run Growth," *Journal of Political Economy,* 94(5), 1002–37.

Sims, C.A. (1980), "Macroeconomics and Reality," *Econometrica,* 48, 1–48.

Stokey, N.L. (1991) "Human Capital, Product Quality, and Growth," *Quarterly Journal of Economics,* 106, 587–616.

Young, A. (1991), "Learning by Doing and the Dynamic Effects of International Trade," *Quarterly Journal of Economics,* 106, 369–405.

Part V

Economic cooperation with the DPRK

Challenges and opportunities

17 NGO contributions to the transition from humanitarian to development assistance in DPRK[1]

Erich Weingartner

DPRK context

When non-governmental organizations (NGOs) first arrived in North Korea to respond to famine conditions after the floods of 1995, they discovered a situation at odds with their prior experience. The Democratic People's Republic of Korea (DPRK) is not an underdeveloped, subsistence economy buffeted by frequent natural disasters. Nor is it a collapsed socialist system in the throes of transitional "shock treatment." Nor is this a chronic war zone, where forcibly displaced people starve in refugee camps, while life continues more or less normally in other parts of the country.

North Korea's socialist transformation after World War II left intact most of the existing structures of agricultural feudalism and Japanese industrialism. The DPRK's "*juche*" ideology (inadequately translated as "self-reliance") has nurtured a fortress mentality which promotes a "military first" policy as the only way to safeguard the socialist development and survival of the nation.

Of course, the DPRK was never as economically self-reliant as its propaganda would have us believe. The DPRK claims it was agriculturally self-sufficient before the natural disasters, but North Korea is not an agricultural country. It has one of the lowest ratios of arable land per population in the world. It was subsidized by allies such as the Soviet Union and China, and traded at favorable bartering rates with the Council for Mutual Economic Cooperation (COMECON) countries. The collapse of the Soviet Union and China's opening of trade relations with South Korea increased the DPRK's isolation and severely depressed industrial and agricultural productivity. Farm machinery and transportation facilities deteriorated rapidly. A decrease in agricultural inputs such as locally produced chemical fertilizer led to declining yields in food production.

The mid-1990s' floods were not so much the cause of the famine as they were the "final straw," coming after reserves had been depleted and industrial production failed to offset mounting food deficits.

Limitations of NGO activities in DPRK

The first humanitarian agencies that arrived in the DPRK were the objects of great suspicion. North Koreans are taught to distrust the motives of foreigners, and to fear spies and subversive influences. Contact with the outside world carries the danger of ideological pollution – so-called "yellow winds."[2] To this day, the local population is shielded from exposure to foreign relief workers.

All encounters with outsiders are "managed" by professionals who are trained to minimize disruptive influences. This places severe limitations on the ability of NGOs to conduct their assistance programs. These limitations become even more crucial as NGOs begin the transition to more development-oriented programs. The most critical factors are the following:

- *Lack of appropriate counterparts.* Most NGOs prefer to partner with local organizations which are themselves non-governmental. Only the International Federation of Red Cross and Red Crescent Societies (IFRC) has a local member organization with which it has a full working relationship. Most other groups are dependent on the Flood Damage Rehabilitation Committee (FDRC), a government agency. All interaction with local Korean people is carefully circumscribed. Relationships with line ministries, professional associations, educational institutions, cooperative farm management, and the like are intermittent, short term and usually without continuity.
- *Access problems.* UN system agencies currently have access to 167 of 211 counties. Even in accessible counties, however, there are considerable constraints on movement. Deviations from original travel plans are extremely rare. Within counties not all areas are equally accessible, with fewer visits paid to the poorest locations. Joint monitoring among agencies or the opportunity to visit each other's projects is rare. Severe restrictions are placed on media visits, further hampering the ability of NGOs to generate funds for continued programs.
- *Difficulty of measuring impact.* Obtaining feedback on end use of supplies remains problematic, particularly for non-food aid projects where agencies have limited monitoring capacity. Opportunities for post-implementation evaluations have been rare. Lack of information remains a highly critical limitation. Since the government reveals information only on a "need-to-know" basis, critical data is withheld at both ends of a humanitarian project.

Consequences for NGO work

Judging by the behavior of DPRK authorities, the value of NGOs is measured in "hard" terms at the level of material inputs, rather than in "soft" terms such as professional expertise and personal contributions. NGOs are therefore tolerated as a necessary annoyance as long as large institutional donors – usually governments – insist on supplying at least a sizeable portion of aid via NGOs.

To solve its problems, the DPRK needs to move beyond its dependence on humanitarian aid and gain the confidence of donors for longer-term development. International aid for reconstruction and rehabilitation, industrial development, trade and investment opportunities is vital. To obtain help, the DPRK needs to become a trusted member of the world community. Among other things, this requires learning how the rest of the world operates.

NGOs offer a window to the outside world for the DPRK, and thus provide an educational opportunity. In this light, the impact of NGOs could be measured in terms of what the DPRK authorities have learned from them about the way the world – especially the Western world – functions.

Fortunately, the learning process has gone both ways, and those NGOs that have persevered over the long term – despite the limitations – have found numerous creative ways to achieve success in small but significant ways. Whatever else can be said about the difficulties in the DPRK, experience has shown time and again that Koreans operate very firmly on the principle of relationship. Perseverance and persistence, based not on recrimination but on mutual respect, will be rewarded. The longer a relationship exists, the greater is the likelihood of a mutually profitable outcome.

A time for change

After six years of food aid, agricultural inputs, and medical assistance, donor fatigue is setting in. Awareness that the food deficit problems in the DPRK are only partly due to natural disasters has caused donors to question the utility of continued food aid interventions in the absence of structural changes and a comprehensive development plan. Food aid causes dependencies, solves none of the underlying causes of the deficit, and uses up resources that might better be spent for the rehabilitation of industry and international trade.

It seems difficult to see how much longer donors can justify continued large-scale food shipments. On the other hand, donations for development programmes have been grossly inadequate. In 1999, the World Food Programme (WFP)'s DPRK appeal of US$141.6 million was 125 percent subscribed. The Food and Agriculture Organization (FAO)/United Nations Development Programme (UNDP) appeal for US$113.4m was only 2.1 percent subscribed. In 2000, a reduced WFP appeal of US$106.25 million was 92.5 percent subscribed, whereas a radically reduced FAO/UNDP appeal of only US$56.4 million still received donations covering less than 5.4 percent of the budget.[3]

The explanation that development assistance involves different aid bureaucracies and has more stringent conditions attached is only part of the answer. It also is true that the same donors who have so far provided massive food shipments have been reluctant to contribute to any programs that would build up the DPRK's self-reliance.

This follows an analysis that the current economic difficulties have been the principal motivating factor moving the DPRK in the direction of positive engagement with its enemies and diplomatic relationships with the rest of the world. The fear that a strengthened and therefore self-reliant DPRK would revert to its hostile autistic behavior, thereby threatening the security of its neighbors and the region, is a major deterrent to a rational development strategy among donors. Limiting assistance to food aid, according to this analysis, keeps North Korean beneficiaries alive, while at the same time keeping their government dependent on aid and therefore genuinely focused on continuing to improve international relationships.

This strategy contradicts the stated aim of encouraging the DPRK to transform its economy in line with market principles. How confident can DPRK officials be that internal reforms will be rewarded by donor support? The logical expectation that development aid should increase as humanitarian aid is reduced does not follow in the real world. As food aid to the DPRK declines, development aid continues at more or less the same inadequate levels.

The question in North Korean minds is not whether the time is ripe for the DPRK to be weaned from humanitarian assistance and urged to accept the more solid fare of development programs. Rather, it is whether donors like Canada will switch North Korea to starvation budgets whenever they dare to do so.

Development-oriented projects operated by NGOs

Recovery and rehabilitation activities have been part of UN and NGO projects and programs from the beginning of humanitarian intervention. Operating on shoestring budgets, they have reaped a rich harvest of experience through trial-and-error experimentation. The following is an incomplete – but indicative – listing of such activities.

Support for domestic production facilities

Both resident and nonresident agencies have procured locally produced commodities for humanitarian distribution. Some NGOs supply ingredients for the production of fortified foods for special beneficiary groups, like pregnant and nursing women. German Agro-Action (GAA) provided flour and sugar to local bakeries for the production of biscuits, and soybeans for the production of soymilk to augment school children's nutrition. Action by Churches Together (ACT) was the first to support local production of selected medicines by contributing pharmaceutical raw materials to the Pyongyang Pharmaceutical Factory, at one-third the cost of imported medicines. Children's Aid Direct (CAD) and Concern Worldwide (CW) have procured winter clothing, boots, and shoes for children and farmers from factories inside DPRK.

The benefits of domestic production have been identified as follows:

- reduced commodity costs;
- maintenance of local employment and expertise;
- rehabilitation and upkeep of local production facilities;
- opportunity for modernization of knowledge and skills;

- education in international practices, standards and protocols;
- support for pride and confidence in local efforts as opposed to a "West is Best" mentality;
- support for appropriate technologies and cultural values (recipes for foods, traditional medicines, Korean designs).

Construction of new facilities

World Vision International (WVI) and others have assisted in the construction of noodle factories to supply food for local communities. WVI also introduced hydroponic greenhouse technology for the growing of vegetables and fruit. A Korean-Australian expert spent a number of months in the DPRK to train local technicians in hydroponic agriculture. Children's Aid Direct (CAD) financed and oversaw the construction by local work teams of greenhouses for use by nurseries and kindergartens. Construction materials (iron bars and u-clamps) were manufactured on contract inside the DPRK. Active involvement of other provincial authorities ensures long-term management of the system. The Swedish NGO, PMU Interlife, has constructed a repair workshop for spare parts and farm implements and offers technical advice on the maintenance of farm equipment.

Education and local capacity building

North Koreans have always maintained that the role of international agencies must be to enhance the ability of local Korean practitioners (not the international partner) to deliver quality services. This has stimulated the development of programs which seek to modernize current practices through the distribution of information and education tools in the Korean language.

The booklet *Facts for Life*[4] has been translated into Korean by United Nation Children's Fund (UNICEF) and distributed by NGOs and UN agencies in all parts of the country. The NGO-sponsored Food Aid Liaison Unit (FALU) and the International Federation of Red Cross and Red Crescent Societies (IFRC) have held workshops on nutritional requirements of pregnant and nursing women in several provinces, and have distributed an educational booklet for local professionals. Health education materials for teachers to use with children aged 4 to 7 are being developed by Children's Aid Direct (CAD) in partnership with the Institute of Health Education in Pyongyang to promote safe hygiene practices. Caritas International equipped vocational training schools with modern machinery, accompanied by a Korean-speaking professional who trained teachers in the use of the equipment.

Within the unique framework of national and international Red Cross societies, training and capacity-building have been an important complement to humanitarian assistance in all IFRC programs. National and international staff work together to prepare training materials for disaster preparedness, first aid, safe use of essential medicines, modern medical, surgical and obstetric case management practices, principles of safe water and sanitation management, etc.

An interface is therefore maintained between international and national expertise and practice. Long-standing relationships built up at the local level have created an environment within which the IFRC may collect data for impact assessment and for the analysis of conditions in-country.

Introduction of appropriate technology

Collaborating with the Korean Technical Research Institute, which has ten years' experience in the field of solar energy, Adventist Development and Relief Agency (ADRA) Switzerland has helped design, construct, and install 100 solar kitchens in children's institutions and hospitals, as well as a pilot solar hot water system. The Swiss Agency for Development Cooperation (SDC) worked with a local factory to produce small, energy-efficient wood stoves suitable for heating rooms in hospitals and schools. Korean engineers made several adaptations to the initial Swiss design to permit the use of coal as fuel.

Upgrading the health sector

A number of NGOs have worked in the health sector. The German NGO Cap Anamur (CA), for example, has emphasized the rehabilitation of health care facilities and the modernization of case management practices of local health care providers. CAD rehabilitated electrical, heating, water and sanitation systems at Hamhung City Pediatric Hospital. Training in use and maintenance of diagnostic equipment also are being provided. Along with the supply of water treatment kits and the establishment of sanitary latrines and water source protection measures, CAD educated child care workers about the importance of safe water and sanitation to reduce the risk of water-borne diseases among nursery and kindergarten children.

Innovations in the agricultural sector

Projects to promote soil fertility management through crop diversification have been initiated by Concern Worldwide (CW). Input support is complemented by a training component which aims to broaden local understanding of crop diversification techniques and the use of green manure. Building on the partnerships established through assistance of double-cropping and sweet potato cultivation, the Italian NGO CESVI has modernized local knowledge about goat breeding, for example, by introducing a rotational grazing system and alternative grazing materials, measures for improved environmental protection and soil preservation, prevention of animal diseases, and hygienic milk processing, and meat production.

To improve quality of seed for the production of winter wheat, German Agro-Action (GAA) projects focus on the rehabilitation of seed production and management facilities, and training in the principles of cultivation. Over a two-year period, ten cooperative farms will produce enough quality seed to be able to distribute to other farms in their provinces. Two Korean agronomists will receive training in Europe for seed production, processing and storage, seed certification, and seed quality testing.

Environmental protection and rehabilitation

CW has combined inputs and training to achieve an increase in successful fuel-wood tree propagation and fodder production, and a greater awareness of the harmful effects of uncontrolled exploitation of natural resources. A two-year GAA project focuses attention on overall energy balance in farming cooperatives, and the introduction of renewable energy sources. Sustainable resource management and conservation practices in watershed and catchment areas and forests will be implemented. In particular, the needs of households are taken into account, given that women are particularly burdened with a multitude of tasks linked to the availability of natural resources for household energy, safe water, animal fodder plants, etc. Land use is to be planned and implemented by the local cooperatives, with training for two North Koreans in natural resource management.

Obstacles to implementation of development projects

Numerous obstacles continue to deter development interventions. The following obstructions have been identified by resident NGOs and UN agencies:

- DPRK security considerations which limit the movement of foreigners (and North Koreans) in the country;
- continued donor concerns over DPRK's military establishment;
- limited access to relevant ministries within the government at the central and local levels;
- limited understanding by the DPRK of the difference between foreign investment and development;
- lack of counterpart NGOs or civil society organizations in the DPRK;
- lack of transparency in the implementation of humanitarian programmes;
- absence of reliable statistical data on macro- and micro-economics;
- overextended capacities within government, which is dealing simultaneously with economic restructuring, political reform and North–South reconciliation.

It is worth noting that many of these oft-repeated lamentations lay the blame for the lack of progress at the feet of the DPRK government. While all are valid in their context, one also should acknowledge the obstacles on the donors' side:

- preference by many donors for humanitarian inputs;
- differential interpretation by various donors on what constitutes development funding;
- insufficient coordination among institutional donors on the issue of development strategies.

NGOs themselves cannot entirely escape responsibility. Failure to establish development-oriented programs can be a function of NGO aims and purposes which are incompatible with the objectives of local authorities. The following factors contribute to NGO difficulties:

- lack of preparation for conditions in the DPRK;
- low level of Asia experience and ignorance of DPRK history and culture;
- tendency to see intervention as a short-term commitment;
- extremely rapid turnover rate, which works against developing rational *modus operandi* in the NGO–government relationship;
- seriously inadequate financial and human resources.

NGOs must exhibit a willingness to work under difficult conditions, to take guidance from local communities, and to make long-term commitments of resources and personnel. Full-scale "development" (i.e., larger-scale interventions) will require sustained, concrete and transparent policy dialogue, the development of meaningful partnerships, and a common understanding of what development implies in the context of DPR Korea.

Managing the transition

The international community must approach development from a Korean vantage point. Some may find this politically unpalatable, but foreign aid workers cannot force Koreans to adopt an alien model of development. Agencies which seek to make a difference need to gain the confidence of DPRK authorities. One way to build confidence is to find common ground between the goals and priorities of the aid community and the stated goals and priorities of the DPRK. Once there is agreement on objectives, there may be room to make adjustments in implementation parameters that will be acceptable to DPRK authorities, while at the same time satisfying a minimum level of expectation from the aid community.

The initial refusal by DPRK authorities to contemplate "development" assistance from NGOs was based in large part on Korean pride. In earlier decades, the DPRK itself operated numerous development assistance projects, for example, in Africa. When NGOs, many of which have extensive African experience, compare conditions in the DPRK to those in Africa, Koreans take offense. They also object to the attitude among NGO workers, many of whom are very young, that they are better judges of what is good for Koreans than the highly educated and usually much older North Korean experts.

When designing development projects, NGOs must therefore learn to recognize the value of indigenous contributions and capacities. There are many institutions, research institutes, and training centers that will continue to be central even if and when large-scale political change occurs. These should be nurtured now to start the task of building for tomorrow.

The same goes for human and intellectual resources. It would be extremely simplistic to write off all North Korean counterparts as agents of a repressive and illegitimate regime. As transformations in other societies have shown, it is inevitable that a substantial percentage of individuals belonging to the current elite will survive whatever transition occurs. In fact, they must be assured of survival in order to allow the transition to happen.

An inventory of DPRK capacity would be extremely helpful in determining where long-term investments should be made in order to lay an appropriate foundation for development. This requires an ongoing effort to build confidence at all levels among all players. Then there must be an understanding among the DPRK government, donors, UN agencies, bilateral and international organizations, and NGOs on what the priorities are and how they may be best achieved.[5]

Development projects initially will probably need to concentrate on agriculture and related sectors, partly because these have shown a degree of success, and partly because the government has designated them as priorities. Introducing new breeds and varieties and minimizing dependency on imported inputs should eventually reduce dependency on food aid.

Development implies sustainability. Under the current system, few interventions are "sustainable," with social sectors suffering from the command economy system.[6] Without government-led program interventions to stimulate economic growth, this situation will not change radically. Donors should be ready to consider ways in which the social sectors could be supported if and when economic programs are initiated by the government.

The massive amounts of humanitarian aid that have been poured into the DPRK over the past five years can be turned into an asset if material aid is used as a tool for building relationships and confidence, and is accompanied by the transfer of knowledge. This argues for a gradual transition, where food and agricultural assistance (valued by DPRK authorities) continues hand-in-hand with an increasing emphasis on rehabilitation and development, especially in those areas with the highest potential for generating information and ideas.

Notes

1 This chapter is excerpted from *North Pacific Policy Papers* 7, published by the Program on Canada-Asia Policy Studies, Institute of Asian Research at the University of British Columbia under the title "NGO Contributions to DPRK Development: Issues for Canada and the International Community," Vancouver, UBC, September 2001.

2 This refers to the airborne pollutants – yellow dust particles – which blow from the Gobi Desert across the Korean Peninsula each spring. The "yellow wind" analogy is often used in public education to refer to unwanted external ideological influences. See Weingartner and Weingartner (1999).

3 See United Nations (2000: 126, 128); United Nations (2001: 5, 110, 13).

4 *Facts of Life* (1993) is the most authoritative expression, in plain language, of what medical science now knows about practical, low-cost ways of protecting children's lives and health. Translated into 175 languages in partnership with 165 leading medical and children's organizations, *Facts for Life* is used in more than 100 countries.

5 For example, following up on a proposal made at the Agricultural Rehabilitation and Environmental Protection (AREP) Roundtable Meeting in June 2000, UNDP is negotiating with the DPRK government to launch studies on two new sectors (energy and transport), building upon the considerable work already done on agriculture and the environment.

6 Essentially, this type of economy entails a lack of real charges for goods and services provided by the state, and thus results in a lack of reinvestment in infrastructure.

References

United Nations (2000) *Inter-Agency Consolidated Appeal for the Democratic People's Republic of Korea,* New York and Geneva: United Nations.

United Nations (2001) *Inter-Agency Consolidated Appeal for the Democratic People's Republic of Korea,* New York and Geneva: United Nations.

UNICEF, WHO, UNESCO and UNFPA (1993) *Facts for Life: A Communication Challenge,* Geneva: joint publication of UNICEF, WHO, UNESCO and UNFPA.

Weingartner, E. and Weingartner, M. (1999) "Humanitarian Aid to North Korea: Peacebuilding by Example," paper presented to the 7th Annual CANCAPS Conference, Halifax, Canada.

18 Europe's new role in Korea

Ronald Meinardus

Introduction

For three reasons, the choice of my presentation's title is problematic. In explaining why, I will at the same time describe my subject.

First, the definition of what we mean by Europe is not immediately clear. Are we talking about Europe as a geographical entity, or as a political organization comprising fifteen member countries today, and several more in the future? I will speak of the European governments, engaged in an unprecedented process aimed at developing joint continental policies, even in the fields of foreign and defense affairs, where letting go of national sovereignty has proven to be particularly difficult. So, in this chapter Europe in most cases refers to the political organizations of the European Union (EU).

A second problem regarding the original title is the term Korea. Politically there exist two Koreas, and – not the least for reasons of limited space – it is not my intention to deal with the EU's relations with both Korean states. I will concentrate, instead, on the policies and actions of the European Union regarding inter-Korean relations.

Finally, the title implies that there is a new role for the EU in Korea. European diplomats would dispute with this notion. While there has, indeed, been a novel and in some ways spectacular increase in the EU's role in inter-Korean affairs, the aims and the methodology of European policies *vis-à-vis* the peninsula, developed as far back as 1999, have remained remarkably consistent.

That said, it might have been better to give my chapter the title: "The European Union's Role in Inter-Korean Relations".

The interests of the European Union in the Korean Peninsula

There exists no colonial legacy, no military presence of any importance, no common borders, so one could assume European interests regarding the Korean Peninsula are limited to the economic sphere. Until not long ago, this was a correct perception. More recently, the situation has changed.

According to Ambassador Dr Frank Hesske, the head of the European Union's delegation in Seoul:

> As the EU begins to exercise an increased role in international political affairs it stands to reason that events on the Korean Peninsula are a matter of great importance. The question is not whether the EU should play a role but more which role it should undertake in Korea."[1]

"Europe's deep involvement in matters concerning the Korean Peninsula … reflects the extent to which Europe has a global role to play," the diplomat adds.

Regarding efforts to define a joint EU foreign and security policy, Korea may be termed a promising object. Seen from Europe, the peninsula is well suited for policy-making. Unlike other geographical areas closer to home, there are no specific national interests of the member states that stand in the way of reaching a common policy.

"Because of the strong US influence and the fact that it was never a European colony, the Europeans consider it 'neutral' territory, i.e., where no one member state has any special interests in it or undue influence," writes a scholar who has analysed on a diplomatic working level the inter-European decision-making process regarding Korea.[2] Therefore, it is comparatively easy for the Europeans to identify a common denominator, and then present this to the world as the EU's position. In a sense, the Korean issue also has become a test case for the EU to act as a global player, an ambition certainly shared by most of the European leaders. "In the globalized world the EU will have a more important political role to play," Javier Solana, the EU's Foreign Policy coordinator, said after the conclusion of the successful mission to North Korea in early May 2001. Asked by a journalist, what the reasons were for this political self-confidence, the Spaniard answered: "After enlargement, the European Union will have four times the population of Japan, and two times the population of the United States. We have an obligation."[3]

Beyond this more general desire to be a participant in the political and diplomatic processes in one of the global hot spots, the EU has declared a fundamental interest in the preservation of peace and stability in North-East Asia. A leading Finish diplomat, who played a role in the formulation of the EU's Korea policy, describes this interest as follows:

> Any major conflict in this region would be expected to immediately cause serious consequences for the international system, particularly the financial system, and from this viewpoint especially the European Union has at least indirect interest in the stability and security of North East Asia.[4]

The EU member states have considerable economic interests in Korea, mainly of course in the South, where European investors have outpaced their competitors from Japan and the United States.

The European Union's objectives regarding inter-Korean affairs

In his talk mentioned earlier, Ambassador Dr Hesske emphasizes that "for once, the European Union can proudly claim that a structured EU policy *vis-à-vis* the

Democratic People's Republic of Korea (DPRK) [exists] . . . and was not inspired by the perspective of short-term political gains."[5] He then specifies that a "coherent strategic vision of Union policy toward DPRK" was formulated as early as summer 1999.

Clearly defined objectives are of crucial importance for any coherent strategy. The European Council made public these objectives regarding the Korean Peninsula on 19 July 1999. In a five-page paper that may well be termed the basic law of the EU's Korea policies, the Council defines six major political objectives, with three referring to South Korea, and the rest to inter-Korean relations and North Korea. The latter three are: (1) enhancing support for international efforts to maintain stability and find a lasting peace settlement on the Korean Peninsula; (2) continuing to press DPRK for more responsible behavior, particularly on security and human rights; and (3) reviewing bilateral relations in the light of DPRK's response to the policy of engagement.[6] The document then lays down the operational goals for the diplomatic engagement with Pyongyang, taking into consideration and reflecting the specific political and diplomatic conditions of the moment.

While the main objectives of the European Union have remained unaltered since 1999, the foreign policy decision-makers have in more than one instance adjusted their operational aims. In the summer of 1999, the EU urged both Korean sides to continue their dialogue, to drop all preconditions and to consider raising the inter-Korean talks to the highest level. The Europeans also expressed their support for the Four-Party Talks aimed at finding a lasting peace on the peninsula. As to the bilateral relations between the European Union and Pyongyang, the EU invited the DPRK to take steps to reduce regional tensions, and urged the North Koreans to discontinue missile activities (testing, exporting) and respect human rights. It is no coincidence, that these latter points also topped the European agenda at the political dialogue between the European Union and North Korea that was started in December 1998.

The implementation of EU policies regarding North Korea

From the very beginning, the EU followed a "carrot and stick" policy regarding North Korea, making the further development of the relations with Pyongyang dependent on North Korean "good behavior" in matters of European concern. In every document the EU has published regarding its engagement with the DPRK, this principle of conditionality is emphasized:

> To the extent that the various concerns which it has expressed to the DPRK are addressed over time, the EU would expect bilateral relations to be progressively improved. Any economic or political benefits which the EU might extend in this context will be related to progress from the DPRK in the various areas of EU concern.[7]

In words and in deeds the European Union has been guided by a *quid pro quo* strategy in its dealings with North Korea. Even though it does not use this term, in practice the diplomatic principle of reciprocity has always played an important role for the European Union. Looking back at the past two to three years, we may conclude that the Europeans have offered the North Koreans economic and diplomatic rewards in return for political concessions.

With regard to inter-Korean relations, 2000 was a very special year. The general consensus was that the unprecedented summit between the political leaders of the North and the South opened a new chapter in the history of the divided Korean nation. There was also widespread agreement among observers that the dramatic rapprochement was to a great degree made possible by the sudden readiness of Chairman Kim Jong Il to negotiate on the highest level with his South Korean counterpart. In the course of the summit, there were several indications that the communist regime would at last adjust its outdated policies and introduce changes, mainly in the economic sphere. Even though the extent of these changes remains a matter of controversy, the fact that the summit took place was proof enough for many that North Korea was ready to open up.

Inter-Korean negotiations on the highest level have always been a stated objective of European policies. In accordance with its policy to reward North Korea for progress in matters of European concern, the EU did not hesitate to "reward" the DPRK: decision was taken to increase the import quota for North Korean textiles by 60 percent from 2001. The European Union then included Pyongyang in its development assistance program. A fact-finding mission visited North Korea soon after with the aim of ascertaining those sectors where economic assistance was most urgent, among others the energy sector. Finally, "the frenetic pace of diplomacy between Europe and the isolated North"[8] culminated with a number of EU member states establishing formal diplomatic links with North Korea (the UK on 12 December, the Netherlands on 15 January, Belgium on 23 January, Spain on 9 February, Germany on 1 March, Luxemburg on 5 March and Greece on 8 March).[9]

The EU's Presidency's mission to Pyongyang and Seoul

The quality of the relationship between the European Union and the Democratic People's Republic of Korea reached a "dramatically enhanced level"[10] in early May 2001, when the acting President of the European Council visited the two Korean capitals. Not only was the trip, headed by Sweden's Prime Minister Göran Persson a first for the European Union, it also was the highest-ranking political visit from the West ever to take place in Pyongyang.

This unprecedented visit had been prepared carefully. In early March, the Swedish State Secretary for Foreign Affairs, Hans Dahlgren, traveled to Pyongyang, and two weeks later, his North Korean counterpart, Deputy Foreign Minister Choi, Su Hon, visited Stockholm during a tour of European capitals. This episode alone demonstrates the advancement of European–North Korean diplomatic exchanges on a high level.

"The aim of the visit is to express support for the process started by the South Korean president, Kim Dae Jung, a process aimed at bringing to an end one of the last conflicts with origins in the Second World War," Prime Minister Persson was quoted as saying. Sweden's Foreign Minister, Anna Lindh, added a further dimension to the European intervention, linking it directly with the hardening of US policies towards North Korea under the Bush administration: "It's becoming clear that the new US administration wants to take a more hard-line approach toward North Korea. That means that Europe must step in to help reduce tensions between the two Koreas."[11]

To what extent the EU's mission in a region traditionally considered the strategic backyard of the United States was indeed a reaction to the change of US policies has been an issue of considerable controversy in public and political debates before and during the delegation's visit. While there is no clear answer to this query, fundamental differences of opinion between Europeans and Americans on how best to deal with the communist regime in North Korea surfaced in the early stages of the Bush administration: "There are real differences of principle on how to conduct global affairs between us and the EU," a researcher at the Heritage Foundation was quoted as saying in this context.[12]

In spite of public expressions of transatlantic disharmony in an important foreign policy matter, all sides applauded the EU's high-level intervention in Korea after it was completed successfully: "This is part of the whole process that we have supported and encouraged, of nations of the world working with North Korea as North Korea emerges more into the world," a spokesman for the US State Department said. South Korea's President reacted with enthusiasm, after being briefed by the Swedish Prime Minister about the results of the visit. Kim Dae Jung termed the diplomatic mission "a proud page in European history," and said that "with the support and encouragement from this EU delegation ... the process of peace, reconciliation and cooperation on the Korean Peninsula ... has now become an irreversible inevitability."[13]

According to the EU presidency, the mission to Pyongyang and the five hours of discussions with Chairman Kim Jong Il were successful in at least four areas: (1) Pyongyang let it be known that it will maintain the missile testing moratorium until 2003; (2) the North Korean leader confirmed his willingness to hold a second inter-Korean summit; (3) the North expressed commitment to the process of reconciliation with the South; and (4) the North Korean regime agreed to enter into a dialogue with the EU on human rights.

One further reason for the confidence on the sides of the EU (and the government in Seoul) was the unprecedented lenience of the North Korean authorities with foreign journalists. The forty-member EU delegation was accompanied by seventy-five reporters, the largest group of foreign journalists ever permitted to enter the North together.[14]

Prospects for European engagement in Korean affairs

A few days after the successful diplomatic mission to Seoul and Pyongyang, the European Commission announced its decision to establish diplomatic relations between the DPRK and the EU. In a statement, the EU expressed the hope that this move would facilitate the European efforts in support of the inter-Korean reconciliation process, as well as its economic and humanitarian assistance towards Pyongyang.

In terms of *quid pro quo*, this may well be termed a political reward for North Korea's cooperation in holding the summit talks. At the same time, the European Union was careful not to sound overly optimistic. "We are at the beginning of a road which is long, winding and stony," European Commissioner for External Affairs, Chris Patten, said.

At the same time, the details of the EU's technical missions to North Korea were made public. One of the missions would provide advice and training for North Korean government officials, mainly in the field of international economic matters, and the second would undertake a survey of the energy sector. The North Koreans reciprocated by agreeing to the first steps in the bilateral human rights dialogue, scheduled to be held in Sweden in mid-June 2001.[15]

After the summit one of the first priorities of the European Union was to send emissaries to Tokyo and Washington to brief the allies on the outcome of the mission. In Washington the EU official said that Europe's ties with North Korea could not develop further should Pyongyang continue to export missiles.

The EU leadership discussed the missile issue with Kim Jong Il while in Pyongyang, but there is general understanding that this is a matter that must be dealt with and solved in US–DPRK negotiations. Politically, not only the future of inter-Korean reconciliation, but also the prospects of European–North Korean relations depend to a large degree on progress achieved in talks between the governments in Washington and Pyongyang. In early June 2001, the United States announced the conclusion of its policy review regarding North Korea, and low-level US–North Korean contacts followed shortly. The European Union has reacted positively to these developments, and publicly retracted earlier statements of a rift between Washington and the Union regarding North Korea.[16]

I would assume that the revitalized transatlantic harmony regarding North Korea's policy will last as long as the Europeans are convinced that Washington is genuinely in search of political solutions with Pyongyang. Should doubts arise as to the sincerity of these efforts, it may well happen that political pressure in the EU will compel the European Union to once again take a more active role in the Korean question.

In the meantime, the EU will go on with its policy *vis-à-vis* Pyongyang, expanding its relations step-by-step in a well-coordinated and reciprocal manner. By so doing, the Europeans not only are assisting the North Koreans to overcome their dramatic situation, they are also promoting reconciliation and eventual reunification between the two Koreas.

Notes

1 Speech given by Ambassador Dr Frank H. Hesske, Head of the European Commission delegation in Seoul at a luncheon organized by the Friedrich-Naumann-Foundation, 25 April 2001.
2 Stephanie Anderson, (2001: 4).
3 Joint press conference in Seoul on 4 May 2001.
4 Makku Heiskanen, (2001).
5 Ibid.
6 European Union, 2198th Council Meeting, Brussels, 19 July 1999 (10135/99 Press 227) "Korean Peninsula – Conclusions."
7 Ibid.
8 Associated Press, 9 March 2001.
9 This leaves two EU members without full diplomatic relations with Pyongyang: France and Ireland. There have been talks between the North Koreans and the governments of both European states this year, but so far these have not come to a successful conclusion.
10 Ambassador Dr Frank Hesske, speech.
11 *International Herald Tribune*, 26 March 2001a.
12 *International Herald Tribune*, 28 March 2001b.
13 Available HTTP. <http://www.state.gov> and <http://www.cwd.go.kr> (accessed 1 May 2002).
14 According to a Western diplomat the freedom of movement of journalists in Pyongyang on this occasion was unprecedented. In his discussions with the Europeans, South Korean President Kim Dae Jung termed the cooperative handling of the Western journalists an "important signal, and a signal to the world that North Korea was coming out." Confidential Report of the EU Presidency and Council Secretariat on the visit of Prime Minister Persson, High Representative Solana, and Commissioner Patten to South Korea on 3 and 4 May 2001.
15 Associated Press, 5 May and 30 May 2001.
16 Reuters, 14 June 2001.

References

Anderson, Stephanie (2001) "The Changing Nature of Diplomacy: The European Union, the CSFP and Korea", Carlisle, unpublished manuscript.

Heiskanei, Makku (2001) "The Role of the EU in Northeast Asia", in *Northeast Asia Peace and Security Network*, Special Report, 1 May.

International Herald Tribune (2001a) "EU to send Mediators to Promote Korea Talks", 26 March.

International Herald Tribune (2001b) "EU Mission Seen as Rebuke to Bush", 28 March.

Part VI

Where do we go from here?

19 Where do we go from here?

John Merrill[1]

The US policy of engaging North Korea began around the time of the Seoul Olympics – during the Reagan administration. This "Modest Initiative" – designed to support President Roh Tae Woo's policy of *Nordpolitik* – emphasized comprehensiveness and reciprocity. We had a list of half a dozen concerns, including confidence building measures (CBMs) and conventional threat reduction. We said that as North Korea addressed specific concerns, we were prepared to take reciprocal steps and ratchet up relations towards normalcy. The Bush administration's policy review in June 2001 reached a similar conclusion – reaffirming engagement and support for President Kim Dae Jung's "sunshine policy." There are some differences with the previous administration's policy, but there is also a desire to achieve engagement, and to address problems in the US–Democratic People's Republic of Korea (DPRK) relationship. The Bush administration believes there is value in doing this. North Korea, too, should show its interest in engagement.

We keep coming back to engagement because there is no real alternative. And, at least in some areas, engagement does appear to have produced results. North Korea has begun cautiously opening its economy and edging into the mainstream of international society.

It is a mistake to think of North Korea in one-dimensional terms. It should not be pigeonholed into some ready-made category. The DPRK is a complex political, economic, and social system shaped by its history, culture, and geo-strategic setting.

North Korea also is a hard "read." To begin with, there's not a lot of reliable information, and what there is often opaque. Unless you're watching carefully, it's not easy to see what's going on. But it is possible to venture some informed guesses. What's important is to focus on high-level, authoritative statements, recurrent themes, and the symbolism of Kim Jong Il's appearances and activities. The Bush administration has made it clear that we're ready for dialogue "anytime, anywhere, and without preconditions." The US government remains very open to resumption of dialogue without preconditions and with both sides free to raise issues of concern. Unfortunately, not much is happening right now either in North–South or DPRK–US official-level dialogue.

Nonetheless, I remain guardedly optimistic. Chairman Kim Jong Il seems to be back in a mode of summitry and diplomatic outreach. In the last few months, he's hosted a top-level European Union (EU) delegation, had a summit in Moscow with President Putin, and will soon play host to Chinese President Jiang Zemin. That Chairman Kim has personally identified himself with North Korea's opening to the outside world is significant – hopefully, a signpost pointing to where we go from here.

Kim's Russian trip had many interesting aspects. Only seven months after his January 2001 Shanghai visit, Chairman Kim had an opportunity to observe first-hand Russia's efforts at economic opening and reform. He reaffirmed the DPRK's self-imposed missile launch moratorium at least until 2003. He reportedly told President Putin that his offer to abandon the North's long-range missile program altogether was still an option if someone else would launch its satellites. Some of the infrastructure projects he discussed, such as connecting the Russian and DPRK rail systems to provide a rail-bridge from Korea across Russia to Europe, would require resumption of inter-Korean dialogue. I don't think this project is just a pipe dream – Chairman Kim personally took twenty-five days to traverse the Russian part of the route.

Even negative factors in the current situation appear to offer some incentive for North Korea to act. The North Koreans know as well as anyone else that only sixteen months are remaining in President Kim Dae Jung's term. They also know that South Korean public opinion is increasingly skeptical about prospects for cooperation with the North. It is worth noting that North Korea has refrained from criticizing President Kim Dae Jung and has toned down its rhetoric about the Republic of Korea (ROK). In mid-August 2001, it dedicated a monument in Pyongyang commemorating the inter-Korean summit.

It's unfortunate that North Korea could not send anyone to this conference. It's probably mostly due to the political situation, but maybe there also was a scheduling conflict. North Korea was involved with its own economics conference last week – the second meeting of the DPRK economics society. (There aren't enough economists in North Korea to go around.) The meeting was held in Wonsan – an east coast seaport that's been mentioned as a possible free-trade zone and that's along the route of the proposed east coast rail link to Russia. The meeting came right after Chairman Kim's return from Russia and on the eve of Jiang Zemin's visit. The conference called for maximizing profits, building an information-based economy, and meeting the requirements of Kim Jong Il's "Seed Theory."

This last point is important. As originally conceived in the 1970s, Seed Theory applied only to literature and the arts. It simply said that a work of art was an organic whole that grew out of a central theme. It was part of a burst of innovation in the arts at that time. In the last year, the North has begun saying that Seed Theory should be generalized and applied to all spheres of activity, including the economy. It provides a potential ideological justification for change – the North can say it remains deeply rooted in Kim Il Sung's thought, even as it branches off in new directions in its economy.

North Korea is not the land that time forgot. It's begun to change. And, at least in the economic sphere, the pace seems to be picking up. There are many things to consider. How can the United States and its allies encourage change and channel in positive directions? Should training opportunities be provided to develop the North's human capital, especially in the areas of economics, law, and business? What can the international community do to promote the development of North–South joint venture projects such as the proposed industrial park at Kaesong – a garrison town just above the DMZ? How can the long list of infrastructure projects mentioned by other speakers be moved ahead? Would it be worthwhile to think about defense industry conversion as in the former Soviet Union?

Note

1 The views expressed here are those of the author and do not necessarily represent those of the US government or the Department of State.

20 Where do we go from here?

A Russian perspective

Georgi Toloraya

The message of this chapter is very simple, although it is based both on twenty-five years of experience in dealing with North Korea and on the more recent results of Chairman Kim Jong Il's visit to Russia.

The message is as follows: North Korea has changed more during the last couple of years than during the previous half century. It is now reaching out to the world. It should be encouraged, and at this point the United States can do more than any other nation to help bring about positive changes.

The recent journey of Chairman Kim across Russia (July–August 2001), which I had the honor to witness, offered important clues to future developments. Among them are the following:

- This visit opened the window to the non-communist world for the North Korean leadership. It gave them a first-hand experience of how a former communist superpower, despite all the negative qualities, goes through the transition to a market economy and democracy and seeks its place in the global economy. This is particularly important because the Soviet Union was the "spiritual father" of the Democratic People's Republic of Korea (DPRK) and the Korean system was created much along the lines of the Soviet model.
- The DPRK clearly indicated its desire to be treated as an equal partner by the world community, to negotiate its new role and positions *vis-à-vis* other countries, breaking out of shell of isolation to become a "regular player" in international relations.
- Pyongyang tried to demonstrate that it is a responsible partner which respects international law and stands for peaceful resolution of conflicts. In Moscow, Kim Jong Il denounced international terrorism and confirmed the missile test moratorium.
- North Korea showed genuine interest in gaining access to the benefits of international economic cooperation. Kim Jong Il committed his country to the large-scale project of creating the railroad land bridge from the Korean Peninsula to Europe (based on his talks with his Russian hosts, he issued a directive on the route and gauge of the future railroad).

- North Korea indicated its desire to solve existing problems in its relations with the countries it considers as its major adversaries and to develop dialogue and cooperation with South Korea.

What "road map" could North Korea follow if this evidence is an accurate indication of the future?

First, Kim Jong Il's government would need firm, realistic guarantees of its security, respect for its sovereignty, and promises of non-interference. Without these it would be impossible for the North Korean power hierarchy to attempt any changes, even in their economy, for fear of provoking a government collapse assisted by outside forces.

Second, having received proofs that the regime is secure and will not be challenged from the outside, North Korea would be able to embark on a much deeper form of economic cooperation with South Korea and the world (probably, along the lines of the South Korean and Chinese export-oriented model). This would provide the foundation for internal economic changes.

Third, these economic changes would bring about alterations in property relations and the socio-economic structure, emergence of a new (or maybe old) elite, which would signify a new North Korea much more predictable politically and economically profit-seeking.

Fourth, these changes in North Korea would become the basis for new security arrangements in the region. The centerpiece of the new international structure would be the peaceful coexistence of the two Koreas on the road to reunification.

One of the major problems is that neither international political scientists nor politicians have ever offered the North Koreans any tangible "blueprint" of how their country should look in an international context. In the absence of such a plan, North Koreans see all demands for "reforms and openness" as purely subversive. Speaking here in my personal capacity and as a scholar, may I suggest to the academic community that such research should be undertaken. Also in my personal capacity, I would take the liberty of suggesting some "recipes" with regard to practical policy for North Korea.

We are witnesses to a unique moment when the whole future of the Korean Peninsula rests largely in the hands and political will and wisdom of one man, President George W. Bush. He can actually do for North Korea what another Republican President, Richard Nixon, has done for Maoist China. That means granting full diplomatic recognition and giving DPRK formal and substantial guarantees of security and respect for its government.

The first step would be confirmation of the October 2000 joint statement and resumption of high-level dialogue without preconditions. The process could result in a formal treaty and cessation of hostilities.

Japan will then probably follow suit. It would be only fair if Japan would render certain economic assistance to the North to "close the past." That could revitalize the North Korean economy and help change its basics.

A tremendous boost in economic cooperation between North and South would follow (the trans-Korean railroad link with the trans-Siberian road might be a catalyst). North and South Korea could then negotiate military détente, formally recognize each other's governments and set up official and unofficial frameworks of relations.

The new peace structure on the Korean Peninsula could then be cemented by a multi-party conference, bringing together both Koreas and the parties with substantial interests in Korea: the United States, China, Russia, Japan, and probably the United Nations and European Union as observers.

Such developments would finally end the era of confrontation in Korea and would usher the peninsula into a new era of peace and prosperity. I fervently hope that these idealistic schemes could succeed, in part or in full. This long road, however, starts with a single step. Let us take it.

21 The United States and North-East Asia

A new era beckons

Donald P. Gregg

My direct experience in Asia began in March 1952, when I flew to Japan during the Korean War. I have lived in Asia for more than twenty years, and have been focused on that region almost continuously for half a century. Almost all of my work concerning Asia has been carried out under the shadow of war; the Korean War, the Vietnam War, and finally the Cold War, which lingers like the dirty remnants of a melting glacier on the Korean Peninsula.

In all this time I have never seen a greater opportunity for the United States to play a key role in ending the Cold War in Korea. Doing so would help bring to North-East Asia a new era of stability and reconciliation it has never before enjoyed. This is a unique opportunity for us, and our ability to take full advantage of this situation can be inhibited only by the restraints and obstacles that we place in our own way.

How has this opportunity arisen? Much of the credit goes to the leaders of Russia, China, Japan, and in particular, South Korea. These men have come to see that they share a common problem: how to assist North Korea to develop a new pattern of relations with them and with the United States that will result in improved economic conditions inside North Korea, and greater stability on the Korean Peninsula. President Kim Dae Jung has, by his active personal diplomacy, created for South Korea the best relationships it has ever enjoyed with its neighbors. China also deserves credit for helping both North and South Korea to become members of the United Nations in 1991, and for providing extensive food aid and economic advice over the past decade. Russia under President Putin is now also playing a more active role, particularly through Putin's recent hosting of Chairman Kim Jong Il in Moscow, an event that was warmly applauded in Seoul.

Until recently, the Bush administration remained aloof from these developments while they conducted a review of North Korean policy options. They wisely came to the conclusion that the United States ought to pursue an American dialogue with North Korea. An initial US–North Korean meeting was held in New York in June 2001 in which the American side laid out the issues it wanted to discuss. No formal response from Pyongyang has been received.

Chairman Kim Jong Il has conducted successful visits to both China and Russia during this period, and also hosted a large delegation from the European

Union. North Korea has moved to establish diplomatic relations with several European countries, as well as Australia. Chairman Kim put relations with South Korea on hold during this period. First, he waited to learn the result of the Bush administration's policy review, and then apparently he wanted to strengthen his international standing by making the other international visits.

The stage has thus been set for new moves between Seoul and Pyongyang, and between Pyongyang and Washington. Here are some observations on the current state of affairs. Kim Jong Il is in firm control of North Korea. He felt secure enough to make a visit to Russia that took him away from North Korea for more than two weeks. He traveled entirely by train, which would have made it impossible for him to return quickly to North Korea if a crisis had erupted. North Korea remained tranquil during his absence. Chairman Kim's confidence in his position derives chiefly from his close relationship with North Korea's military establishment, which he has strengthened, particularly over the past two or three years. North Korea's credibility rests largely with its ability to wreak havoc on the millions of people who live in Seoul. In a short war the North could commence hostilities but it could neither sustain nor win such a conflict.

Today North Korea is a state that cannot feed its own people and is heavily dependent on large-scale humanitarian aid provided by forty-nine other countries. This aid, plus heavy fuel oil that the United States provides as part of the 1994 Agreed Framework, amount to about US$400 million per year. North Korea's other sources of foreign exchange come largely from missile sales and other murky activities that are hard to quantify. In any case, North Korea cannot support itself as it stands today. I believe that the North Korean leadership realizes this, and has reluctantly concluded that it must change the way it relates to the outside world. Although the North Korean leadership will never admit it, their long-standing policy of self-reliance ("*juche*" in Korean) has failed.

If this analysis is correct, the immediate question is "Why not let North Korea collapse?" The answer is that the consequences of such a collapse would be devastating to South Korea's economy and demographically destabilizing to China's North-eastern region. South Korea has taken heed of what happened in Germany in 1989 following the collapse of the Berlin Wall. Extrapolating from the costs of German reunification, the South Koreans are virtually unanimous in their belief that a collapse of North Korea would be an unmitigated disaster that they could neither afford in economic terms, nor deal with as a society.

It is estimated that more than 200,000 North Koreans have already fled the miserable conditions in their own country, and are living illegally in the large ethnic Korean community in North-eastern China. The Chinese are fearful of the massive refugee exodus that would be triggered by a North Korean collapse, and are determined to do all they can to prevent such an event from occurring. This is one of the main reasons for the continuing flows of food aid and practical advice from China to North Korea. China may not be anxious to see a united Korea emerge on its border. But that eventual possibility is vastly preferable to the destructive impact that would be visited on the entire region by either an explosion of war or an implosion resulting from utter economic failure in North Korea.

During a private meeting with President Kim Dae Jung, held in Seoul in mid-April 2001, the President spoke frankly about the consequences of collapse in North Korea. He said that he had long been aware of the horrors that a second Korean war would bring to the Korean people, but that he had recently acknowledged the impossibility of dealing adequately with a collapse of the Pyongyang regime. The President said that resentment and mistrust of North Korea on the part of the South Korean people remains pervasive, even as they hope for better North–South relations. He fears that such feelings would impede any major effort to help a failing North Korean regime. The result, President Kim said, would be chaos and the possibility of large-scale armed conflict. In closing, the President said, "Engagement is our only option."

The effective diplomatic steps carried out by South Korean President Kim since his 1998 inauguration have changed the political climate in North-East Asia from one of rancor and suspicion to consensus. In late February 2000, before the Pyongyang summit had been announced, the Russian ambassador to South Korea made the following public statement at a conference in Seoul.

> Russia's relations with the Republic of Korea have already passed childhood and entered maturity. It should be mentioned with satisfaction that the Republic of Korea has become one of our most significant partners in the Asia-Pacific region ... In this rare moment of history, the major powers in North-East Asia are free from open regional rivalry and military confrontation ... One should not miss this "window of opportunity".

The Pyongyang summit held in June 2000 received strong support from all of South Korea's neighbors. In my view, that meeting heralded a paradigm shift in North-East Asia, and possibly marked the start of an era of reconciliation for the entire region. A six-month hiatus in the North–South reconciliation process has been widely attributed to the change of administration in Washington. The next moves by the Bush administration will be watched closely, and will do much to set the pattern of our future relations in the region. Here are a few modest suggestions:

I believe that it is not helpful to the advancement of US interests in North-East Asia to give the impression that we believe either that North Korea is a major justification for building a national missile defense system, or that North Korea can only be dealt with successfully by building such a system.

This impression currently is widespread in the region largely because of two events that took place in 1998. In July 1998, the congressionally-sponsored Rumsfeld Report was issued. It assessed the ballistic missile threat to the United States as being stronger and more imminent than the Clinton administration had acknowledged. Six weeks later, the North Koreans launched their multi-stage Taepodong rocket, which dismayed the Japanese, surprised most technical experts, was longer-range and more technically advanced than anticipated, and seemed to be the perfect example of the threat that the Rumsfeld Report had envisioned. (Any cause-and-effect relationship between those two events has yet to be established.) North Korea was already designated as a state sponsoring terrorism for egregious acts committed in the 1980s, and thus became the poster child of rogue nations, at least in the minds of some. Since the election of President Bush last year, the military capabilities of North Korea, Iraq, and sometimes Iran have been cited as the main justifications for America's development of a national missile defense system.

There is no denying the fact that in August 1998 the North Koreans fired a rocket that surprised Washington, and the severity of our reaction may have surprised the North Koreans. The announced purpose of the rocket was to launch a small satellite that would have broadcast North Korean revolutionary music from space. (The world was spared this musical assault as the final stage of the rocket failed.) The USA, however, saw the rocket in terms of the missile threat outlined by the Rumsfeld Report. The North Koreans, I believe, were quick to see how deeply upset we were, particularly the Congress, and adroitly moved to take advantage of our concern. In other words, by over-reacting to the North Korean rocket we made ourselves vulnerable to what some called North Korean blackmail tactics. This is a pattern that I hope and trust will be broken by the Bush administration.

Since the August 1998 firing of the Taepodong rocket, the cessation of North Korean missile testing has been a central objective of both the Clinton and Bush administrations. In September 1999, the North Koreans agreed to hold off on further missile testing in return for the lifting of American economic sanctions. And it is highly significant that Chairman Kim Jong Il, in his recent visit to Moscow, affirmed that he would delay further missile tests until the year 2003. This seems to be a clear signal that he hopes that the dialogue with the United States will be resumed in the near future.

I thus suggest that we stop referring to North Korea as a rogue nation, and that we put North Korea and Iraq into entirely separate categories. Iraq, to my knowledge, has shown no interest whatsoever in changing the way it does business. It shoots at our aircraft, refuses all International Atomic Energy Agency (IAEA) inspections, and remains recalcitrant. Iraq is oil-rich, rabidly anti-Israel and extremely difficult to influence through any dissident Iraqi groups.

North Korea, in contrast, is desperately poor, and has shown clear signs that it wants better relations with its neighbors. Most significantly of all, it has South Korea, America's close ally, as its next-door neighbor and ethnic twin. In reviling North Korea as a rogue state, we do ourselves no good with the South Korean people, who take this as evidence that we are willing to jeopardize North–South reconciliation for the sake of national missile defense. There is clearly a case to be made on its own merit for a missile defense system of some sort. There is no benefit to applying pejorative labels to North Korea when no other country in the region will subscribe to them.

In moving to resume a dialogue with Pyongyang, I believe that the United States would be wise to follow President Kim Dae Jung's lead and attempt to deal with the easy things first. A good place to start would be to discuss hooking up the North–South railroad line that was cut during the war. The South has already done much to prepare for this move, which is both highly symbolic and substantive. Russia and China have expressed support for this project, and it was widely reported that Chairman Kim and President Putin were to have talked about revived intercontinental rail travel during their meeting in Moscow. Working on the railroad would open up the demilitarized zone (DMZ) for joint US–North Korean mine clearing activities, and also might pave the way for discussions of preserving the DMZ as an ecological showpiece in which both the North and South would have an interest.

Tackling the easy things first would mean placing the issue of conventional troop deployments near the DMZ somewhat lower on the US–North Korean agenda. Convincing North Korea to weaken or decrease its forward troop and artillery deployments along the DMZ will be one of the most difficult issues to resolve. North Korea's conventional troop deployments are its main claim to credibility. It would be unrealistic to ask Pyongyang to weaken itself at the outset of a dialogue with a new administration that it does not yet know or trust.

The Bush administration has already taken significant steps to play an effective role in bringing North Korea out of its dangerous isolation. Its policy review validated both President Kim's "sunshine policy" and a resumption of the American dialogue with Pyongyang. President Bush has been well advised to reach out positively and personally to President Putin of Russia and Prime Minister Koizumi of Japan. They are popular leaders of major countries who show evidence of holding power for significant periods of time, and are men who can exert considerable influence on North Korea. President Putin's role in hosting Kim Jong Il in Moscow was handled constructively and showed his firm support for the resumption of North Korea's dialogues with both Seoul and Washington.

Secretary of State Colin Powell's recent visit to Asia also was very constructive. He was positively received in Beijing and skillfully paved the way for President Bush's visit to China in 2002. In Seoul, Secretary Powell made a highly significant statement regarding North Korea. He said, "There are opportunities with the North that we couldn't have dreamed of twenty-five to thirty years ago. We have to make sure that we try and seize these opportunities." This statement shows clearly that the Secretary is aware of changes in the North, and that he is not condemning Pyongyang to permanent isolation for its past sins.

I have watched North Korea closely over the past several years. It has become clear that what it wants from the United States is a statement that we respect its national sovereignty, and that we hold no hostile intentions toward the Kim Jong Il regime. Once we have reached the point where we can say that to North Korea and mean it, I hold great hope for a constructive American relationship with North Korea. These ties will be welcomed by Korean people everywhere, and by Korea's neighbors as well. Such a constructive relationship would place us "on the right side of history" in North-East Asia, making us a key element in the saga of reconciliation that began last year at the summit meeting in Pyongyang.

Finally, I submit that by working closely with China and Russia to bring North Korea out of its dangerous isolation, the Bush administration also can establish positive new working relations with those countries. These new relations will be helpful in dealing with other difficult regional issues, such as Taiwan and the continuing presence of US forces in North-East Asia.

Index

Page numbers in **bold** refer to Figures and Tables.